AF587465

INDONESIA:
A New Beginning?

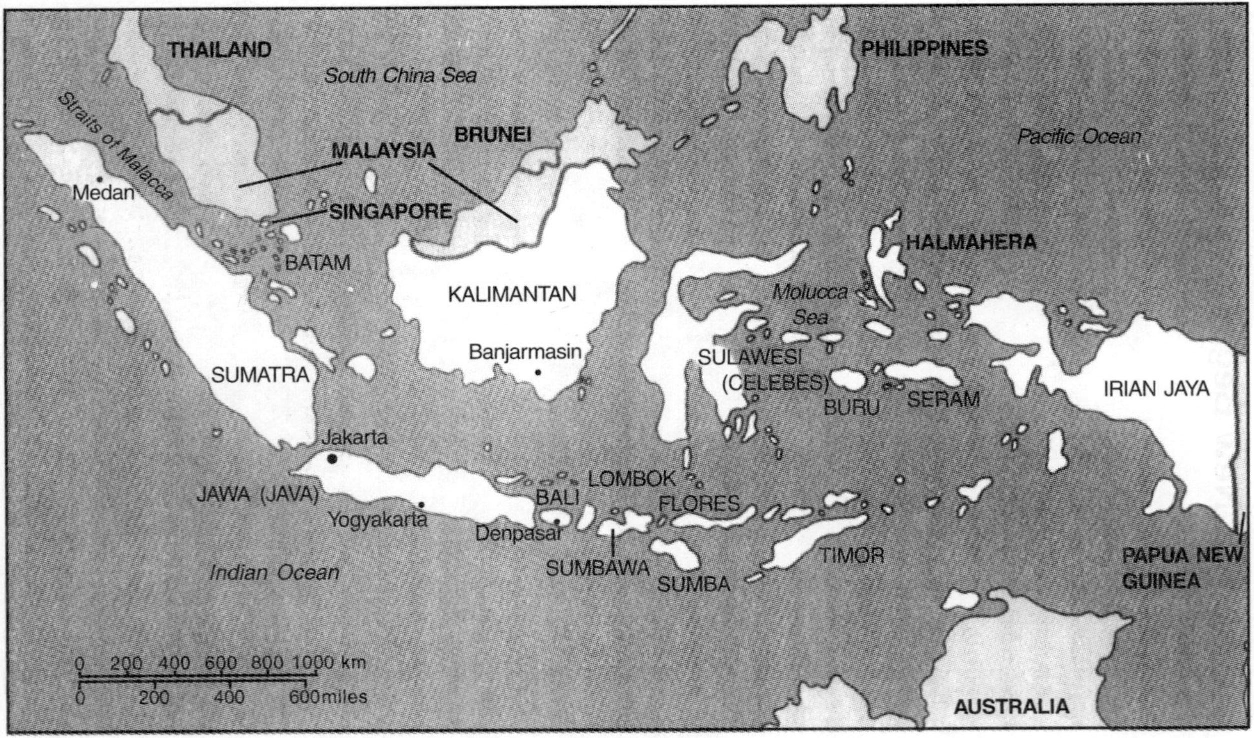
THAILAND
South China Sea
PHILIPPINES
Straits of Malacca
BRUNEI
Pacific Ocean
MALAYSIA
Medan
SINGAPORE
HALMAHERA
BATAM
KALIMANTAN
Molucca Sea
Banjarmasin
SULAWESI (CELEBES)
SUMATRA
IRIAN JAYA
BURU
SERAM
Jakarta
LOMBOK
BALI
FLORES
JAWA (JAVA)
Yogyakarta
Denpasar
TIMOR
PAPUA NEW GUINEA
SUMBAWA
Indian Ocean
SUMBA
0 200 400 600 800 1000 km
0 200 400 600miles
AUSTRALIA

INDONESIA

INDONESIA: A New Beginning?

Edited by
Satish Chandra
Baladas Ghoshal

STERLING PUBLISHERS PRIVATE LIMITED

STERLING PUBLISHERS PRIVATE LIMITED
A-59 Okhla Industrial Area, Phase–II, New Delhi–110020.
Tel: 6916165, 6916209, 6912677 Fax: 91-11-6331241
E-mail: ghai@nde.vsnl.net.in
www.sterlingpublishers.com

INDONESIA: A New Begining?

ISBN 81 207 2425 9

Printed in India

Published by Sterling Publishers Pvt. Ltd., New Delhi–110020.
Laserset at Vikas Compographics, New Delhi–110020.
Printed at : Sai Printers, New Delhi - 110020

CONTENTS

FOREWORD

India and Indonesia have very close historical and cultural ties that date back to thousands of years, and there is a long-standing understanding and goodwill between the two countries. It is therefore not surprising that President Wahid made his first public speech after his election to the presidency at the Gandhi Ashram in Bali.

Indonesia, which has opened a new chapter in democratic governance, is seeking to re-evaluate its international linkages, both political and economic. In the not too distant past, President Sukarno and Pandit Nehru together were instrumental in launching the Non-Aligned Movement (NAM), which lasted well beyond their individual life-times. With the end of the Cold War and the emerging pattern of realignment of security, political and economic cooperation, the two countries can together bring about an entirely new perspective on the status of the Indian Ocean zone in the international order.

In South Asia, India's relations with Bangladesh, Nepal and Sri Lanka have perceptibly warmed up in recent times; relations with Bhutan and Maldives are very close. Relations with China are on the mend. The winds of economic progress and the need to address real problems like poverty and fiscal deficit may well catch up with India-Pakistan relations before long. SAARC looks more promising than it ever did before. The emergence of ASEAN as a coherent economic bloc, and Indonesia's position within this formation, creates opportunities for our two countries to act as a bridge for an entirely new and dynamic movement in the Indian Ocean region. In fact President Wahid, in a recent interview, has gone to the extent, of supporting the participation of India in the 'ASEAN plus four' meetings, recognising its role along with Japan, China and South Korea. I welcome his call for Asian renaissance which needs to be pursued.

In the international arena, it is not difficult to forecast that the 21st century will see Asia become the focus of attention, both strategically and economically. Japan and China are already recognised as major powers. They could well be joined, among others, by India, Korea and Indonesia. Managing the ambitions of a number of countries which are in close propinquity will not be easy, and it is desirable that the process begins now. It is equally evident that in the post-Cold War world, economic interests are likely to dominate the foreign policies of governments. Economic blocs are already a reality, and enlightened self-interest requires taking strategic positions as early as possible, before positions harden too much. I would suggest that the emergence of a confident Indian Ocean zone consisting of mutually supportive partners would be a positive and healthy development and India and Indonesia are ideally placed to take up this initiative to bring this about.

We are all aware of the kind of agonies that the Indonesian economy, polity and society at large have gone through in the past few years due to the financial and economic crisis that engulfed many countries of the East and Southeast Asian region. The crisis adversely influenced the very social fabric of Indonesia and the restructuring process presently underway has to deal with not only the economic downslide but also tackle the social maladies that have emanated. The social unrest has risen due to closure of banks, factories, companies, other institutions, etc., and their consequent impact on unemployment levels. Politically, the country is in transition to full democracy.

The Indonesian economy is on the road to recovery just as the other crisis-hit economies are. In 1999, its GDP growth turned positive. This was possible due to improved performance of different sectors of the economy such as agriculture and manufacturing. Higher capacity utilisation, increased export earnings and lower volatility in the exchange rate were some of the important factors that contributed to the recovery. These were brought about with the help of different policy steps aimed at economic restructuring as well as unproved demand in the global export market.

India should seriously explore the possibilities of intensifying its trade and investment relationship with Indonesia for mutual benefits. Presently, India's importance for Indonesia as an export destination or an import supplier is not very significant. Indonesia too, does not figure prominently in India's export and import baskets. The total trade between the two countries stood at $ 1299 million in 1997. The two-way investment linkages have also remained low. One may emphasise that Indian companies need to be prompted to go and set up their manufacturing units in Indonesia and also enter into either buy-back arrangement or target the global market. This would be one way in which India could show its solidarity with the Indonesian economic restructuring process. This would particularly be welcomed when the Indonesian economy has suffered from a liquidity crunch.

The agricultural sector could be a major area of cooperation. We know Indonesia grows a variety of crops including rice, rubber, corn, tea, coffee, soyabeans as well as several tropical, fruits and spices. India too, is abundantly endowed with these commodities. Joint commodity marketing and cooperation in the area of processed foods could perhaps forge beneficial ties between the two countries on a sustained basis. Similarly, acquaculture could be another area for cooperation.

The new government has already ushered in many new measures to transform Indonesia into a vibrant democracy. Removal of all state controls on the press is a welcome step, particularly in this age of the Information Revolution. That the present government has given top priority to reform of the legal system and the establishment of a credible and impartial judiciary is another notable initiative.

President Wahid, in his efforts at establishing truly democratic governance has taken the necessary steps to confirm the primacy of civilian rule and make the armed forces accountable to the civilian government.

The civilian institutions in Indonesia are in the process of being rebuilt. Indonesia appears to be moving towards a political system which is not dissimilar to ours. A democratic parliamentary system of governance, independent judiciary, free press and attendant institutions provide ample space to diverse sections of the population to share in, and work for the realisation of, common aspirations. This is our experience in India. Other systems do not provide this platform. I understand that the outlying provinces have begun openly expressing their resentment against an autocratic kind of rule. Many of the provinces are clamouring for greater autonomy and a greater share of revenues between the centre and the provinces. The emergence of independent East Timor has given rise to similar calls in Aceh and Paptia (till recently known as Irian Jaya). Violent outbreaks of religious and ethnic clashes have been witnessed in Ambon and other regions. While law and order and the rule of law should be enforced by the security forces, democratic governments have to explore all possibilities of removing the roots of discontent. We in India can understand these problems faced by Indonesia quite. readily and sympathetically and can appreciate the political compulsions they generate.

In this context, I would suggest that Indonesia may find it worthwhile to examine some of our constitutional provisions governing the relations between the centre and the states, or the provision creating the Election Commission and other institutions intrinsic to the democratic functioning of the Indian polity.

An area which has been accorded high importance in the economic agenda of the Indonesian government is upgradation of human resources. This is another field in which India has, over the decades, created a large pool of highly skilled personnel like engineers, doctors, management graduates, software professionals, accountants, scientists, etc. India also possesses a reservoir of medium skilled manpower resources.

There is great need for, and interest in, expanding the facilities for Indonesia studies in Indian Universities. Both sides need to take a fresh look, at how this access can be expanded and expedited since this is a relatively easy, though long-term measure through which understanding of each others' societies can be enhanced.

One example of such interactions is the India-ASEAN Eminent Persons Lecture Series, conducted by the Research and Information System (RIS) for the Non-aligned and Other Developing Countries, on behalf of the Government of India.

India and Indonesia have always maintained good relations with each other. Our earlier relationship was based on shared ideological convictions, which was perhaps enough in the bipolar world that existed at that time. The relationship that now has to be established will be considerably more complex and deeper. Mutual understanding and respect will have to become an important feature in this relationship. For this purpose, sustained effort will have to be put in by both sides to understand each other, both as nations and as peoples.

It is time now to widen and deepen the scope of our bilateral relations beyond just economic interests. The cultural ties between India and Indonesia are age-old. There are also common concerns about the future security environment in Asia and an honest elimination of nuclear weapons. There is virtually no conflict of interest. On the other hand, there is a great degree of convergence of interests. Given the geopolitical and economic complementarities, it becomes obvious enough that this bilateral relationship should be one of the pillars of the foreign policies of the two countries.

I hope and wish that cooperation between India and Indonesia will flourish in the years to come and will contribute to the prosperity and stability of the Asian region as a whole. It is in this context that I would compliment the Society for Indian Ocean Studies for having brought out this volume on "Indonesia: A New Beginning?". I am confident that the volume will help in injecting a creative and constructive spirit in our relations with Indonesia.

K.C. Pant

Deputy Chairman

Planning Commission of India

1
Introduction

Satish Chandra & Baladas Ghoshal

As the largest country in Southeast Asia occupying a strategic location astride the sea routes between the Indian and the Pacific Oceans, Indonesia has always attracted the attention of scholars, diplomats, military practitioners and policy- makers. Whatever happens to Indonesia has a direct bearing on the inter-state relations and regional security of Southeast Asia. Indonesia's internal political instability in the early 1960s together with an aggressive foreign policy pursued by its first president, Sukarno, had brought about a confrontation with Malaysia, vitiating regional security environment. It had also led to economic stagnation. Again, it was Indonesia's restraint, good neighbourly policies and a strong commitment to regional cooperation under a new leader, after the fall of Sukarno in 1966, that made the birth of ASEAN possible, and contributed to regional stability in Southeast Asia for over three decades. Indonesia's strongman for thirty-two years, President Suharto, while he had governed autocratically, had brought brisk growth in the country for more than a decade beginning from the 1980s. In terms of social indicators, Suharto's record was quite impressive — so much so that in the early 1990s the World Bank hailed Indonesia as one of the most successful stories of political and economic development in the developing world. Unfortuantely, all that was marred by his refusal to bring about political liberalisation and arrange for an orderly succession, as well as mounting charges of corruption and nepotism involving his family. More importantly, Indonesia's weak political, economic and legal institutions could not withstand the forces of turbulent change engendered by the essentially volatile nature of global capital and money markets. The outcome was the economic crisis of 1997, wiping out all the gains Indonesia had made over the last two decades. The consequent social turmoil eventually precipitated Suharto's ouster from power, giving rise to hopes that after thirty-two years of firm government, a new Indonesia — open, transparent, liberal and democratic — would emerge.

Three years have passed since Suharto fell from power. Have these hopes for a new Indonesia been fulfilled? Will Indonesia succeed in its journey toward establishing a democratic society? Will the civilian elite be able to reduce the army's *'dwifungsi'* role and establish its supermacy over the military? With all the separatist movements, ethnic and religious, accompanied by violence, wreck the country, leading to its break up? What role would Islam play in the emerging political scenario? What is the position of Hindus in a multi-religious society? Will Indonesia be able to recover from the economic mess and the debt burden? What are the implications of Indonesian instability for the region and its security? These are some of the questions that are troubling many who are interested on Indonesia. This is only natural because of the close historic, cultural and economic relations between India and Indonesia since the time of the great Mauryan ruler, Ashoka, and the spread of Hinduism and Buddhism. The Andhra and Chola states of South India had close maritime contacts with Indonesia, and Indian traders remained active in the area till the 18th century, despite Dutch efforts to create a monopoly and discrimination against all other traders. When Islam came to Indonesia from the 14th century onward, religious divines and leaders from Gujarat and Bengal played a definite role.

Contacts between India and Indonesia were revived after the two countries attained independence. This interest has continued despite setbacks during the Cold War era. India is concerned about political and economic developments in Indonesia and the direction in which it is moving. Being Asia's second largest democracy, the multi-racial, multi-cultural, multi-religious, character of Indonesian democracy and its maintaining and upholding by tradition of being moderate and tolerant in religious matters is important not only in South and Southeast Asia but across the Islamic world where the forces of moderate and liberal Islam are facing the forces of fundamentalism and terrorism.

It is with the view of finding answers to the above questions that the Society for Indian Ocean Studies brought together in May 2000 a group of scholars who are familiar with Indonesia to deliberate on these issues. Papers presented at the seminar which was supported by the Ministry of External Affairs, Government of India, have since been revised to bring them up to date. A number of fresh papers have also been commissioned to cover as wide a field as possible. The situation following the removal of Abdurrahman Wahid by the MPR, and the election of Megawati Sukarnoputri as president has also been taken into account.

The first paper of *Shri S.K. Singh*, 'India and Indonesia — A Perspective', recalls the age old historical and cultural relations between India and Indonesia. S.K. Singh notes that during the Indonesian struggle for freedom, India was able to provide some material and considerable psychological assistance to Indonesia which was then fighting under Sukarno for liberation from the colonial yoke. Even at this early stage, the two people realised the advantage of building mutual strong political and strategic cooperation and friendship. On becoming free and sovereign nations, in the Bandung Conference they collaborated to sow the seed of non-alignment. However, while the South Asian and Eastern archipelagic landmass formed the logical confluence and cross road of trade between China and Japan on the one hand, and the western part of the Indian Ocean on the other, on account of historical developments followed by the cold war, it was only in the late seventies that India reviewed and re-explored its relations with Southeast Asian countries to enable it to seek an increased share of trade and investment by gradually moving away from its earlier inward looking and import substitution model of industrialisation.

India's "look east" policy which began in the nineties must be seen as a part of the country's recognition that Southeast Asia is India's "proximate neighbour". In the context of Southeast Asia, Indonesia is viewed by India and the world as the principal anchor of the ASEAN, just as India is the largest and the sheet anchor of SAARC in South Asia.

Emphasising that both countries were ethnic, multi-racial, multi-linguistic, multi-cultural, broadly open to tolerance and patience and possessing a clear intangible policy for survival, S.K. Singh, citing the example of the breakup of Yugoslavia and the revival of the spectre of the 19th century Balkan Wars, felt that Asia could not be complacent. However, he was certain that Indonesia would emerge from its current national building problems with its sovereignty and territorial integrity unaffected.

In conclusion S.K. Singh argues that Indonesia's economic and political changes had to be seen together. Western powers, specially the United States, recognised quickly their stake in preventing Indonesia from descending into total chaos. They recognised that chaos in Indonesia could threaten the nascent economic recovery then underway elsewhere in the Asian region. They also recognised that chaos in Indonesia would affect passage through the important sea lanes under Jakarta's control, and would jeopardise the commercial interest of the USA. By inference S.K. Singh implies that India also had a stake in safeguarding the passages across the sea-lanes which, in turn, was dependent on the continued territorial integrity of Indonesia.

The second paper, "Political Transition in Post-Suharto Indonesia" by *Baladas Ghoshal* highlights the opportunities and challenges that the change over from authoritarianism to democracy present to the new leadership. The change gave a blow to the authoritarian forces in the country, freed Indonesians from a claustrophobic and oppressive political system, and thus created possibilities for a more open and accountable system. However, the absence of a democratic tradition in the country, a weak civil society without experience in social and political mobilisation, as well as in party building, a continuing culture of corruption in the judiciary and the bureaucracy; and slow progress in bringing Suharto era culprits to account resulted in mounting public discontent. Growth of regionalism with separatist movements due to the weakening of the central authority and declining state capability, and ethnic and communal violence has manifested itself in ongoing bloodshed in Aceh, Moluccas and Kalimantan. Restless soldiers, religious tensions, a static economy and heavy debt, and finally the removal by the MPR of a President whose stubborn, erratic and confrontational behaviour and style together with the lack of sight had become an impediment to good government — all have made the transition a challenging and a difficult one. Ghoshal's main thesis is that Indonesia now shows all the characteristics that a transition from authoritarian political system to a democratic one entail a simultaneous process of decay and renewal. While there has been general breakdown of law and order situation in the country as a result of declining legitimacy of institutions that Suharto had put in place in order to keep a tight rein on his people, yet at the same time one can also witness both at the national and local levels, emergence of groups and forces of renewal slowly laying the foundations of a civil society and democracy.

Evaluating the government under the leadership of Abdurrahman Wahid as president, Ghoshal notes that Wahid tried to put substance into effective governance through his belief in social empowerment and the vital roles of religious and cultural leaders in peacefully resolving tensions and conflicts at the grassroots level. Even while he was trying to establish a new style of governance through devolution and decentralisation of power in sharp contrast to Suharto, he also needed to adjust himself to the demands of a head of the government whose actions must conform to certain rules and procedures and must be transparent and accountable. Despite his deep commitment to democracy, transparency and accountability, Gus Dur had all along been acculturated to function as a *'Kiyai'* who is considered as a father to his followers and who functions in earnest sincerity, but in a fashion, which may not strictly follow democratic norms. The style that suited him when he was the dissident leader of a non-governmental organisation (*Forum Demokrasi*) did not work while he was president. However, the desire for a more just system of doing things permeates every aspect of national discussion. It is truly the hallmark of a new Indonesia.

Ghoshal considers that the takeover of Megawati as president does not mean that political uncertainty in Indonesia is over. He notes that she displayed few political skills and articulated little in the way of original political ideas as vice-president. Though she has charisma, her taciturn and aloof style of functioning endears her to few but the most enthusiastic supporters. She enjoys the backing of the military (TNI), and unlike Wahid's belliose attempt to assert civilian control over the military, she believes in a gradual approach in withdrawing the TNI from politics. Unlike Wahid, again, she may be able to establish a better raport with the bureaucracy helping her to administer more effectively. However, the problems of dealing with the secessionist movements in Aceh and Irian Jaya where the army wants to reassert control, and the radical Islamic movement demanding a new Islamic order are likely to prove severe tests.

In conclusion Ghoshal suggests that Indonesia's process of 'reinvention' and transition is going to be long drawn out. The future course of the country may be decided by a struggle between the new democratising impulse of the reformers and the forces of chaos that seek an advantage in provoking the religious social and separatist tensions that have now risen dangerously to the surface across Indonesia.

Tracing the development of the state system of Indonesia, *Ganganath Jha* points out that though the founding fathers tried to evolve a parliamentary system of government, but presidential system emerged, and powers of the legislature were eroded. The first two presidents, namely Sukarno (1945–65) and Suharto (1966-98) were extremely powerful and dominating. They increased the powers of the presidency enormously and the mechanism of checks and balances were diluted. Despite difference in outlook and policies, surprisingly there was commonality as far as the institution of presidency was concerned. By using emergency powers and media, Suharto evolved a system in which the legislature had no alternative but to support him. The new president, Abdurrahman Wahid, is popular and scholarly but has inherited a system which needs thorough overhauling, and the institutions of democracy strengthened. He has also to cope with the unrest in different parts of the country on ethnic, religious, and economic grounds.

Ganganath Jha says that the most striking feature of Indonesian politics is that it has not declared any state religion. Although the Muslims are in overwhelming majority and most of its neighbouring states have declared their state religion in order to maintain their national unity, Indonesia has abstained from doing so. Malaysia and Brunei, the two immediate neighbours, have declared Islam as the state religion but Indonesia preferred to remain secular. The preamble of 1945 Constitution assures religious freedom by declaring protection and promotion of faith in the God Almighty and endeavoured to create a just civilised humanity. The various governments have been pursuing a religious policy, which respects the right of every religious group. They have officially recognised religions, namely, Islam, Protestantism, Catholicism, Buddhism and Hinduism. The break up of different religious communities in Indonesia in mid-nineties indicated that Muslims comprised 87.2 per cent, Protestants six per cent, Catholics 3.5 per cent, Hindus two per cent and the Buddhists one per cent.

Indonesia gives emphasis on 'Unity in Diversity', to unite the people in a common fold. It has heterogenous ethnic and linguistic groups. More than three hundred languages are spoken, and their culture and life styles differ. The majority is of Malay stock, split into dozens of smaller sub-groups, with varying family structures and social systems. The prominent ethnic groups are the Javanese, the Sundanese, the Minhasans, the Bugis, the Makassars and the Balinese. Again there are the Dayaks, the Bataks, and the Dani and the Asmat of Melanesian stock.

However, the policy which proved controversial was transmigration of the people from densely populated areas to less populated zones. Java and Bali inhabit sixty-five per cent of Indonesian population. Java alone has hundred million people. This island however occupies only 6.8 per cent of the total land of the country. Sumatra, which is comparatively bigger in size, has fourty-one million and Sulawesi thirteen million population. Indonesia endeavoured to diversify its population from densely populated areas to new zones. Between 1960 and 1973, they transmigrated people from Java to other islands. Initially, 17,116 families were settled in Irian Jaya and 8,155 in Maluku but a number of people were also transmigrated to Kalimantan, East Timor and Aceh. The number of transmigration was 367,997 between 1979–84. As the government supported it, transmigration continued. Unfortunately, it has not resolved the problem of population density in Java. As job opportunities are available mostly in Java, poor and impoverished people continued to come to Java, and the problem remains the same.

These migrations provide a background to the ethnic riots in Irian Jaya, Sulawesi and Kalimantan though economic and cultural factors cannot be ignored. Thousands of people have been massacred in Irian Jaya where a call for *jihad* has been given. The beheading and massacre of civilians by Dayaks in Central Kalimantan has shocked the world.

Highlighting the trouble spots in Indonesia, *V.Jayant* says that the basic Java-Sumatra divide runs deep and strong across Indonesia, and there are several burning problems that need to be sorted out; at least four major 'Trouble spots' are now crying for solution. They are East Timor, Aceh, Ambon and Irian Jaya.

Basically, they may be different manifestations of the same problem, but they have all reached various stages of 'explosion'. The East Timor issue has burst out in the open and the international community, through the aegis of the UN was forced to intervene and restore order. A transition is now taking place and a UN sponsored peace keeping force is maintaining calm in this troubled island. At least it is nearer a solution.

Aceh has moved to the centre stage right now. An underground freedom movement has been active there since the 1960s, but when Gen. Suharto established himself in power, he wiped out all dissent. To this day, there are complaints of genocide, massacre and suppression of political rights in this highly sensitive island.

A religious or communal divide has taken shape in Ambon in Irian Jaya because of the Christian-Muslim divide. There have been frequent skirmishes and clashes between the local tribals and army units stationed there.

The Suharto regime gave away the mineral wealth in Irian Jaya and the mining rights of gold as well, to influential local and foreign companies. This resulted in frequent clashes between the local population and the 'intruders', with the military invariably backing the companies. The extent of damage to the environment and the killings of innocent tribals in the island have still not been fully assessed. It is only when the whole picture emerges that the Indonesian authorities and the international community will wake up to the realities.

Dilip Chandra's focus is on the future of political Islam in Indonesia. Dilip argues that inspite of the rise to power for the first time of a Muslim *Kiyai* (religious teacher), in the person of President Wahid, predicting the political future of Islam in the strife torn nation is extremely difficult. For instance, inspite of pronouncements of the unity of the *Umma* by the top leaders of the two key Islamic organisations, Nahdatul Ulama (*NU*) and *Muhammadiyah,* their differences persist. *Muhammadiyah's* strident criticism of Gus Dur and its demand for him to step down from the presidency, reflect the lack of confidence on the part of its leaders and followers in the ability of a *Kiyai* to lead the *Umma* and the nation. The consequent belligerence of Gus Dur vis-à-vis his Muslim opponents served only to further undermine the unity of the *Umma.* Notwithstanding such differences, ascendancy of Islam in society and even in politics in Indonesia is likely to continue and gain further ground in the days to come. Dilip Chandra attributes this phenomenon to several factors. For one, many of the Western educated Islamic leaders of the new generation have found important places in the government. For another, despite the differences within the Islamic *Umma* the very rise of a *Kiyai* to the highest office of the state itself is a significant victory for Islam. Given its massive following and influence in the densely populated provinces of central and east Java, *NU* traditionally believed to be the moderate face of political Islam, could well visualise for itself a key role as the moderate civil-political alternative in a political scenario fast polarising between the two main political actors left in the field, i.e., army and Islam, the secular democrats having lost much of their initial advantage after the overthrow of the military regime of Suharto. Dilip Chandra seems to be of the view that in a possible scenario of confrontation between the two, the secular democrats/ nationalists and other civilian forces would join hands or rally behind the only civilian alternative, and that such an alliance would be easier to form with the *NU* — the moderate section of Islam — in the lead.

Dilip Chandra also highlights the importance of the societal role of Islam. He refers to the phenomenon of neo-Sufism making inroads in Indonesia. The key features of this neo-Sufism or *taswuf positif,* as some like to call it, are their stated link with *Sharia*-based Islam, pursuit of an inner dimension religious life distancing itself from the hierarchy, authoritarianism of the conventional *Tarekats* (Orders). This new Sufism responds specially to the conditions of an Indonesian liberalism. Dilip Chandra concludes by saying that although the political future of Islam remains uncertain, its societal role, which started gaining salience in the 1980s, continues to gather strength. However, the greatest threat/ challenge to the Islamic leadership in Indonesia may yet come from the fundamentalist sections, that could seriously undermine the already deteriorating law and order situation in the country.

Tracing the development of Hinduism in modern Indonesia *Martin Ramstedt* notes that the international news coverage of the violent clashes between Muslims and Christians, has obscured the fact that there are also other minority religions threatened by the Islamic resurgence in Indonesia. One of them is Hinduism which is usually exclusively associated with Bali. It is hardly known that it was only between 1958 and 1961 that the religious leaders of the Balinese unanimously declared the "Balinese religion" to be Hindu, and that Hinduism was then adopted by adherents of other ethnic religions comprising *Agamch Budha* (East Java), and various groups of the Javanese *kebatinan* tradition in South

Sulawesi, Central and South Kalimantan and North Sumatra. The development of "Indonesian Hinduism" or *Hindu Dharma Indonesia* has in fact been a response to the religious policy of the Indonesian state which interpreted the *panaca sila,* contained in the preamble of the Indonesian Constitution of 1945, to make "belief in the One and Almighty God" *(Ketuhaman ang Maha Esa)* as the basis of the Indonesian state. It was formulated in such a way that it would hopefully placate the radical Islamic strand within the independence movement, which had wished to see the *shariat* (Islamic law) being made the basis of the Indonesian constitution, without alienating the significant Christian segment of the Indonesian people living for the most part in Eastern Indonesia. On the basis of this principle, the Muslim dominated Indonesian Ministry of Religion formulated a definition of religion *(agama)* that requires a sacred tradition to be monotheistic, universal, and scriptural in order to qualify as "religion". Consequently it did not recognise the country's plethora of ethnic religions because they did not match the official definition of *agama*. The Balinese eventually succeeded in having their ethnic religion recognised as "Hindu" and "religion", after their religious leaders had reformulated the traditional beliefs and practices along the lines of the official definition of "religion". They took recourse to monotheistic versions of Indian Reform or Neo-Hinduism in order to allay accusations of "animism", parochialism, ancestor worship, and "polytheism". When Suharto's purge of Communism increased the necessity to register as a member of an officially recognised religious community, quite a few adherents of the above mentioned ethnic religions resorted to Hinduism between 1965 and 1980.

The heterogeneous Indonesian Hindu community however remained rather fragmented during the period of relative religious tolerance, i.e., between 1965 and 1989. With the onset of the Islamic resurgence at the end of the 1980's, however, pressure that had never quite fully subsided, increased, forcing the Hindu community to bridge its inherent factionalism based on ethnicity, caste, and sect, and to realign itself with the universalist Hindu movement in India. For Hinduism, the most serious measure after 1989 was the sudden cut in financial support on the part of the Indonesian government. Since Hindu institutions could not rely on foreign funding like Christian or Muslim organisations, most Hindu schools and colleges had to be closed down. Similarly, funds were lacking to sponsor local rituals and temples. In addition to the financial discrimination, Muslims started to openly denigrate Hinduism and to harass local Hindu congregations. Discouraged by the rising pressure, many more people converted to Islam or Christianity.

Ramstedt says that pressure on the Hindu community reached a peak after the onset of the financial crisis in the fall of 1997, followed by Suharto's demise in May 1998, and the increasing Islamisation of the Indonesian society under B.J. Habibie's intermediate presidency. The general financial crisis has been hardest on the Hindu community that counted 5,987,134 members in 1997, making up three per cent of the total Indonesian population of two hundred million people. Its membership includes a large number of economically, educationally, and geographically marginalised people. Some of them have looked for better opportunities in other religious communities. Forced conversion to either of the two religion has frequently taken place in hospitals, schools, and other government institutions in Hindu regions outside Bali.

Despite Abdurrahman Wahid's return to a policy of religious tolerance after he had been elected as the new president, continuous Muslim immigration to Bali has also alarmed the Hindu Balinese, contributing to the growing radicalisation of the Hindu movement itself. The increasing "Indianisation" or "Neo-Indianisation" of Hinduism in Indonesia has even further alienated traditionalists in Bali, North Sumatra, South Sulawesi, and Central Kalimantan who have felt encouraged by the "Law on Regional Autonomy' recently passed by Abdurrahman Wahid. Non-Balinese traditionalist have been advocating a separation from Hinduism since the President has recognised *aliran kepercayaan* as "religion" in the first half of 2000.

Thus, the development of Hinduism in Indonesia is at the cross-roads.

Tracing the economic development of Indonesia with reference to investment, banking, oil and gas, *K. Subramanian* divides the economic development of Indonesia into several phases: the period from 1950–65 is a period of gradual attenuation of government control, inflation and economic dislocation which formed the background to the overthrow of Sukarno in 1965; the period from 1967–73 was a period of stability and modest achievement followed by the oil boom which lasted till 1980. Subramanian agrees that compared with other oil exporting countries, e.g., Nigeria and Mexico, Indonesia used its enhanced revenue well. During the 1970's about forty per cent of government budget went to infrastructure for the economy. The government also laid strong emphasis on improving education, health services and family planning. As a result of these, there was progress in reduction of poverty and improvement in social conditions. Economic growth average rose to eight per cent through the 1970's and early 1980 due to strong expansion of public and private investment. When the honeymoon in the oil boom ended in the early 1980s, after some confusion, the Indonesian government entered the export oriented regime. The tariff system was rationalised and *ad-valoram* rate was reduced from two hundred and twenty-five to sixty per cent. Custom duty procedure was simplified. There were also reforms in the financial sector. Thus, during the period from 1983–90 much progress was made in terms of the goal of improving the economy more internationally competitive and less relying on export of oil and gas.

This can be compared to some extent to the liberalisation of trade carried out by India in the nineties.

It was against this background that FDI in Indonesia peaked during the period 1990–94. However, these developments led to growth of regional imbalance. Industrialisation was concentrated in Java with development in many regions remaining low. Also the network of big business families, Chinese and other influences rendered the whole scheme opaque and lacking in accountability. Thus, the system was one marked by arbitrariness and lack of direction or cohesion.

Drawing on a number of studies undertaken by UNCTAD and other agencies, Subramanian argues that despite the outward growth, the Indonesian economy failed to lay the institutional foundation for technological deepening critical to sustain long term growth. Much of the growth came from low value added industries.

Subramanian concludes by underlining the point that despite ASEAN's existence from 1967 development in term of promoting regional linkages or investment and intra-regional growth was very small. In a way ASEAN did not have a common approach or policy when the crisis grew. There was a weak demand to form an ASEAN Fund to support the countries in strain. Japan took initiative but the US merely vetoed the proposal and the IMF was also opposed to the idea. US did not want these countries to come under the Japanese tutelage.

Subramanian traces the parallel development between Indonesia and India in a number of cases. It is clear that closer study of the Indonesian experience may be useful in a situation of the export-oriented growth model being adopted by India. Thus, the relationship between investment and technology, and between money and capital, role of FDI, etc., need to be studied bearing in mind the specific institutional and cultural constraints and conditions obtaining in the countries belonging to a region such as South Asia, Southeast Asia, etc.

The focus of *Bhattacharyya* and *Prithwis De* is Indonesia's foreign trade and the pattern of India-Indonesian trade. From India's point of view, Indonesia represents an attractive export market. Indonesia's objective for the Indian market according to them, is how to increase Indonesia's exports. Most of the Indonesian products sold to India are raw materials and intermediate goods. Indonesia would like to diversify their export basket and include manufacturers. If counter trade mechanism is implemented it could really prove immensely beneficial. It can also involve exchange of products with projects. Indonesia needs to strengthen its economic cooperation bilaterally and multilaterally to eliminate the negative factors of globalisation, such as unfair treatment to the developing countries and unjustified trade.

On investment, Bhattacharyya and De quote the data released by the Indonesian Investment Coordinating Board and show that India's approved investment in Indonesia till March 1999 was merely US $ 748.9 million, constituting just 0.34 per cent of the total approved FDI. The actual amount of Indian FDI in Indonesia currently stands at around US $ 200–300 million. Indonesia's FDI was US $ 115.32 million till December

1998, just 0.22 of the total FDI entering India. According to the Ministry of Commerce Annual Report 1999–2000, out of the total nine hundred and twelve active joint ventures of India dispersed over ninety-one countries, twenty are in Indonesia.

B. Raman looks at the Indonesian armed forces and its future role in the politics of the country by analysing its composition, tasks and threat perceptions, doctrine, concepts and politics of the country, and finally its crisis of legitimacy under the presidency of Habibie and Wahid. The armed forces, called the TNI, justified their *dwifungsi* and their role in politics in the past by projecting themselves as the only state institution with a national perspective and capable of promoting national harmony. They have justified their role in economic management of the country on the ground that the armed forces are the only segment of the state machinery with the required managerial capability. They have also been projecting the armed forces as closer to the people than the political class and the civil bureaucracy. The consequent militarisation of the state reached its zenith under Suharto in the early 1980s.

After being elected as president in October 1999, Wahid gradually asserted his powers of supervision and control over the armed forces and diluted their role at the national level, while leaving their role intact at the regional level. He reduced the number of military officers in the president's office, enforced his right to take all important decisions concerning the armed force and reduced the primacy of the army in the armed forces by giving greater importance to the navy and the air force than they had enjoyed in the past. He removed from the military intelligence its responsibility for the security vetting of the public servants. He has eased out Gen. Wiranto, a military strongman, from the cabinet as well as the armed forces by taking advantage of the adverse report of the Indonesian

Human Rights Commission against him and the army. The army has not resisted all these changes because of its own support for Wahid and clear Western warnings against any resistance and fears of stoppage of IMF assistance if it tried to resist the changes. Raman argues that Wahid's ability to continue successfully on this path would depend on the attitude of radical, but off-mainstream Islamic elements who were upset over the actions against Muslim officers which they viewed as a conspiracy by the Christian West (particularly in East Timor), his ability to keep his family members, who are increasingly being accused of Suharto-style cronyism, under control so that his popularity does not wither away, and on his success to promote a recovery of the economy; and finally a national reconciliation with the religious and ethnic minorities.

Raman concludes by saying that, if Wahid fails, the military may be tempted to take advantage of the resulting situation to reassert its dual role. Going by the developments in the last few months which has put Wahid in a state of siege and placed him in a precarious position vis-à-vis the military, Raman's conclusions are not misplaced. The political instability caused by the stand-off between the president and the parliament together with the deteriorating law and order situation and growing religious, ethnic and separatist violence, has helped the armed to recover some of its lost ground.

G.V.C. Naidu dealing with "Australia and Indonesia" assesses the impact of East Timor on Indonesia. He contends that, ever since its annexation, East Timor has been the most tricky and vexing problem between Australia and Indonesia. Australian acquiescence of Indonesian action for whatever reasons and the extension of a formal recognition to that act smacks of duplicity for it was Australia that was at the helm in pressing Jakarta, when it was most vulnerable, to grant self-determination to the Timorese. Unlike in the past, the issue of East Timor's separation from Indonesia and Australia's role in that, especially at a time when Indonesia was going through one of the most trying times in history, will not be forgotten easily in Indonesia. It has generated genuine fears about the future of Indonesia remaining a single political entity. Indonesians have begun to seriously doubt Australian motives and its likely future policy if other separatist movements like the one in Irian Jaya throws challenge at Jakarta. A major casualty of the Indonesia-Australia stand-off is the 1995 Security Agreement between the two countries, which Indonesia unilaterally terminated. This has also cast a long shadow over future Australian involvement in the affairs of the Asia-Pacific.

Naidu, however, argues that Australia and Indonesia would have to work together to ensure a peaceful transition and the survival of East Timor as a nation. According to him,the onus lies with Canberra in inventing ways to circumvent the East Timor issue and move on to other cooperative issues, sooner than later, so that the current estrangement is ended and a new modus operandi is evolved in the interest of regional peace and security.

Coming to the "Maritime Dimensions of the Southeast Asian Security" and its possible impact on and role for India, Naidu looks into the maritime disputes with focus on the South China Sea, modernisation of the regional navies, and India's interests and concessions especially in the Andaman Sea Region. Geographically, among the ten countries of Southeast Asia, only one, i.e. Laos, is land-locked while all these are either archipelagic nations or have long coast lines and substantial maritime interest. More importantly, barring a few, most of them have unsettled maritime boundaries or have claims for offshore assets, islands and sea-bed resources. Hence, sea power and maritime issues dominate the security concerns of the countries of Southeast Asia individually as well as collectively at the regional level. A clear mainfestation of this can be seen in the attempts to develop the naval forces in the region.

Naidu points out that, because of these strategic location astride some of the busiest sea-lanes of communication in the world and reports of vast resources of oil and gas beneath them, any settlement of the dispute is fraught with serious problems. China is already in possession of the Paracel group of islands and has unequivocally extended its sovereignty claims to the Spratly too. Malaysia, the Philippines, Brunei and Vietnam too have varying claims over the Spratlys islands and most of them have already deployed military forces. PLA-Navy is being modified and the ASEAN countries individually will not be able to match the Chinese military might. They would also find it difficult to fashion a collective approach in the event of a conflict essentially because not all the countries have claims on those islands. A negotiated settlement is increasingly appearing to be difficult as long as China is reluctant to resile from its position. The issue that directly concerns India is the Andaman Sea. India shares its second longest land and maritime boundary with Myanmar, and the Andaman and Nicobar islands lie close to Southeast Asia. Close proximity of the current military leadership in Myanmar and China, and the latter's naval activities in Myanmar close to India-held Andaman has raised concern in India. India has already strengthened its Andaman base and is planning to set up a new command, called the Far Eastern Maritime Command, in the region. Naidu argues that unlike the 1980s, the Indian Navy is no more looked with suspicion by the Southeast Asians, as a result of a number of initiatives, it has undertaken in the last few years. India has also been gradually establishing military links with some select countries of Southeast Asia.

Indian interests in Southeast Asia are growing and hence developments in the region will have considerable impact on India's security concerns. Although India is the only one that operates power projection capable ships such as an aircraft carrier, it is unlikely to get involved in the event of a conflict in South China Sea. Naidu, however, mentions India's unilateral naval exercise in South China Sea and sees the possibility of similar exercises with one or more country of Southeast Asia. However, that would depend on the future development in South China Sea and initiatives coming from the countries of Southeast Asia.

The present study although centred on Indonesia, shows that all aspects, historical, political, cultural, institutional have to be taken into account in order to trace the trajectory of development of a country or region.

The study shows the crucial role of Indonesia for the stability of ASEAN and the wider Asian region. Closer economic, political, cultural and strategic relations between India and Indonesia could be factors in strengthening the multi-ethnic, multi-religious character of Indonesia. India's experience of a liberal democratic regime, based on decentralisation of power to states based on a federal structure, could also provide a kind of a bench-mark for Indonesia's struggle for a new democratic order.

2
Indonesia And India — A Perspective

S. K. Singh

For two thousand years and more, geography and history, culture and commerce, trade and maritime compulsions have brought India and Indonesia together. Continuity of this historical process between the two peoples, their culture, literary and religious affinities have helped structure common interests and perceptions in making cooperation between the two nations a habit. The Indian Ocean has been a major factor impelling them towards greater togetherness.

A quarter of a century ago the two countries demonstrated their capacity to build a lasting understanding, as independent states by determining their bilateral maritime boundary through brief and friendly talks. This boundary has stood the test of time. Their mutual affinity and cooperation have helped in building their bilateral relations and encouraging their two regions, ASEAN and SAARC to come closer together. The mutual attraction of the two peoples has been real and lasting. Their friendship is based on a common philosophy and has, therefore, helped maintain their continuing understanding.

Mutuality of Interests

When the Second World War ended both India and Indonesia were ready, indeed impatient for self-rule and total independence from colonial control. While departing, the British left India partitioned, and in the midst of a virtual civil war, imposing a senseless fratricidal blood-bath across the two vivisected countries. In Indonesia, the Dutch colonial rulers showed a disinclination to depart, amicably or peacefully. The struggle for liberation from colonial rulers, therefore, became violent, and the guerilla war against the Dutch had to be fought for several years. Post-Independence, the young Indonesian guerilla warriors formed the core of the new Indonesian army. As time went on this army claimed, within their own constitutional system, certain political, administrative and military functions in their society and country. India was able, during the struggle for freedom, to provide some material and considerable psychological assistance to Indonesians who were then fighting for liberation from the colonial yoke under Sukarno's leadership. Even at this early stage the two peoples realised the advantage of building mutually strong political and strategic cooperation and friendship.

On becoming free and sovereign nations, in the Bandung Conference they collaborated to sow the seeds of non-aligned thinking. Panchsheela doctrine was enunciated. While India and China used Panchsheela as the basis for their respective foreign policies, Indonesia chose to establish another set of five principles also called Panchsheela, in their Constitution as the nation's guiding philosophy.

The Asian continent can be subdivided into several distinct regions: West Asia including the Gulf; Southeast Asia; South Asia; East Asia; and Central Asia. The two regions spanned by India and Indonesia are South Asia and South-east Asia, and the two regional organisations structured in the last decades, covering the two countries are: the SAARC and the ASEAN. The ASEAN, in these last decades, has emerged as a very successful cohesive and result-oriented regional organisation, and an instrument for real cooperation. The SAARC is still struggling to evolve in the same direction. This progress has not been without occasional hiccups. The one fact worth noting here is that Indonesia is the largest element and the real anchor of the ASEAN; and likewise India is the largest country and the anchor for the SAARC region. Both these large and far-flung nations have very long coastlines and are endowed with large populations and multi-ethnic; multi-religious; multi-cultural; multi-linguistic societies. Their histories, traditions, tolerance and vision for the future have remained constant. Both have been deeply impacted by the ancient Hindu classical epics, Ramayana and Mahabharata, as also the values and principles of Islam. In India, out of the total population of a billion plus, the largest minority is of the Muslims, a community of a hundred and forty million approximately. Indonesia is now the fourth most populous nation of the world and remains basically and broadly an Islamic nation, with Hindu and Christian and other minority communities.

Various Western historians and, geographers have described Islam's impact on Asia as meriting study from three angles; one, overlooking the Indian Ocean, from the Red Sea and the Persian Gulf, and controlling the endless chain of deserts stretching across Asia from Arabia to China; two,

Islam in India, with its influence extending throughout the Indian Ocean region, both east and west of the Cape Comorin; and the third that of Buddhism that went east into China, and deep into the heart of Asia. All this influenced at the same time, a maritime culture and force that over the centuries came to control the seas and lands of the Indian Ocean, and even bordering the Pacific Ocean.

The South Asian and East Asian archipelagos and land mass were described by earlier historians as the logical confluence and cross-roads of trade, lying at the centre of an enormously rich and super-productive region that today comprises the Indonesian East Indies. Geography placed India/Indonesia region on the edge of Asia, half way between China and Japan and India, as also the countries of the western part of the Indian Ocean and around it. The two Asian super powers in both economic and strategic sense that emerged in the earlier eras were China and India. There were times when both were enormously prosperous, and in control of themselves, simultaneously engaged in multi-faceted external activities. The centre of gravity of the Far-East remained, for longer or shorter periods, close to the Malay peninsula and the islands of Sumatra and Java. The two sleeping giants, China and India, were both slow to wake to the apprehensions around them, and also invariably acted slowly and with deliberation.

India's interest in the East Indies was expressed through the work of her sailors, merchants and missionaries, who through the centuries spread the message of Buddhism, Hinduism and Islam in this region, informing and covering the peoples of Archipelago. The Islands remained part Buddhist, some converting over a period of centuries from Hinduism to Islam. Chinese and Indian traders made the islands of the East Indies "a busy crossroad of trade" for many centuries, and created what Braudel calls "the super world economy" of Asia with levels of economic and social development exceeding those of contemporary Europe.

India and Indonesia acknowledge that ASEAN and India are no awkward strangers. We have been neighbours and friends in time and space of existence for as long back as either can remember. Our habits, customs and social mores, our myths, our legends, our cuisine, our arts, crafts designs remain our shared legacy.

Long pilgrim trails wind their way through our lands. Our merchants and traders linked us together for centuries through their functioning in the Indian Ocean and the Bay of Bengal. There were other traders that went across land and mountain routes plying their wares in our towns and markets. In every aspect of India's ethos one can see the footprints of Southeast Asia. The eminent post-Independence historian Sardar K.M. Panikkar, noted that the victory of the Portuguese along the Goa coast in early16th century helped Portugal lay the foundation of Europe's mastery of the Eastern Seas, and this continued for more than four hundred years. The Portuguese were followed by the Dutch, the British and the French in that order, in this area. The maritime links between India and Southeast Asia soon came to be dominated by Europeans, and as a result of these European initiatives and operations, Chinese and Indian traders started fading out until they more or less abandoned what in the Chola period had been their maritime vigour and dynamism. The Europeans dominated this part of the world through the operations of their naval and maritime fleets. And all this went on unabated until the 1950s, when colonial powers declined in our region and finally withdrew from here.

Jawaharlal Nehru agreed with K.M. Panikkar's thesis that Europe came to dominate Asia, only through their naval and maritime organisation and functioning. Nehru tended to see India's relations improving and consolidating with the rest of Asia, specially East Asia, in terms of India building closer maritime relations with all the major Asian countries, specially Indonesia.

It was with a view to build closer relationship with Asian and Afro-Asian nations that he convened the First Asian Relations Conference in New Delhi in 1947 and went on to encourage the holding of the Asian-African Conference at Bandung in 1955. This effort was to define and build a new post-colonial relationship amongst the newly independent countries of the region. These conferences were important milestones; and made it easy for India to re-define its relations with Southeast Asia. The dispute concerning the Himalayan border which created tensions between India and China, as also the Vietnam War, affected the nations of the region by dividing them. Asian nations were already looking outside the region for seeking cooperation and friendship rather than exploring the prospects for a deeper pan-Asian relationship.

In the late 1970s, India reviewed and re-explored its relations with Southeast Asian countries, to enable it to seek an increased share of trade and investment by gradually moving, away from its earlier inward looking and imports-substitution model of industrialisation. The 1970s, as a result, saw a significant increase in India-ASEAN trade. Even this, however, remained limited in scope, and marginal to the corporate plans of Indian industry and trade. While both India and the ASEAN countries became aware of each other's sizes and, importance, trade cooperation remained a low priority for both. India's trade with ASEAN countries in

1971–72 was a mere 1.5 per cent of her total world exports and 0.39 per cent in terms of its total world imports. By 1978–79 these shares had gone up to 4.2 per cent and 5.2 per cent, respectively. With all this, India has remained keenly aware of the importance and value of its links with Indonesia.

India's Look-East policy must be seen as a part of the country's recognition that Southeast Asia is India's 'proximate neighbourhood'. In the context of Southeast Asia, Indonesia is viewed by India, and the world, as the principal anchor for stability in Southeast Asia.

The list of problems faced by India and Indonesia, covers many weighty domestic ones, and a few external ones. Both countries are multi-ethnic, multi-religious, multi-linguistic, multi-cultural, broadly open, tolerant, patient and possessing a clear intangible quality for survival which they recognise has helped build their own philosophical and physical resilience.

Until the decade of the seventies of the 20th century, some foreigners used to ask the rhetorical question: "Will India, can India, survive?" We need not feel either amused or complacent about certain foreigners wondering aloud whether or not both Asia and Indonesia might be diminished through energising certain factors that can combat Indonesian territorial integrity. We must recognise that after the manner in which Yugoslavia has been fractured recently, and continues to suffer through the revival of the spectre of the 19th century Balkan Wars, Asians cannot afford to be complacent. We should not doubt that Indonesia will emerge from its current, nation-building problems with its sovereignty and territorial integrity unaffected; capable of re-structuring the sinews of its national strength and economic prosperity.

The Challenge of Political Stability in Indonesia

The advent of the new millennium finds Indonesia going through a period of change not entirely without pain and apprehensions. Indonesia has remained, and continues to remain, a power entity considered not at all threatening the interest of any of its neighbours. All the major world powers, USA, Russia, China, Japan, India, EU and the countries of ASEAN, SAARC and APEC recognise this benign aspect of Indonesia's power structure.

Twenty per cent of Indonesian GDP comes from oil and gas. Its soil is tremendously productive and, throughout history, the country has produced the bulk of the world's high valued spices. What has kept Indonesia strong, however, is the resilience it has acquired through wisdom.

President Abdurrahman Wahid, characterised by some foreign observers as a man both serious and occasionally eccentric, tried to limit the power of his own presidency and became open, flexible, accessible, tolerant, patient and compassionate. He has tried to contain the visible interference of the military in politics and economy. He has made high profile efforts to forge political and strategic partnerships with China, India, Japan and the industrialised and economically successful East Asian states. At the same time, he allowed his Foreign Minister to go on record to state: "Indonesia should be aware of the endeavour of Western states who have shown an increasing tendency to impose their political agenda on developing countries by employing economic and political, pressures and sanctions." President Wahid even as an Islamic thinker and preacher, advocated a closer relationship between Indonesia and the Jewish state of Israel, having made a well publicised visit to that country.

The recent ethnic, religious and sometimes social violence which has been erupting in Indonesia is indicative of the people's growing impatience. The visible controls over civil society established by the military during the Suharto period have made people impatient and angry. Both the president and vice-president have refused to see the turmoil in Indonesia as a symbol, or a signal, for ethnic separatism.

The need of the hour is to deepen democracy in the country through humane governance, and to face the economic challenge by creating an environment for development which betokens the nation's idealism, resilience and capacity to cope with challenges that have recently arisen, and continue to tax the ingenuity of the government and the nation, in coping.

The Indonesian Armed Forces had inherited the mantle of the original participants in the country's War of Independence against the Dutch when Indonesian youth fought as a citizen's guerilla force. Over the decades, their belief in their right to play a role in the political life of the country was forced on the Indonesians. Sukarno thought of many of them as personal friends and comrades. The second president, General Suharto chose to base power structure entirely on the support of the military. General Nasution who was the Army Chief in the late fifties articulated the thesis that Indonesia must follow a middle-road between the military's total involvement in politics as exemplified in Latin American societies, and their total depoliticisation as in the case of the Western democracies. In due course this came to be known as the doctrine of "*Dwifungsi*" or the dual function of the Armed Forces. In 1982, President Suharto enshrined this term as part of the country's constitutional system.

Western powers had indicated that in case of the military resisting the expansion of civilian authority in the country, there would be no support or assistance available to them from the West. During a visit to Jakarta in January 2000, the US Permanent Representative to the U.N., Ambassador Richard Holbrooke stated rather bluntly: "What we are watching is a great drama, a struggle between the forces of democracy and reform, and the forces of backward-looking corruption and militarism. However, a balance had to be maintained in the process of diminishing the military's power and influence within the national political life because the country's radical Islamic segments did not favour overly harsh action against senior Muslim officers."

Indonesia is important for the safety, stability and prosperity of the Asian region. It is the world's fourth most populous country; controls strategic sea-lanes through which pass forty per cent of the world's commerce, including eighty per cent of Japan's oil supply and seventy per cent of South Korea's. Prior the East Asian and Pacific region plunging into the economic crisis of August 1997, Indonesian economy had an averaged seven per cent growth over the previous twenty-five years despite the fact that the country was riddled with corruption and inefficiency.

Indonesia recognised the need for economic reforms. While Jakarta has been slow to implement the kind of thorough-going and in-depth reform the size and shape of the economic crisis has forced them towards de-investment and further privatisation.

Indonesian economic and political changes have to be seen together. The Western powers, especially United States, recognised quickly their stake in preventing Indonesia descending into total chaos. They recognised that chaos in

Indonesia could threaten nascent economic recovery then under way elsewhere in the Asian region. They also recognised that chaos in Indonesia would affect the important passage through the sea-lanes which were under Jakarta's control, and it would jeopardise the commercial interests of the USA.

Washington has faced the challenge manfully and does recognise the imperative need to accept a role in facilitating Indonesian transformation to a more open economic and political system. For this both Indonesia and the USA recognised the need to define their common interest in ensuring that the following possibilities are realised:

(i) Offer assistance to appropriate non-governmental organisations which could ensure that the three major voting processes during 1999 were continued peacefully and credibly and that these be enabled to contribute to the strengthening consolidation of democracy;

(ii) Declare that the world, including the USA, would keenly watch the process and outcome of Indonesian voting exercise of 1999;

(iii) To avoid permitting international peace-keeping commitments in East Timor which may contribute towards permitting the conflict to remain in place without solving the underlying differences between the parties;

(iv) Put pressure on Indonesia to implement the economic reforms, and to rely on IMF assistance to solve its economic problems;

(v) Promote reforms in Indonesian military and consider re-building ties with the military once it agrees to act responsibly through the three voting processes within Indonesia in 1999.

With this aim in view the US restored Indonesia's participation in the International Military Education and Training Programme so as to help strengthen Indonesian military's professionalism, civilian control and respect for human rights.

To a large extent, of late, political developments in Indonesia have had a positive impact on Indonesian asset markets. As the Indonesian political system functions to create a climate of political certainty, it would be possible to expect relief. The path being taken by the asset markets at the present moment, will not be easy or straight, given the likely twists and turns in the political landscape in the interim period. However, the overall prospects in view of whatever economic help and backing Indonesia may require, should be considered positive in the context of the entire region and the sea-lanes yearning for greater stability. However, all bets will be off if political chaos in this country gets resuscitated and intensified because then the investor and consumer confidence would get badly damaged. The economic, growth forecast so far for Indonesia this year has remained at 2.7 per cent. The economic and non-economic factors in respect of Indonesia must not be permitted to become further negative.

The story goes on; and so does the uncertainty.

3
Political Transition in Post-Suharto Indonesia

Baladas Ghoshal

The forced resignation of President Suharto in May 1998 after a period of economic, social, and political turmoil has opened up both opportunities and challenges for the new Indonesian leadership. On the one hand, it had served a blow to the authoritarian forces in the country, freed Indonesians from a claustrophobic and oppressive political system, and thus created the opportunities and possibilities for a more open and accountable system. On the other hand, the absence of a democratic tradition in the country; a weak civil society without experience in social and political mobilisation, as well as in party-building; a continuing culture of corruption in the judiciary and the bureaucracy; slow progress in bringing Suharto era culprits to account; regional assertions with separatist movements due to the weakening of the central authority and declining state capability; ethnic and communal violence manifested in ongoing bloodshed in

Aceh, Moluccas and Kalimantan; restless soldiers, religious tensions, a static economy and heavy debt; and finally the threat of impeachment of a president whose stubborn, erratic and confrontationist behaviour and style together with the lack of sight is now recognised as an impediment to good government — all have made the transition a challenging and a difficult one. In fact, now nearly three years after the fall of Suharto, Indonesia is still experiencing the birth pangs of democracy and struggling to, what the famous Indonesian literary figure Goenawan Mohammad termed, 'reinvent' at every stage of the transition. As a result, it displays all the characteristics of the transition from authoritarian political system to a democratic one a simultaneous process of decay and renewal. While there has been a general breakdown of whatever institutions Suharto had put in place to keep a tight rein on his people, yet one can witness both at the national and local levels emergence of groups and forces of renewal slowly laying the foundations of a civil society and democracy.

While the rest of the region has somehow recovered from the great Asian economic crisis, Indonesia, the largest country in Southeast Asia, is still under economic and political turmoil causing serious concern about the very survival of the country. The downfall of Suharto in May 1998 was celebrated as heralding the birth of a 'new Indonesia', and a 'second independence' from the oppressive rule of their own ruler and its worst manifestations in the form of "cronyism, corruption and collusion" (KKN). The change brought rising expectation and a hope that it would usher Indonesia towards democracy, good governance, transparency and accountability of its new leaders. More than three years after the changeover, the rising expectations continue but the hope has somewhat dimmed as the country plunges into political, economic, ethnic and religious turmoil halting the movement towards demilitarising its society and establishing democracy in the country.

Indonesia's greatest challenges in the months ahead, therefore, are fundamentally political. Inseparable from the challenge of political integration and the deepening of democracy through humane governance and creation of institutions, which can mediate the various conflicting interests in the country, is the economic challenge of creating a stable environment for a fully integrated and vibrant national economy. At this time of transition, political stability and economic developments are inter-linked. Without one the other will suffer which makes it imperative that both must proceed together. That makes the task of governance more formidable for the new government. While recovering from an economic crisis, Indonesia is trying to complete its transition to a democratic society, and embark on an ambitious programme of decentralisation. "Any one of these challenges would test any country. For Indonesia, the task can sometimes seem overwhelming," to quote Mark Baird, World Bank's country director for Indonesia.[1] Mark Malloch Brown, head of the United Nations Development Programme (UNDP) also considers Indonesia's current problems as a 'democratic birth-pains problem' when he says that one can not expect " . . . this government to solve all the problems. A first government elected under these circumstances has a double crisis. It lacks the legitimacy and the consensus within its own ranks to take certain bold decisions. Yet, on the other hand, because it is the first democratic government there is a huge crisis of expectations. . . it is caught between those weak capacities and those huge aspirations for it."[2]

Arguably what is happening in Indonesia is that freedom has begun to take hold in daily life and to break down layer upon layer of distress and cruelty that was imposed on them by an authoritarian system. The result is messy, since the new freedom has given rise to "million little mutinies," the colliding trajectories of countrymen shaking off the old servile mind-sets of unquestioned submission and conformity to the regime in power. This turmoil marks the road to progress. This is compounded by the fact that since the economic crisis of 1997, Indonesia's per capita annual income has fallen from US $1,300 to US $650, leading to a great downturn in social stability and an increase in political violence resulting from anger, frustration, and primordial fears. Indonesians, by and large had lost their faith and trust in their government.

People's faith and trust, however, could be restored only if there was a government that could empathise with the people and their aspirations; had the courage to decentralise and devolve power to the provinces together with the ability to undertake better communication between the state and its sectarian and ethnic minorities; and could pursue cultural tolerance and fairness in the form of constitutional safeguards for the disadvantaged. Juwono Sudarsono, a leading Indonesian political scientist and former cabinet minister, puts it aptly: "The ideals of democratization must be translated into effective programmes of democratic consolidation incorporating the diversity of religious affinity, provincial identity, as well as linguistic and ethnic origin... that effort can only be done through a strong commitment to social justice reinforced by inter-religious tolerance that matches cultural diversity with national citizenship. These constitute the fundamental elements of coherent, measured and durable democratization across all levels of Indonesian society."[3]

The government that took over in October 1999 under the leadership of Abdurrahman Wahid and Megawati Sukarnoputri as president and vice-president, respectively, was a legitimate one, the result of a fair election and parliamentary processes and was committed to an inclusive style of policy-making, economic recovery and national unity. Under their leadership, Indonesia was becoming more liberal and humane in many ways as the harsh policies of the Suharto's thirty-two years of rule were overturned. There is now a much more vibrant public debate about critical issues facing the country. Civil society groups and media who had been muzzled under Suharto are now flourishing. The treatment of minorities was changing as the official discrimination against the Chinese language and other aspects of ethnic identity was being removed. The government had been non-partisan in addressing religious conflicts in the Maluku and elsewhere. Wahid was trying to put substance into effective governance through his belief in social empowerment and the vital role of religious and cultural leaders in peacefully resolving tensions and conflicts at the grassroot level. His government had generally followed the IMF and World Bank prescriptions for the economy, earning itself the international goodwill and the foreign investor's confidence, at least until mid-2000 when the stand-off with the IMF began over the implementation of further economic reforms. Steps were also taken to increase revenues by continuing with the privatisation programme, by speeding up the selling off assets inherited from bankrupt banks and companies and by increasing the numbers who pay tax and the amount paid. To help spur economic growth and recovery, foreign investment, either direct or portfolio was welcomed, provided the investors wanted to help Indonesia as much as they wanted to make profits. Indonesia's ethnic Chinese were encouraged to repatriate funds thought to be stashed abroad and the diplomatic corps were turned into a super trade agency to help boost flagging exports, thankfully matched by equally flagging imports. The economy generally looked a little healthier as it started to grow again by between four and five per cent in 2000 while inflation was brought under control. Incomes and purchasing power seemed to have returned to eighty per cent of pre-crisis levels, and utilisation of industrial capacity also seemed to have reached an average of sixty per cent. As a result, poverty had been reduced from the high-crisis levels. Indonesians began to feel that their life and prospects were improving. More foreigners could be seen around Indonesia's capital interested in finding out what was going on and about business prospects.

While it enjoyed the trust of the people, it also faced huge expectations that it would bring instant relief to those hardest hit by the lingering recession. Until August 2000, Wahid's government was based on compromises and included a hodge-podge (Indonesian gado-gado) of reformers, holdovers from Suharto's ruling Golkar, and representatives of the military. The government's economic team had different party allegiances that, to the extent that they were pulled in different directions, constituted an obstacle to cohesion, as these people espoused a variety of views. As a result, economic policy-making was half-hearted and was based on adhoc measures. It lacked cohesion and could not address the problems at the root of the ailing economy. After sidelining the military and consolidating democracy, Wahid's government was under increasing pressure to speed up economic reforms or risk losing the fragile gains in stability it had achieved. Renewed growth has reduced the incentive to push ahead with painful changes in Indonesia's financial, legal and tax systems, where local vested interests, corruption and inefficiency continue to deter urgently needed investment. Without real structural change, it was feared, the consumption-led recovery would dissipate and Indonesia will face a long period of stagnation, as have other countries that refused to tackle financial system and corporate problems. There was unease too among business leaders and foreign investors of reports of continuing divisions over policy in Wahid's multi-party coalition government and among his economic advisers.

That situation was expected to change with the installation in August 2000 of a new cabinet, leaner and revamped and whose members were closer to Wahid. While the second cabinet of Wahid was more homogenous than the first one, it had also faced criticisms from the public on the ground that in selecting its members the president gave higher priority to loyalty than to competence and expertise. The cabinet included a couple of dubious ministers whom he continued to irrationally defend to his coalition partners. It also had a very narrow support base in the parliament as the largest party, PDI-P, has only one representative, and second largest, Golkar, had none in it. With the parliament increasingly becoming assertive, both the president and his cabinet became vulnerable to criticism. The threat of impeachment of the president was constantly hanging over Wahid's head like Damocles' sword. During the time that Gus Dur had been in power, he had managed to upset friends and foes, politicians and legislators by making controversial statements. He had risked lawsuits by making unproven accusations of corruption and other wrongdoings by politicians and even members of his first cabinet. To the frustration of his supporters he showed no intention to correct his erratic behaviour or change his style. He had even given his opponents further ammunition by neglecting to correct his habit of using private account to keep large amounts of money that had been donated for government administrative purposes. Two cases — one of US $2 billion for relief work in Aceh by Sultan of Brunei and another Rp. 1 billion from an Indonesian businessman which went largely to the funding of Papua people's Congress in Irian Jaya in July 2000 — were particular instances and which eventually were important ammunition for his removal from the presidency, where Wahid had not taken special care to distinguish between public and private spheres. With the Bulog-gate, Brunei-gate[4] and alleged sex scandals, Wahid's popularity rating went down so much that most people wanted him to quit. The tremendous goodwill and trust with which he began his office turned into serious doubt, even among his well-wishers, about his ability to govern effectively. Misgivings about his increasingly capricious ways and limited ability to grapple with Indonesia's formidable problems had steadily sapped the will of the *reformasi* movement — the collection of students, pressure groups and disguised middle class people who helped to bring down Suharto and to install the first democratic government in four decades.

Reinvention and the Need for Institutional Reforms

Indonesia is now in such a challenging phase of transition that practically all institutions need reform and rejuvenation to create genuine democratic institutions and a democratic culture. Indonesia does not have a tradition of democratic political culture and movements. Even if it tried to practice parliamentary democracy in the early years of independence, the political parties were highly faction-ridden and were based on personalities rather than on organised grassroots support. Political changes in the past had never been the product of any sustained, disciplined and organised political movements with grassroots support, but always had been the result of sudden and short bursts of movements arising from economic crisis and heightened political tension. Such changes need not necessarily lead to democracy. On the contrary, it may even bring anarchy unless channeled and regulated by a responsible and accountable leadership. To consolidate such changes along democratic lines, there is a need for organised collective action based on political party building and routinised patterns of elite recruitment, essential conditions for grassroots democracy. Democratisation requires consolidation of nation-wide organised collective behaviour. It also requires an acceptance and a commitment to respect pluralism reflecting the diversity of religious affinity, provincial identity, as well as linguistic and ethnic origin. Political parties that have been formed in the post-Suharto era have not been able to overcome the shortcomings of the old party system characterised by narrow sectarian interests and lack of organisational capacity. They still rely for the societal support on their leaders rather than on collective action based on party-building, elite recruitment and constructive programme and action at the grassroots level. All the three new major political parties — PDI-P, PKB and PAN — are known not by their disciplined organisational party machinery which is able to mediate the interests of their supporters, but their charismatic leaders —

Megawati, Abdurrahman Wahid and Amien Rais, respectively. The process of 'reinvention' and democratisation, therefore, was going to be long and difficult — until the time when the political parties of Indonesia will be able to transform themselves from 'partai tokoh' (parties of prominent individuals) to parties with disciplined cadres and committed members based on organised collective behaviour.

Policies and leadership are not enough for good governance. Wahid inherited weak governance and market institutions. Strong vested interests from the past continue to hold considerable power, and a highly centralised bureaucracy is also ill-equipped to respond to the public's rising expectations. A strong, professional and impartial bureaucracy is an essential requirement for that. In this respect also, Indonesia had the misfortune of having a weak tradition of impartiality and professionalism in government bureaucracies. More importantly, after the economic crisis hit the country since 1997 much of the civil service is in a state of demoralisation and inertia as a result of cuts in their real salary and perquisites as well as allegations of corruption. An efficient, strong and organised civil service is very crucial at this period of transition not only for serving their inexperienced ministers and to carry through the democratisation process and decentralisation initiatives, but also to see that administratively the country does not fall apart. At the moment, the administration is encountering great problems in coordinating the intricate steps to decentralisation, because provincial planning boards, regional governments and local universities often lack expertise and practical know-how.

Indonesia's judiciary and legal system, likewise, are notoriously corrupt. Justice sector reform happens to be the single largest priority. Everything else, including bank restructuring and private sector workouts, depend on the legal system. Judges but also prosecutors, court administrators, the police and prison administrators need to be part of the reform process. It will require civil service reform, as well as to instill in government officials the concept of public service, accountability and performance-based management. The new government has few effective levers with which to enforce economic reforms and control the military. With Indonesia's armed forces being blamed for past abuses of Suharto era, no official or machinery of government is willing to take any decision or action for fear of becoming a scapegoat. Lack of cohesion in the government imposes limitation on its ability to address the national issues coherently and firmly, providing further grounds to the disgruntled elements within the society to indulge in greater violence in their responses by rejecting the authority of the state. A steady hand on the instruments of governance, therefore, becomes an imperative for stabilisation of the polity and democratisation. For having that grip over the administration, Indonesia requires not only a competent and an efficient bureaucracy, but also one that can adept itself to the changing needs and acquires new skills to perform the desired goals and tasks. Juwono Sudarsono rightly points out the challenges before the Indonesian bureaucracy when he says: "The paradox of democratic reform is that as state intervention is reduced to allow for a higher degree of freedom and efficiency, the public bureaucracy's technical skills must be improved in order to deliver the required public goods: enforceable legal codes, improvement of human capital through selective vocational skills and retraining programmes, competent and effective environmental protection for future generations. The bureaucracy must also provide an effective social safety net for the desperate and the despondent."[5]

A competent bureaucracy is all the more important now as there has been a general breakdown of law and order and visible erosion of authority of the state in controlling its affairs. The iron rule of Suharto is gone but many 'mini Suhartos' have suddenly appeared in the various parts of the country in the form of Mafia gangs and protection rings. As we have noted earlier, the judicial system of Indonesia had been notorious for its inefficiency and corruption. As most members of that service started their career during the peak of the corruption era, they are still part of the corruption syndicate and court the Mafia. Common men have lost their faith and confidence in the legal system of the state and are taking resort to 'street justice' by setting on fire or murdering someone caught in trivial crimes. With crime rates and distrust of the police on the rise, justice in Indonesia is increasingly being meted out on the street, a symptom of the growing anarchy. As a result, vigilante killings have become "an epidemic."[6] In an atmosphere of challenging transition to democracy, Indonesian legal institutions have been struggling to cope, creating an enforcement void that increasingly is filled by vigilantism. Now that Indonesia is a democracy, people feel like they can do anything they want, and the police have done little to generate confidence in their crime-fighting abilities, or to discourage people from taking the law into their own hands. The police also have done little to stem mob violence. Vigilantes are rarely arrested. Even when violence is occurring close to them, the police have been loath to respond. While the country's press is unusually free to speak on any political or economic area, there is also certain restraint on writing on sensitive issues, particularly on Islam for fear of mob violence, which has also become a major excuse for inaction on the part of the law-enforcing authorities. After Indonesia's armed forces being blamed for past abuses of Suharto era, no official or machinery of government is willing to take any decision or action for fear of becoming a scapegoat.

This is what has happened in Kalimantan where the army remained inactive in the first few days of the outbreak of ethnic violence by the Dayaks against the Madurese, and allowed the situation to deteriorate on the pretext that the maintenance of law and order was not under their domain, rather the responsibility of the police, which now has been separated from the armed forces. The army found it convenient to put the blame on the police for inept handling of the situation. It may even be possible that the army remained inactive at the initial stage by design only to prove the inefficiency of the police and its own indispensability in times of crisis so that it can reestablish its supremacy over other political forces in the country. Over the last few weeks, many army leaders, including the army chief of staff, Endriartono Sutarto, have been issuing statements highlighting the failure of the police service to maintain law and order and indicating the possibility of the army again taking over the functions of internal security. Undoubtedly there is a rivalry between the police and army, a divide deepened when President Wahid formally split the two last year. Whatever might be the logic behind their half-hearted attempt to bring the situation under control in Kalimantan, or elsewhere, it is also true that the army today is overstretched and ill-equipped to handle social and political violence on such a large scale as it is happening today in Indonesia. Part of the reason for its failure to maintain law and order in the country is also due to its meagre resources and lack of equipment, particularly after the economic crisis, to be sufficiently mobile and rapid in its reaction to such widespread disturbances. Partly it was also due to the division within the armed forces between those who are willing to adjust to the new environment of a reduced role for the armed forces in the politics of the country, and those who resent the change, the so-called 'rogue elements', and have been trying to undermine the present government by either fomenting trouble or taking partisan role in the on-going ethnic and sectarian clashes. Even high-ranking Indonesian government officials now admit of the factional rivalry within the armed forces and the lack of coordination between the central and local commands. As for the police in Indonesia, as the fundamental institution in maintaining public order, it is basically overstretched and undermanned to play an effective role in protective security. There are now only 200,000 in the police force, one policeman to thirteen hundred persons in the population.

While the above symptoms of decay and breakdown of institutions have created a growing sense of scepticism among the country's elite groups about the prospect of democracy, one can also witness a lot of creativity and rejuvenation at the grassroots level. Practically all the forces that were pushing for change during the anti-Suharto agitation have joined the government, leaving the opposition quite weak and confused. This has led to the emergence of outside groups who are now taking the actual lead in laying down foundations for a civil society capable of pushing for change. Throughout Indonesia, previously uninvolved teachers, workers, journalists, poets and novelists are breaking away from the corporatism of the Suharto regime, and are creating a whole range of new institutions. These aim to fight corruption, resist violence and work for human rights. They call them Corruption Watch, Parliament Watch, Military Watch and their numbers are increasing. One such organisation is Commission of Missing Persons and Victims of Violence (Kontras), and it is helping people at both national and local levels to set up many such institutions and initiate them to political activism. They are now beginning to question the arbitrary actions of not only political leaders, but also an authoritarian bureaucracy, which was the hallmark of the Suharto regime. They are not prepared to take anything for granted, not even the parliament, which they believe needs to be supervised, as that institution in the past had always been an appendage to the rulers. At the local level, these new groups are making an attempt to control the village military officials (Babinsa) who in the past were all-powerful in each and every aspect of the life in the villages, and are now charging 'security fees' (protection money). They reject today military interference in land conflicts or in the village head elections.[7] In the broader picture of Indonesian politics, they might not have made a major imprint as yet because of the miniscule size of such groups. Seen from a longer perspective, however, the emergence of such citizens watch groups will go a long way not only in the creation of a healthy civil society, but also in laying the foundations for grassroot democracy in Indonesia.

The Armed Forces and Scale Down of *Dwifungsi*

The declining state capability in the allocation of resources and the maintenance of order has major implications for the unity and stability of the country. In the past, the armed forces of the country were regarded as the main instrument for keeping the various centrifugal forces under control. In the post-Suharto period, the military, in particular the army, is facing a huge crisis of confidence amongst the people as accusations continue to grow over its alleged rights abuses in the past. The TNI, formerly called ABRI, now is perceived neither as a friend of the people nor as a moderator within the political landscape. Instead of being a solution to the problem, it has now become a part of it. While the TNI will increasingly find itself ill-equipped to play its old role in the new world, it is unwilling to relinquish its privileges and power. The military is divided over its dual functions. One group wants the military to end all of its socio-political practices. Any military personnel occupying non-military positions must quit TNI through early retirement or else they must leave their position. Another group wants the military to shun day-to-day political practices, including the seats in the parliament (DPR), but to retain it in MPR, which is not involved in political activities. Still another group wants the THI to shun not only politics, but also business activities as this diverts military's attention from its primary functions as the defender of the country's security. For them, business ethics and military ethics are not complementary and hence the military must stay away from business. There is yet another group of officers, who want the military to shun politics without having to lift rulings on the dual function. All in all, TNI officers want military personnel to improve their professionalism. So long the military remains politically active, establishment of civilian governance becomes tenuous. A nagging tussle between the civilian government's attempts to sideline the military and latter's desire to cling on to the levers of power will continue for quite some time to come. On the one hand, military personnel would have to adopt themselves to reform policies. On the other hand, civilian officials also must reform themselves by improving their administrative capability, avoiding corrupt, collusive and nepotistic practices and ending their old habit of looking for political support from the military. In a revealing interview with the *Jakarta Post*, the then defence minister Juwono Sudarsono conceded that the military may in some case be a source of insecurity, as some individuals or groups within the military seek to line their own pockets by participating in and/or protecting illegal mining operations.[8] The mines which have been forced to temporarily close down operations are often those who had lost favour with the military by refusing to pay for protection, or attempted to stop it "helping itself", or are selling concessions which are not theirs to sell. Indeed, since the fall of Suharto, the military has become even more active in areas such as illegal logging and mining and also in protection racket for illegal enterprises in those fields. Information on the scale of involvement is patchy due partly to the fact that these operations take place in remote areas, but it has been a common secret for many years. The isolated nature of these operations makes it even more likely that financial exploitation (with Wahid's and now Megawati's inadvertent blessings) will take place. The forty per cent or so of the troops living outside camps and mixing directly with the civilians have the chance to supplement their meagre income in a variety of other ways. They are sometimes behind organised gambling, prostitution and drug trafficking. They also have been hired out to factory workers facing industrial unrest. Such octopus-like economic grip of the military spread over the country cannot be removed so easily in the near future. To quote Juwono: "Removing the military from economic interests is a big adjustment process . . . it must be steady and comfortable . . . . We must be willing to tolerate a degree of corruption for the foreseeable future. . . perhaps as many as five more years. If we move too quickly there must be repercussions."[9]

The challenge before the government is to scale down the *dwifungsi* role of the armed forces in the politics of the country in order to make the democratic process more credible. At the same time it has to be undertaken in such a manner so as not to provoke a backlash from the TNI. Presently, the task before the government is to re-equip and reform the military, to put it again in the words of Juwono Sudarsono, the first civilian defence minister and the person who was mostly responsible for steering the transition, "not as an instrument of stability at all cost or repression but as part of the infrastructure of democracy subject to graduated civilian authority, standards of military professionalism, the rule of law and respect for human rights."[10] The removal of Wiranto from Wahid's first cabinet and subsequent reshuffle within the armed forces' hierarchical structure had helped Wahid, at least for a certain period, to establish his own control over the organisation. He formed a coalition with reform-minded generals within TNI who were prepared to give up its *dwifungsi* role to make the organisation more professional and devote itself to its traditional security functions. However, over the last year with Wahid's stand-off with the legislature and the possibility of impeachment, he had lost much of his control over the TNI, when during a reshuffle at the top hierarchy of the armed forces he could not install people of his choice to important command positions. The first sign of loosening of Wahid's grip over the military was the fate of reformer Lt. Gen. Agus Wirahadikusuma who, under pressure from old-guard generals, was dumped from his powerful position as head of the strategic command (KOSTRAD) even though Wahid himself made the appointment. Moreover, as the country plunged into further violence and instability, the generals were able to retake some of their lost grounds and reassert their position. The military was successful in taking a moral ground of constitutional legitimacy when it resisted President Wahid's efforts in early February to declare a state of emergency and freeze parliament[11] to save himself from the prospect of impeachment. Not only that, to show their unhappiness with Wahid, all thirty-eight military representatives stood up in parliament in February to endorse the memorandum of censure and finally the impeachment proceedings against him. In the last few months of his presidency, the relations between the military and Wahid had been "very precarious". The military leadership made a systematic and concerted attempt to give the impression to the political publics that while they were trying hard to make Indonesia's much-maligned TNI more professional, Wahid "wants to abuse the military to support him in power."[12] To demonstrate their commitment to the constitution of the country, the army leadership had taken a position that in the confrontation between Wahid and the legislature it would protect the office of the president and not the person. Behind their profile of being correct and neutral in the dispute between the executive and legislature by posturing to remain on the side of the constitution, which undoubtedly has restored the fallen image of TNI to a considerable extent, the armed forces leadership simultaneously was deliberately undermining the authority and power of Wahid and coming closer to Megawati, his nemesis and one who was believed to be favouring a honorable position for the armed forces and against drastic move of curtailing its powers and privileges.

Indonesia's military had been seeking greater legal authority to deal with Indonesia's internal unrest and stability. The military is also torn between what it views as its mandated role to preserve the integrity of the Indonesian Republic and strong political and social pressure to reduce its role to purely external defense. While it seeks a compromise that would allow it greater flexibility in dealing with Indonesia's social turmoil, the military will not remain on the sidelines indefinitely. With the police incapable of dealing with the internal unrest and the political leadership immersed in internal factionalism and power plays, the military sees a good opportunity to return to its former role of ensuring internal security and stability. In seeking to reassert itself as an internal security force, the military was backed by Susilo Bambang Yudhoyono, himself a retired general and Indonesia's coordinating minister for political, social and security affairs under Wahid and now under Megawati. In essence, a tacit agreement is now being formed between the military and political elite. This compromise gives the military more autonomy in dealing with Indonesia's security while the political leadership deals with its own issues. Effectively, it creates a dual regime, one political and one military. This may allow the military to quell unrest in areas of Indonesia and allow the political elite to position for power without fear of direct military intervention. However, it will quickly prove an untenable situation. Any move the military makes to deal with separatist actions, illegal migrants or rebellion will have political ramifications. Further, while the military controls the guns, the government controls the budget. Ultimately, be it in Aceh, Irian Jaya, Borneo or even the streets of Jakarta, the separation of the political and military agendas will increasingly prove a failure. This will lead to increased competition between the military and civilian leadership, as each seeks to promote its own agenda above the other. While the political elite remains fractured, the military is pulling together to create a unified front. However reluctantly, the military will once again insert itself firmly into Indonesia's politics, even if only initially to ensure social stability.[13]

As a result, even if the necessity of the military to scale down its *dwifungsi* becomes more compelling, the process itself will not be very smooth. It will take time for the TNI to wean itself from the lever of power and privilege. This was evident in the October 2000 MPR session when despite an earlier agreement to do away with the TNI's reserved seats in the parliament after 2004, it was unanimously extended until 2008. The National Assembly (MPR) also made it harder to bring retroactive charges against top commanders for atrocities. The task of extricating the military from politics and making it more professional is complex. The TNI will continue to exert "a formidable political presence," as the Brussels based Internal Crisis Group had put it, through its territorial organisation which in the past had helped it to consolidate its power at every level of the society and which is still intact. While that reality was clearly understood by Wahid and now by Megawati, the challenge is to modify, or dismantle, the deeply entrenched system without crippling the frontline of national defence. About two-thirds of the army is split into small units and dispersed all over Indonesia in a way that parallels the civilian administration. The five layers of TNI command start at provincial level and reach right down to the village, where non-commissioned officers staff it. More powerful than their bureaucratic counterparts, the military can determine who holds local political posts, from village head to regional secretary. In many cases, provincial governors and other administrators are also army personnel, leading to the virtual militarisation of the society. All departments of government having large funding and budget sources, as well as territories within the country that has exploitable natural resources, like Riau, Aceh and North Sumatra, have always been dominated by the military. According to Cornelis Lay, a lecturer at Gadja Mada University, Jogyakarta, the TNI's willingness to intervene in local politics is largely determined by the economic potential. "The result is that all territorial institutions from top to bottom — even their battle units — become very independent 'business empires'."[14]

While the armed forces will not be able to make a comeback to its old position because of the changed circumstances, domestic as well as international, it will continue to act as a critical factor in the political process of the country until an effective civilian administration capable of running a diverse and strife-torn country like Indonesia emerges. Laksamana Sukardi who was removed by Wahid from his cabinet for his reformist zeal is right when he wrote: "And even the military rollback can not be viewed as permanent if no progress is made on the other fronts that are crucial for moving the country forward politically and economically.

There are already signs that confidence among the top brass of the military is being restored as they watch the civilians spinning their wheels in the mud. Although the danger of a military takeover seems low at the moment, it remains a real possibility in Indonesia, and one that could grow more likely if the government's performance over the coming months is as poor as we have seen in the last few months."[15] Juwono Sudarsono also claimed in a recent interview that legal changes to the status of the military would not ensure a return to barracks until effective civilian administrators can replace military personnel. Juwono is worried by the fact that a severe shortage of funds has eroded the military supply chain and weakened the command over troops in the field.[16]

Ethnic, Communal and Regional Conflicts

A more formidable crisis relates to Indonesia's unity and territorial integrity — whether the country can remain together when it is engulfed in violence and threatened by ethnic and religious separatism. Religion, nationalism and feelings of victimisation have triggered conflict across the archipelago, and some fear the breakup of the world's fourth most populous nation. Whereas Indonesia has been forced to come to terms with an independent East Timor, it faces ongoing strife in Aceh, Irian Jaya, Kalimantan and elsewhere. These are mainly, but not only struggles for autonomy, if not independence. Aceh was the last powerful state to be incorporated into the Netherlands Indies and its independence had previously been guaranteed by international treaty. Even after Indonesia's independence, its first president, Sukarno, had granted a special status for Aceh within the Republic. Therefore, Aceh may have a case for restoration of sovereignty, whereas other potential separatist movements have only a case for ethnic self-determination. Papua's case is even stronger in international law, mainly because of question over the Act of Free Choice in 1969. Aceh still lacks serious international sponsors, and the prospect for an independent West Papua are made less attractive by the problems in Papua New Guinea, and the difficulties in the development of a Papuan leadership and political structures to sustain a modern state. Nevertheless, people in both regions feel utterly alienated from Indonesia by the treatment they received over the last thirty years under the Suharto regime. Megawati was possibly right when she said that if places like East Timor, Papua or Aceh had experienced a benign enlightened democratic Indonesia, they might well have wished to remain a part of it.

Pulled from above and torn from within, the very concept of Indonesian nationhood has come under serious challenge from ethnic and communal conflicts that are raging the country. In one of the most savage outbreaks of ethnic violence to strike in Indonesia in recent years, the indigenous Dayaks in Kalimantan province had beheaded and hacked to death scores of Madurese migrants, including women and children. The fighting followed a series of brutal ethnic clashes that have erupted across Indonesia. The country has struggled to deal with a breakdown of law and order after more than three decades of authoritarian rule and also with the fallout of the former government's forced migration policies. Under Suharto, the government forcibly moved people from every corner of the nation to relieve overcrowding and to dilute the political strength of local ethnic groups. Tensions frequently arose between the newcomers and indigenous population, particularly over jobs and other economic concerns. During the Suharto years they were kept in check by military repression. However, now that Indonesia is struggling with democracy, the military and police have stopped (more precisely overstressed) employing the same tough measures. Although Dayaks and Madurese have coexisted for years, tensions have escalated in recent years over economic issues. Economic rivalry is a factor. Dayaks accuse the Madurese of monopolising stalls at the market and controlling the local bicycle taxi business. Many of the Madurese competing for lower rungs of the economy were recent immigrants fleeing the poverty of their native Madura, desperate for work. The Madurese also established farms on what traditionally had been Dayak land. Dayaks remain the most marginalised Indonesian ethnic community. They rely on the forest and a traditional way of life. The Madurese are generally hot-tempered and resort to violence to resolve disputes. The prosperous newcomers tend to think of the Dayaks as stupid and lazy. The powerless Dayaks see the Madurese as greedy and arrogant. An American journalist covering the mayhem in Kalimantan puts it best: "These economic tensions, added to the age-old stereotypes of the Madurese as clannish, threatening and rude, made it easy to roil the Dayaks. Combine that with the Dayak claim that all Madurese men carry knives, which they are all too willing to use and the Madurese become in Dayak eyes a perfect scapegoat for their woes. It is easier after all to blame the Madurese next door for Dayak problems than the central government in Jakarta."[17]

Violent sectarian conflict has also rocked another province, Moluccas, also known as Maluku. In Ambon, in the Maluku province, violence is based on Christian-Muslim hatred stemming also from the local indigenous people's antipathy towards the outsiders (Bugis, Madurese and Buton

— BMB) that, like many other genuine grievances, were again suppressed under President Suharto. Clashes between Muslims and Christians have prompted calls for an Islamic jihad, or holy war. Tension in Indonesia is based not just on economic hardship, but, as we have mentioned earlier, on transmigration policies of the past thirty years, plus traditional ethnic rivalries. Religion forms only the tip of the iceberg of social conflict in North Maluku. Under-development of the region despite the richness and abundance of its natural resources and hence low levels of education, injustice within the bureaucratic system of the regional government are also major contributors. Sectarian violence obviously is a huge humanitarian tragedy. It has also implications for economic recovery. In many areas, cast adrift by the government, refugees have returned to their families and original villages. In places like Madura, that puts a dramatic strain on an already overburdened local economy. In other places like Sulawesi, officials worry that traumatised and angered by ethnic violence, they will bring their new resentments with them. The refugees created by ethnic violence could be the country's next time bomb. These floating communities, are expelled from their homes in the brush-fire wars, then trapped in disheveled or unfamiliar provinces or even long-forgotten hometown. They contradict the hope that Indonesia can cohere as a pluralist state, with more than three hundred ethnic groups spread across 13,000 islands and speaking some four hundred and fifty languages. They only confirm the fears of those who think the nation might shatter into dozens of fragile 'independent' states.

More than any other province, Aceh is posing the most serious challenge to the unity and integrity of the country. An oil-rich province on the northern tip of Sumatra, Aceh has seen growing demands for a referendum on self-determination in reaction to years of harsh anti-rebel military operations and perceived economic injustices. The Acehnese, like people in many other resource-rich provinces of Indonesia, have long complained about unfair treatment from Jakarta. In particular, this concerns the lopsided distribution of national wealth among the regions. Java, they feel, receives a disproportionate portion of the revenue, much of which is earned by other provinces. The national development efforts are largely concentrated on Java, while revenue-earning provinces are perceived to be lagging behind in development. Aceh is also fiercely Islamic and therefore wants to be guided by the Muslim Sharia Law. The religious issue has been addressed by Jakarta's recognition of the Acehnese rights to have the essential prescriptions of Islamic law applied in their daily lives. Wahid had promised the Acehnese greater autonomy from Jakarta, a move that should ensure that it would, among other things obtain a much fairer share of the revenue it earns from the exploitation of its considerable natural resources. With the military accused of gross human rights abuses in the provinces during the past several decades, Wahid had ordered a thorough investigation of the alleged cases. He had also declared the end of a 'security approach' to deal with the Aceh problem, and instead followed reconciliation and political settlement of the problem. This was evident in the peace agreement signed in Geneva on 12 May last year. Temporarily it may have diffused the situation in Aceh, but it is still regarded as too little too late by the Acehnese. Since then a number of peace talks were held, and despite the ceasefire between the government and the rebel forces, killings and abductions continue in the province with each of the parties suspecting other's hand in the matter. Efforts to find a peaceful solution remain bogged down, in part because GAM itself is divided into eight different factions, and there is little confidence in the ability of the Indonesians to coordinate an effective civil action plan on the ground. Human rights advocates accuse the military of disregarding both the ceasefire and the entreaties from President Wahid to find a peaceful way to resolve the conflict.[18] They contend Indonesian soldiers and police officers are engaged in a brutal, out-of-control campaign to squash the separatist movement through kidnappings, torture and more recently, targeting humanitarian workers. However, activists in Aceh suggest that the rebels, known as GAM (Free Aceh Movement) is also guilty of human rights violations and extortion of money from the local people and businesses.[19] Indonesian and Western intelligence reports indicate an estimated two thousand armed guerrillas — some from as far away as the traditional hotspot of Pidie on the northern coast — have moved into North Aceh district in recent weeks in a calculated move to boost rebel tax collections and to bleed the state of much-needed revenue by forcing the shutdown of the Exxon Mobil Gas fields. The subsequent cut-off in supplies to the giant Arun liquefied-natural-gas facility is costing the government US $100 million a month in lost LNG shipments, not counting losses from the shutting down of related industrial plants. As a result, under strong pressure from the military, the Indonesian government has finally ordered tough new military action against separatist rebels in the northern province of Aceh. The order to the police and military to restore law and order in the province was given in a decree signed by Wahid, who was hesitating to deploy the anti-guerrilla unit because of memories of a series of brutal military crackdowns in the 1990s, traumatising Aceh's population and fuelling the move for independence from Jakarta's heavy-handed rule. The decree deliberately avoids using the words military operation. Yet, it is well known that for months, army generals have been putting pressure on the government to sanction a crackdown on the separatist movement. The announcement was made despite an appeal to the president earlier this week by a delegation of Acehnese leaders to scrap the plans for a military crackdown. The government has officially described the latest move as an effort to bring about a comprehensive solution to the Acehnese problem. The rebels recently were gaining strength, especially as it became increasingly clear that direct peace talks were making little progress. With 30,000 troops already in the province, there are genuine fears the bloodshed will now increase rather than peace being restored.[20]

Decentralisation and Devolution of Power

To deal with such sectarian violence, religious and ethnic separatism, Indonesia needs not only structural and institutional changes as wider autonomy and financial redistribution between the centre and the outer provinces, but also clear-cut, firm and immediate policies that can address the roots of the problem. The government's ability to formulate clear-cut policies or to undertake restructuring was hampered by the lack of cohesion within itself and President Wahid's conflict with the military that had prompted repeated rumors of a coup serious enough for the United States to warn the military to respect the elected government. Even with the new cabinet not much progress has taken place in Jakarta's dealings with the provinces. Whatever may be the constraints before the government to arrive at an amicable solution to the regional problems, it is losing time and the danger of secession, particularly of Aceh, is becoming more and more real as the militants gain further popular support for independence. If Aceh throws a challenge to the central government, Irian Jaya, Maluku and Riau would soon follow suit. Under those circumstances, the fear of Indonesia disintegrating may not be misplaced. Indonesia's unity and integrity, however, can still be salvaged only if the government comes out immediately with a clear-cut plan for power- and resource-sharing arrangements between the centre and the provinces, be it federal or any other name that Indonesians might suitably choose.

Wahid wants to empower the people at the local level through his decentralisation plans, which are in force from January this year. While the central government is impatient to implement autonomy hoping that a fairer distribution of national wealth will reduce separatist sentiments and regional violence, there is a complete lack of institutions at local level to absorb such autonomy.[21] Autonomy alone cannot effectuate economic justice and community peace unless there are institutions, procedures and legal framework to operate such decentralisation. With the autonomy programme, much of Jakarta's former power over finance and administration has been passed down to some three hundred regencies and municipalities. It is a radical shift in the way Indonesia is governed, and thus has created "almost complete confusion among all parties involved about the meaning and the direction of devolution."[22] In the absence of proper institutions and regulatory mechanisms, implementation of autonomy may result in decentralisation of corruption, rather than empowerment of the local government. The autonomy programme also encourages resentments and jealousies as it disenfranchises some local bureaucrats.[23] There is now a great uncertainty about the fate of more than two million central government civil servants that are present in every province and every district. Rather than preserving Indonesia's unity, the effect of the new laws may be widespread social resentment. Hastily implemented new system will leave a few resource-rich areas better off. Yet, much of the rest of Indonesia will suffer from a precipitous drop in income. The result could be economic chaos that could engender "a widespread breakdown in law and order", as well as intensification of the existing conflicts.

Warning Sign of Economic Decline

The ongoing sectarian clashes, regional and social unrest posed a serious threat to monetary stability in Indonesia. It had weakened the exchange rate of the Rupiah against the US dollar, from about Rp. 7000 late in December 1999 to almost Rp. 11,500 until the third week of July 2001, when Wahid's removal and Megawati's accession to power brought back the market confidence in the currency and to Rp. 9,000 to a dollar. A weakening of the local currency automatically pushed up the prices as the country's production system still heavily depends on imports. Apart from such uncertainties, the government is still saddled with the reform of the banking sector as well as corporate and debt restructuring, problems left by the Habibie government. The legitimacy and goodwill that Wahid's government enjoyed initially came under serious challenge for its failure to improve the economic conditions of the ordinary citizens. Indonesia's three-year, US $5billion loan programme with the IMF has been stalled since December 2000, when the agency withheld a US $400 million pay-out because the government missed targets on privatising key banks and failed to issue fiscal guidelines on a move toward a decentralised government. The IMF was also worried about a government plan under Wahid to change the central-bank law, which was believed to be threatening the bank's autonomy in setting monetary policy.[24] In the last few months of Wahid, the relationship — which was closely watched as a measure of international confidence in Indonesia's economic policy-making — became acrimonious with Indonesia accusing the IMF of being too pushy in its dealings with the country. Two top-level meetings in January-February 2001 failed to find a way to get the programme back on track. Late February, the World Bank warned that Indonesia risked falling into a new economic crisis if its relationship with the IMF collapsed, or if the country's political stability was at stake.

Ordinary Indonesians have already suffered economic hardships for more than three years and their patience are wearing thin. Economic slowdown will provide cause for further social unrest and will push Indonesia to instability and uncertainty. As far back as July last year the *Jakarta Post*, the country's leading English language daily, had rightly warned in an editorial: "Indonesia's problems are currently mainly in the economic field, where the turmoil is keeping investors away, and putting heavy pressure on the national currency, the Rupiah." A longer period of currency volatility would have cast a big shadow over the sustainability of the nascent recovery, as the consumer-led growth might peter out under a tight monetary policy. The World Bank report, however, stated that the "most likely scenario," was that the country would continue to "muddle through" with "some slippage in structural reforms, but with continued macro-economic stability that would help sustain poverty reduction."[25] With Wahid out and Megawati into the presidency and with the hope of improved political stability and economic policy-making and reforms under her, Indonesia may possibly again get back the market confidence of the investors and international lending agencies and that might brighten the prospect of economic recovery and the resultant political stability.

Indonesia and ASEAN

The crisis highlighted the fundamental elements of the Indonesian model that needed to change. It has equally presented the country with a rare opportunity to strengthen policies, rebuild institutions, reinvest in people, and create a more resilient and inclusive society than it has ever been. The challenge before the government is to hold the nation together, keep regional and religious tensions within bounds and let its people enjoy some fruits of both liberalism and democracy. Another formidable challenge is to maintain a delicate balance between crime and punishment relating to the question of trial of Suharto and his cronies, military that abused the human rights of Timorese, Acehnese or Javanese. While there will be constant domestic and international pressures to bring the offenders to book, a blind pursuit of justice might make things difficult for the government to stabilise the economy and the polity. Whatever direction it takes in the coming future, Indonesian crises will impinge on the regional development and security in a number of ways:

First, while one can perhaps imagine a situation in which other economies in the region perform better than Indonesia for some period of time, it is, however, inconceivable that the region as a whole could prosper in the years ahead without an open, stable and vibrant Indonesia. Any political and economic instability in Indonesia will automatically have an effect on the economic development of the whole region, which, in turn, will not only affect the Southeast Asian states' capability to allocate resources to its people, but will also bring uncertainties in the strategic environment of the region. Indonesia's neighbours treat it indulgently out of fear not so much of its strength but of its weakness, and of the spectres that evokes: in the short term, economic stagnation; in the long term, waves of refugees, pirate-infested seas and a power vacuum. Neighbours therefore fear the knock-on effects of prolonged instability in Indonesia.

Second, a political and economic collapse in Indonesia will lead to a major exodus into the neighbouring countries like Malaysia and Singapore, and would undermine their social and economic stability. Indonesia's neighbours are worried. In February, Malaysia's deputy Prime Minister, Abdullah Ahmad Badawi, gave warning of " a new wave of boat people" if things go wrong. In the same month, Malaysia's defence minister, Najib Tun Razak, warned that Indonesia risked 'Balkanization' into warring, splintered territories and posed the biggest security threat in Southeast Asia. "Since the economic crisis, the country (Indonesia) has been experiencing severe instability, with the possible breakup of the state — the Balkanization of Indonesia . . . . The mind is boggled with the kinds of scenarios that could soon engulf the region, following this," Najib said.[26] He called for international efforts to prevent any breakup of the world's fourth most populous country, an archipelago of 13,000 islands that straddles vital shipping lanes. "The biggest security threat facing the region is the breaking up of Indonesia and we can not allow that to happen," he further said. Malaysia has voiced fears that the political upheaval and ethnic violence in Indonesia are triggering waves of illegal immigration and pose regional social and security concerns. Malaysia has already ordered border patrols to be stepped up to stem an expected influx of people fleeing violence in Indonesian-ruled Borneo, an island also shared by Malaysia and tiny Brunei. The governments of Australia and Singapore have similar fears. The conflicts in Aceh and in Maluku, while domestic in nature, have inevitable consequences on inter-state and regional relations. To escape repression, victimisation or unrest, Acehnese or Madurese have fled their territories and entered Malaysia and Singapore complicating their relations with Indonesia. More importantly, as many Acehnese belonging to GAM (Gerakan Aceh Merdeka) have been living in Malaysia over the years and the fact that their movement for an Islamic slant, has given rise to suspicion about the Malaysian encouragement to Acehnese separatism, resulting in occasional misunderstanding and irritation between Indonesia and Malaysia. Third, if the Acehnese succeed in their struggle for independence, there are fears as expressed by both the Filipino and Thai foreign ministers in the last informal summit of ASEAN that it will surely embolden the Pattanis in Thailand and the Moros in the Philippines to push for a similar movement. None of Indonesia's neighbours, therefore, wants to see Indonesia fracture, as it could trigger similar movements elsewhere, as well as add a dangerous element of uncertainty into the region. The prospect of Islamic fundamentalist governments sitting astride stretches of the Straits of Malacca would be a security planner's nightmare. Given the difficulties of patrolling the area, Malaysia and the Philippines also worry that Islamic militants will find it easier to operate in their southern islands.

Fourth, Indonesian stability is intimately connected with the peace and regional order in Southeast Asia. Indonesia has the fourth largest population in the world. It has immense natural resources and a strategic location, for it controls all or part of a very major waterway between the Pacific and the Indian Ocean. The US Pacific Command transits these "SLOCs" (Sea-Lanes of Communications) in order to support operation in the Gulf. The Japanese need these waterways to transit their oil tankers. More than half of all international shipping trade traverses these waterways. Indonesia made ASEAN possible. ASEAN's formation was a result of Indonesia's adapting a more cooperative approach to its neighbours. Over the last three decades, ASEAN has developed a pattern of cooperation so strong that it has altered the geopolitics of East Asia. The cohesion among ASEAN countries have added to the stability of the East Asian region by allowing smaller countries to band together to form a counterweight to larger regional powers. Though by far the largest member of ASEAN, Indonesia has been careful to ensure that ASEAN has remained an organisation of equals. A blow to Indonesia would undermine the integrity of ASEAN as an institution, as well as regional security. An Indonesian instability will also add to the greater incidence of piracy in the waterways of the region. Since much of the world's piracy occurs in Indonesia's shipping lanes, a breakdown of authority could give it free rein. It is easy to see why Colin Powel, America's new secretary of state, has singled out Indonesia as a country that bears close watching.

The Emerging Perspectives

Despite the signs of turmoil, President Wahid looked unruffled until the last day and exuded confidence in his ability to lead his nation through the transition from authoritarianism to democracy. He attributed many of the country's problems to the machination of his political detractors in the 'central axis force' (the group that actually offered him the presidency but felt cheated when he upstaged them by not fulfilling their agenda) and supporters of former President Suharto who are alleged to be fomenting unrest to escape justice and destabilise his government. While he might be sincere in his belief in the empowerment of the people through devolution and decentralisation of power, he needed to put them into substance in order to bring about a change in the political culture. Even while he was trying to establish a new style of governance in sharp contrast to Suharto, he also needed to adjust himself to the demands of a head of the government whose actions must conform to certain rules and must be transparent and accountable. Despite his deep commitment to democracy, transparency and accountability, Gus Dur had all along been acculturated to function as a '*Kiyai*' who is considered as a father to his followers and who functions in earnest sincerity, but in a fashion, which may not strictly follow democratic norms. He occasionally took resorts to practices that circumvented the regular channels of bureaucratic norms and procedures. The style that suited him when he was the dissident leader of a non-governmental organisation (Forum Demokrasi) did not work now that he was the president. As the editorial in *The Economist* (London) had put it best: "His jokey way of shrugging off trouble once seemed charming. It has become a refusal to face criticism, punctuated by ill-tempered bouts of ineffectual authoritarianism."[27] Wahid derives his support from the Muslim social organisation, *Nahdlatul Ulama* (*NU*), which his grandfather founded, and he himself led for a long time until he formed his own political party, PKB, in 1999. His formal leadership of *NU* gave him a kind of feudal power, which he claimed he could use to foster democracy. "It can no longer be taken for granted that his democratic instincts lie deeper than the feudal ones."[28] As a result, calls for Wahid's resignation grew louder and stronger over the last few months before his removal. He had added to the instability by unleashing militant supporters, Banser (the military wing of the youth movement of *NU*), in his defence.

He had survived the last August MPR session, which questioned him on some of the above issues and his sacking of two of his cabinet ministers, by promising that he would he would mend his ways and that he would transfer some of his powers to his vice-president, Megawati. He had reneged on both those promises. The attempt by the members of parliament to impeach him for his alleged involvement in two financial scandals failed at the beginning of the year, not because of any inherent strength on his part, but essentially for the lack of any immediate alternative to him at the time. Nevertheless, the forces ranged against him had used those two minor corruption cases to cripple his government. He also survived for some time because of the existence of some lonely optimists who, while admitting his mistakes, argued that the problems he had inherited were so huge and the forces arrayed against him so powerful, that no reformer could have been expected to do better. Under the circumstances, instead of delivering ultimatums and weakening him with protests and threats of impeachment, they argued, reformers should have united behind him. After all, a change in the presidency would not bring the drastic improvements that Indonesians yearn for. Unseating Gus Dur, they further argued, would only sharpen the political divide in the country and more likely to usher in a new period of political instability. As against them, Wahid's detractors were convinced that longer he stayed in power, the more egotistical, willful and enfeebled he would become.

There was a third perspective, which urged Indonesians not to waste their energy on infighting, but to concentrate on assiduously, and cooperatively rebuilding what remains of Indonesia. Julia Suryakusuma, an Indonesian sociologist, argued that most Indonesian leaders, past and present, are reflections of the people, and, more specifically, of the political elite. "People are baying for change in leadership. This is also what happened in 1966, with the late President Sukarno, the father of Mrs. Megawati, in 1998 with Mr. Suharto, in 1999 with former President Habibie and now with Mr. Wahid," she noted. "If this is the only way we can use our newfound 'freedom' — to change our leaders by whatever means, without changing, for example, our political system and behaviour," she lamented: "then all we are doing is substituting one leader who reflects the people with another leader who reflects the people."[29]

So Wahid was under siege. Wahid was given three months to respond to the charges. He rejected the parliamentary censure on the ground that it had no constitutional right to do so, but for the first time apologised to the body for any "inappropriate behaviour."[30] The basis of the memorandum was not very strong, as the report of the house investigating committee had only concluded that the president "could be suspected of having played a role" in the Bulogate and "had given inconsistent statements" on Bruneigate. In any case, given the confrontationist mood of both the president and parliament impeachment proceedings looked almost a 'foregone conclusion'.[31] More importantly,

Megawati had already shown her readiness to take over the presidency as long as it was done according to procedures prescribed by the constitution. To counter his detractors moves, Wahid had issued a couple of blunt warnings to parliament not to try to impeach him and said hundreds of thousands of his supporters were now ready to march on the capital, Jakarta, to protect him. Such threats did not carry much conviction with his opponents essentially because the bulk of the armed forces and the police leadership were not prepared to support him. Hence, this is what had happened, when he, out of desperation and as a last move to cling on to power, declared a state of emergency and suspended parliament, no one took serious note of it. Even the country's judiciary went against him and called his move unconstitutional, paving the way for his dismissal. Two years ago, thanks mostly Gus Dur's democratic drive, the military was forced to define a so-called 'new paradigm' that left its social and political role behind. Yet, ironically, it was Gus Dur himself who unwittingly pushed the TNI back to centre stage. Wahid believed that the constitution empowered him with the status of 'supreme commander of the armed forces' that would give him a free hand to do whatever he pleased with the military. This turned out to be his biggest mistake and paid dearly for it. He threatened military leaders that they either support his plan to declare a state of emergency or be ready to be replaced by more accommodative and pliable generals. It was the last straw for the military leadership and they could not swallow the 'humiliation'. Eventually it was the corporate interests of the TNI that united them against Wahid.

Leadership Change and the Prospect for Political and Economic Stability

The drama that was unfolding over the presidential crisis in Indonesia over the last seven months has now reached a denouement with the MPR (Supreme Legislative Council) overwhelmingly voting for the removal of President Abdurrahman Wahid, and electing the current vice-president, Megawati Sukarnoputri, as the second popularly elected president of the country. While the international community has welcomed Megawati's accession to power and the country's currency suddenly gained against the dollar from Rupiah 11,500 to Rp. 9,500 overnight, Indonesia is yet to recover from the political uncertainty that it has fallen in over the last one year. Much before the first censure motion was moved against Wahid in February this year by the country's parliament, which has been using its newfound freedom and power to call the president to account for many of his actions, he was already under siege. A highly respected moderate Muslim scholar known for his inclusive and democratic ideas had begun his presidency, as we have noted earlier with a tremendous amount of goodwill and support while democratic reform had begun under his predecessor, Habibie, it was to Gus Dur that Indonesians looked for laying a firm foundation on which a truly democratic society could be built. However, soon he began to waste that goodwill away through his erratic behaviour, contradictory statements and inept handling of the country's political and economic affairs. Within few months after he took over, even his friends and well wishers turned out to be major critic of his rule. Thousands of people have died in various parts of the country due to ethnic, religious and social strife. The country's currency was experiencing a steady decline in value affecting its economic recovery and restructuring of its foreign debts. There was a general breakdown of law and order and visible erosion of authority of the state in controlling its affairs. He did not want to shed his intellectual arrogance and autocratic ways, and also failed to acknowledge that the power of the presidency has waned and that parliament might be fractious and immature but could not be ignored.

One cannot, however, ignore some of his achievements. He was quite successful at the initial stage to reduce the role of the armed forces, which for the first time openly accepted civilian control and transformed itself from a tool of those in power to that of the nation and the state. However, as the country's political and economic situation began to deteriorate, he began to lose control over the armed forces, which had now been able to resurrect somewhat its lost image and position. He was able to purge the presidential palace and the office of some of its air of regal grandeur and preferred to be addressed as 'Gus Dur" rather than as 'Mr. President'. He had the courage to propose the opening of relations with Israel and recognising the basic right of Communists in Indonesia to reorganise.

Now that Megawati has taken over, does that mean the political uncertainty in Indonesia is over? She has, however, already secured broad support of the parties opposed to Wahid. At the same time she has displayed few political skills and articulated little in the way of original political ideas while vice-president. Her taciturn, martyr-cum-saviour image has made her out to be aloof and arrogant, endearing her to few but the most enthusiastic supporters. One area that works in her favour at this point of time is her close relation with the Indonesian military (TNI). She has already received backing from Indonesia's generals who see a Megawati presidency as assurance that their institutional interests will be protected. Both Megawati and the TNI share the same outlook toward secular nationalism and oppose radical Islam. And unlike Wahid's bellicose attempts to assert civilian control over the military, Megawati believes in a gradual approach in withdrawing the TNI from politics. Unlike Wahid again, she may be able to establish a better rapport with the bureaucracy helping her to administer more effectively.

Since she has never been a Muslim cleric, is a woman, and has been accused of consorting too closely with ethnic-Chinese minority, she may find it slightly harder to carry this message with authority. Further, she might well inspire the fragmented Islamist opposition, though it remains weak, to unite against her and eventually might spark the rise of a radical Islam. Megawati undoubtedly has charisma, but is rather weak on ideas and political skill. Her organisational abilities still remain untested. A Megawati presidency might make a bigger difference to the way the army treats the regional assertions. Wahid tried to find non-military solutions to Aceh and Irian insurgencies and is committed to decentralisation. Megawati does not seem to favour too many concessions to the regional demands, and would rather prefer a stronger central authority. Her concept of a united Indonesia, stemming from her father's legacy, matches with that of the army, which might put her into a confrontation with the Acehnese and Irianese. She might also turn the army loose on Islamic extremists such as the *Laskar Jihad*, which has injected itself into sectarian violence in the Maluku islands. All in all, a change from Wahid to Megawati as the president of the country automatically does not bring the desired results. On the other hand, it may set a precedent for any disgruntled groups to force the future presidents out before their constitutional term expires. Like Benazir Bhutto of Pakistan, she is also vulnerable to the overwhelming influence of her husband on her life.

The Indonesian crisis need not be seen only in the negative; instead, one can paint a fresh image that captures the human spirit and dramatic change that could serve as a starting point for thinking about the country. Indonesia today is trying to build the foundations for a political system that is not simply more just and even-handed, but seen to be so by the Indonesians and the world at large. This desire for a more just system of doing things permeates every aspect of national discussion. It is truly the hallmark of a new Indonesia. If Indonesians succeed in their struggle for transforming their society and polity from authoritarian to democracy, it will also have major effect on the stability and security of Southeast Asia. The emergence of civil society and their attempt to influence the agenda of the state will qualitatively alter the nature of state-society relations in Indonesia. Once that happens in Indonesia, it will inevitably influence the regional relations, for the new regionalism would have to operate not only at the inter-governmental level, but also at the level of the civil society. Developments in one country will influence developments in another country that will make the region not only more interdependent but may also complicate inter-state relations.

To sum up, Indonesia's process of 'reinvention' and transition is going to be long drawn out. The future course of the country may be decided by a struggle between the new democratising impulse of the reformers and the forces of chaos that seek an advantage in provoking the religious social and separatist tensions that have now risen dangerously to the surface across Indonesia.

References

[1] Mark Baird, " Others can help Indonesia if Indonesians help themselves", *International Herald Tribune*, 3–4 March, 2001.

[2] Quoted in *Far Eastern Economic Review (FEER)* 8 March, 2001.

[3] Juwono Sudarsono, *Problems and Prospects of Democratization in Indonesia*, Keynote address at the opening session of the International Seminar on "Towards Structural Reforms for Democratisation" in Indonesia Ministry of Education and Culture, 1998. p.4. Juwono is cautiously optimistic about democratisation in Indonesia and is rather apprehensive about 'political backsliding' when he says: "The real danger is political backsliding, there is too much brainstorming but nothing except storms. The civilian authority must be successful . . . . Political parties must be institutionalized. We are good at creating movement, but not at getting organised. We need a leader like the Indian sitting bull, but all we get are bull shifter leaders." *Jakarta Post*, 15 July, 2000.

[4] One of the scandals involves the alleged embezzlement of Rupiah 35 billion (US $3.5 million) from Bulog, the national agricultural commodities agency, by Wahid's masseur, Suwondo, who allegedly requested the money from the agency saying Wahid needed it for humanitarian relief in Aceh. Bulog officials have said that Wahid had months earlier asked if Bulog funds could be used for aid projects in Aceh. Wahid had admitted that he considered doing so, but at the end decided against this. Instead he admits accepting US $2 million from the Sultan of Brunei toward this end. Critics charge that it was improper to accept this money, the basis of the second allegation. See, *Far Eastern Economic Review*, 15 February, 2001.

[5] *Ibid*, p.2.

[6] Quoted in Rajiv Chandrasekharan, "As Anarchy Spreads in Indonesia, Vigilante Justice Prevails," *International Herald Tribune*, 19 April, 2001. Government officials do not record the number of deaths, but human rights organisations estimate that

more than a thousand suspected thieves were slain by mobs in 2000. In Jakarta, one hospital morgue alone has recorded two hundred and five victims in the past year and a half. On Java, the most populous island in Indonesia, police estimate that at least hundred people were lynched in 2000 after being accused of being witches. Some of the victims, including women as old as seventy years, had their eyes gouged out and their limbs severed. *Ibid.*

[7] On the emergence of such citizens' groups, See *Jakarta Post*, 7 July, 2000.

[8] *Jakarta Post*, 15 July, 2000.

[9] *Ibid.*

[10] Juwono Sudarsono, Address in Washington, D.C. on 11 April, 2000. Department of Defence, Republic of Indonesia. p.1.

[11] The only occasion when the president used such a power was in 1959 when Sukarno suspended the constitution and deployed emergency powers.

[12] Quoted in John McBeth, "A Minefield Called Jakarta", *FEER*, 22 February, 2001. pp.21–22. McBeth quotes a senior general: "We now have the perception that he wants to abuse the military to support him in power, which is in contrast to the military's current position of reforming itself to be out of politics. He is trying to make the military his political tool."

[13] Indonesia's Army commander has vowed that the military will step in to 'save this nation' if political turmoil and escalating ethnic and separatist violence threaten the unity of the country. The military 'must guard the nation if a chaotic situation erupts' said General Endriartono Sutarto. He said the military could take over responsibility for internal security if the national police force, which has admitted that it is undermanned and poorly equipped, is overwhelmed by events. He also said the armed forces would prevent any of Indonesia's increasingly disaffected provinces from trying to secede. 'If there are only two options — to conduct a military operation or lose a region — we will firmly chose the first option,' he told soldiers at a training base in West Java. Any move by the generals to take over the duties of the police would contravene current government policy of separating the two. *The Straits Times* (Singapore) 12 March, 2001

[14] Quoted in Barry Wain, "Demilitarizing Indonesia", *Asian Wall Street Journal*, 4 June, 2000.

[15] *Jakarta Post*, 23 June, 2000. In the same article Laksamana was critical of Indonesia's electoral system when he said: "Indonesia does not elect individual candidates — so no accountability between our elected leaders and their so-called constituencies . . . . Democracy in Indonesia is designed to give maximum power to elites to broker backroom deals. The voter plays a minor and temporary role in the process. The people can express their choices through voting, yet anything is possible in the MPR." The reference was obviously to the anomaly between the people's verdict which gave Megawati's party, PDI-P, the largest number of votes as well as seats in the parliament, yet the MPR preferred to choose a minority party leader, Abdurrahman Wahid, as the president of the country. The election of the president, according to Sukardi, was constitutional, but not democratic.

[16] Juwono, op cit.

[17] Simon Elegant, "The Darkest Season", *Time* 12 March, 2001. pp.14–20. Elegant quotes Kma Usop, a Dayak cultural leader and a Professor at Palangkarya University to highlight Dayak prejudice and widespread resentment against the Madurese. "The Dayaks are in a panic, they are feeling marginalised. They have been provoked for many years. The Madurese are violent. They fight in the market and in the farms. We don't have similar problems with the Buginese, Chinese and Javanese."

[18] "Indonesian authorities will launch "limited security operations" against rebels in the troubled province of Aceh, former minister of defense Mahfud MD said. Speaking to reporters after meeting with President Abdurrahman Wahid, Mahfud said the operations would be "limited" and assured that they would not take the form of the harsh anti-rebel military drive, known as Military Operation Zone (DOM), imposed in Aceh for nine years until August 1998. The limited security operations, Mahfud said, would only target members of the Free Aceh Movement, who have been fighting for the independence of Aceh since the 1970s... . Mahfud's statement came a day after the government declared the GAM as separatists whose clear aim is to separate Aceh from the unitary

Republic of Indonesia. Besides preparing for limited security operations, Mahfud said that the government would also issue an amnesty for all GAM members who leave the organisation and pledge loyalty to the Republic of Indonesia... He said that the preparatory steps currently being taken by the office of the coordinating minister for politics, social and security affairs, would include comprehensive socio-cultural as well as militaristic approaches.... Despite the current truce, more than two hundred people have been killed in violence in the province this year alone. The two sides remain politically disparate, with GAM demanding independence and Jakarta saying it will only grant limited autonomy." *Jakarta Post*, 12 March, 2001; also see *Kompas*, 12 March, 2001.

19 See, Rajiv Chandrasekharan, "Aceh Aid Worker Tells of Execution-Style Killings", *International Herald Tribune*, 14 December, 2000. Also see, Dini Djalal, "A Bloody Truce", *FEER*, 5 October, 2000. More worryingly, the separatist movement is being wracked by a growing criminal element that is apparently succeeding in its efforts to impose a local form of taxation. "Residents say each village household must pay Rupiah 1000 monthly to GAM; in towns, GAM collects upto10 times that amount. Businesses are reportedly forced to pay millions of Rupiah, depending on their size." *Ibid*. Many, perhaps most, Acehnese want independence, but they dread being governed by what they view as a floundering leadership. GAM is comprised of several factions and has no structure that makes it difficult for local people to demand accountability — and for mediators to produce a comprehensive plan. The result is confusion and disillusionment.

20 TNI chief, Admiral Widodo said Presidential decree (Inpres) No. IV/2001 on efforts to restore law and order in Aceh was a political umbrella for the TNI to perform their duties there, so that the TNI would not have to ask the government to impose the military emergency status in Aceh. "I have just asked my boys to perform their duties professionally. I have also asked them to ensure that they are there to create peace not to make war with innocent people," Widodo said, adding that the operation will last for six months, before being evaluated on whether it should be continued or stopped. Back in Aceh, GAM commander Tengku Abdullah Syafiie warned that his forces

would fight back hard if Indonesian troops intensified a security crackdown against separatists. See *Jakarta Post*, 21 April, 2001. Back in Aceh, GAM commander Tengku Abdullah Syafiie warned that his forces would fight back hard if Indonesian troops intensified a security crackdown against separatists. "This decision was a terrible mistake and the government will suffer for it," Abdullah told *The Jakarta Post*'s correspondent at his hideout in restive Pidie regency on 19th April. Abdullah further threatened that "the more troops they send to Aceh, the more they will be returned as sacks of clothes. We cannot let them kill our people." *Ibid.*

21 During the Suharto era, the huge Indonesian archipelago was run from Jakarta. The president made all-important decisions. Ministers, provincial governors and lower level officials were supposed to execute policies, not make them. As a result, a culture of looking towards their 'leader' developed in public policy-making and administration. This had a debilitating effect on the Indonesian society in general, as it gave rise to a system of governance where decisions were forced on the people at the provincial and local levels, but also discouraged any initiatives or ideas based on local needs. The culture of looking towards the centre and the leader still continues, as habits cannot change overnight. The local governments and districts have no clue how to govern.

22 Hans W. Vriens, "Hasty Power shake-Up Worsens Indonesia's Woes" *International Herald Tribune*, 13 March, 2001. Jakarta has not clearly defined the different roles and responsibilities of the central government, the provinces and regions. Ironically, the advocates of autonomy feared that a genuine federal state would make the thirty-two provinces of Indonesia too powerful and encourage them to seek independence. To avoid this breakup, the chief architect of regional autonomy, Ryaas Rasyid who has now resigned from Wahid's cabinet on policy differences, decided to hand many powers directly to the three hundred and sixty-four regions, and gives the provinces only a vague mediating role. One consequence is that mining companies no longer can negotiate their contracts with the once powerful ministry for mines and energy in Jakarta. Instead they have to deal with the top local officials in the area in which their mine is located. Tax rates in Indonesia are already so high

that no significant new mining investment has come in during the last few years. As a result, the mining industry is expected to shrink by thirty per cent in the next five years.

23 Simon Elegant of *Time* has reported that soon after the killing began in Kalimantan, police arrested three men for paying Rupiah 20 million to incite violence between Dayaks and Madurese. Two of the men were civil servants appointed by Jakarta who had lost their jobs as part of the autonomy scheme.

24 *Asian Wall Street Journal*, 28 February, 2001. Rizal Ramli, coordinating minister for economic affairs, however, announced that Indonesia will assuage the IMF's concerns over the central bank law by setting up an independent panel of experts to review proposed changes and ensure that they will not undermine the central bank's autonomy in setting up monetary policy. The central bank itself, however, has expressed concern that some of the proposed changes to the law have the potential to undermine the bank's hard-won independence and return to its previous situation of effectively under government control. "The result of the amendments may not be the best for the country or for monetary policy," Bank Indonesia deputy governor Achjar Illjas said in an interview in late February, adding that he believes the current law already has adequate provisions to hold top central bank officials accountable for their performance. Quoted in *Ibid.*

25 Quoted in *International Herald Tribune*, 1 March, 2001. Also see, *Asian Wall Street Journal*, 28 February, 2001.

26 *The Times of India* (New Delhi) 28 February, 2001. Najib said Indonesia had unwittingly forsaken domestic stability in the name of Western-defined democracy since fallout from Asia's economic crisis led to the ouster of long-time dictator Suharto. Many Malaysian, who share a language and religious traditions with Indonesians but are far better off economically, view their large neighbour as a warning of what could go wrong if Malaysia's historical tensions between ethnic and religious groups explode. Najib said that Suharto's government had ensured law and order and economic progress. According to him Indonesia now needs "managed reforms and not radical changes."

27 *The Economist* 17 February, 2001.

[28] *Ibid.*

[29] Julia I. Suryakusuma, "It's Time Indonesians Shouldered the Blame," *International Herald Tribune*, 14 March, 2001.

[30] "At this moment, I personally ask for the forgiveness from parliament and the people of Indonesia for any inappropriate behaviour." Quoted in *International Herald Tribune*, 29 March, 2001.

[31] Amien Rais, quoted in *Ibid*. The *Jakarta Post* summed up the sentiment of many across the country in an editorial on 28 March, 2001, under the headline, "What Next?" It said Wahid had either missed or chosen to ignore the point that he no longer had the support of most members of parliament.

4

Indonesia's Political System and Complexities

Ganga Nath Jha

Indonesia, situated at the crossroad of the Pacific and the Indian Ocean, is the largest country of Southeast Asia. It covers about 5,193,250 square kilometres of territory, of which 2,027,087 sq. kms are landed and 3,166,163 sq. kms are sea territories. Again, it is the largest archipelago of the world with 17,508 islands and a population of two hundred and ten million. Though the founding fathers tried to evolve a parliamentary system of government, the presidential system emerged, and powers of the legislature were eroded. The first two presidents, namely Sukarno (1945 – 65) and Suharto (1966 – 98), were extremely powerful and dominating. They increased the powers of the presidency enormously and the mechanism of checks and balances were diluted. Sukarno, the father of the nation and the protagonist of three "A" movement, the archipelagic concept, guided democracy and *Pancasila*, wanted to restore the glories of the Majapahit period. He was not prepared to tolerate any opposition to his policies. When he was ousted from power in 1965, the armed forces took over the administration. His successor, General Suharto, gave importance to development and order. He promoted the ideals of *Dwifungsi*, which entitled the army to perform a dual role in civil administration as well as in defence matters. He also extended the territorial frontiers of Indonesia by annexing East Timor. He changed the course of foreign policy and cultivated close relations with the United States. He further strengthened the institution of presidency by using emergency powers and the media. He evolved a system in which the legislature had no alternative but to support him. The situation started changing only after the economic crisis (1997–98) when there were series of demonstrations and bloodshed against the leadership of Suharto. Some of the army generals also felt that President Suharto must resign. As a result, Suharto resigned on 21 May, 1998, and was succeeded by B.J. Habibie.

As there was unrest against the leadership of Habibie too, he took urgent steps to hold election, which was held in the following year. More than forty-eight political parties took part in the election, but none of them got an absolute majority. Habibie wanted to come back to power with the support of the military, but Golkar and the then Commander-in-Chief, General Wiranto, did not oblige him. Thus, a coalition government of pro-democracy parties led by Abdurrahman Wahid emerged.

The Indonesian Constitution

The Republic of Indonesia was born on 17 August, 1945, and the Dutch colonial masters left on 27 December, 1949. After getting independence Indonesia tried to be assertive in the politics of the region in particular and Third World in general. President Sukarno made *Pancasila* the ideological and philosophical foundation of the Republic and its ideals were incorporated in the Constitution declared on 18 August, 1945. *Pancasila* is a Sanskrit word, which was also considered the philosophical foundation of Indian foreign policy. However, for India this word was incorporated in the policy documents much later. Indonesia wanted to incorporate the ideals of *Pancasila* both in foreign policy and domestic matters right since its inception.

The Constitution of 1945 explained five principles of *Pancasila* as the following:[1]

a) Belief in the one and only God.
b) A just and civilised humanity.
c) Unity of Indonesia.
d) Democracy guided by the inner wisdom of deliberations of the representatives.
e) Social justice.

The Articles of the 1945 Constitution enumerated the ideals and goals for which the nation was born. The founding fathers were inspired by the urge for unity, common goals, and democracy built upon the age-old Indonesian concepts of *Gotong Royong* (mutual assistance), of deliberations of representatives (*Muswarah*), and consensus (*Mufakat*). Preceded by a preamble including *Pancasila*, the Constitution had thirty-seven Articles defining the role of the Chief Executive (President), Legislature (MPR and DPR), and the Judiciary. The founding fathers envisaged the foundation of a unitary state with sovereignty vested in the legislature. However, subsequent developments favoured the adoption of a presidential system in which the president was very powerful. Both Sukarno and Suharto believed in the personality cult and strengthened the powers of the president enormously.

The sovereignty of the people was symbolised by the *Majelis Permusjawaratan Rakjat* (MPR), also known as People's Consultative Assembly. The total number of appointed members to the MPR was fixed at one-third of the total, and total the number of MPR members were to be twice the number of the members in DPR. Accordingly, the members of the MPR had been fixed at thousand out of which four hundred and twenty-five were elected, seventy-five appointed by the armed forces, and the remaining five hundred were government appointees.[2] The MPR met every five years to elect and re-elect the president who was legally accountable to this House.

The legislative powers were, in fact, vested in the *Dewan Perwakilan Rakjat* (DPR), also known as the House of Peoples' Representatives which included representatives of regions, and political and functional (*karya*) groups. According to the 1969 Act, the number of members the DPR had been fixed at four hundred and sixty, of which three hundred and sixty were elected and hundred nominated. However, this figure was increased in 1975 to five hundred of which four hundred were elected and hundred were appointed members. Each member of the DPR pledged that he would always uphold the message of the people's sufferings, that he will adhere to and defend *Pancasila* as the basis and ideology of the state, the 1945 Constitution and all existing laws and regulations in force in the Republic of Indonesia, that he will endeavour to the best of his ability of promote the welfare of the Indonesian people and be loyal to the country, the nation and the state of Indonesia.[3] The DPR proved to be a rubber stamp during 1965–99, but is emerging as an important institution of rule-making ever since Abdurrahman Wahid came to power.

The most striking feature of Indonesian politics is that it has not declared any state religion. Although the Muslims are in overwhelming majority and most of its neighbouring states have declared their state religion in order to maintain their national unity, Indonesia has abstained from doing so. Malaysia and Brunei, the two immediate neighbours, have declared Islam as the state religion but Indonesia preferred to remain secular. The preamble of 1945 Constitution assures religious freedom by declaring protection and promotion of faith in the God Almighty and endeavoured to create a just civilised humanity. The various governments have been pursuing a religious policy, which respects the right of every religious group. They have officially recognised religions, namely, Islam, Protestantism, Catholicism, Buddhism and Hinduism. As a result, there are 26,769 Protestant churches, 13,361 Catholic churches, 34,408 Hindu temples, 2,552 Buddhist Viharas and 537,837 Muslim mosques.[4] The break-up of different religious communities in Indonesia in mid-nineties indicated that Muslims comprised 87.2 per cent, Protestants six per cent, Catholics 3.5 per cent, Hindus two per cent and the Buddhists one per cent.[5]

Indonesia gives emphasis on "Unity in Diversity", to unite the people in a common fold. It has heterogeneous ethnic and linguistic groups. More than three hundred languages are spoken, and their culture and life styles differ. The majority is of Malay stock, split into dozens of smaller sub-groups, with varying family structures and social systems. The prominent ethnic groups are the Javanese, the Sundanese, the Minhasans, the Bugis, the Makassars and the Balinese. Again there are the Dayaks, the Bataks, and the Dani and the Asmat of Melanesian stock.

Various ethnic groups have preserved their customs and traditions. The majority population is of Islamic faith, with a deep impact of Sufism, which came to Indonesia along with the spread of Islam. Opinions differ about who first brought Islam to Indonesia, but it is acknowledged that Sufi saints played the most important role. The traditional Hindu and Buddhist rulers of the times were tolerant of the activities of Sufi saints and this approach was reciprocated subsequently when Islam became a powerful force at the government level. It allowed Hindu and Buddhist traditions to be amalgamated with the new evolving religion and culture in Indonesia. It is recorded that when the kings of Samudra, Pasai and Perlak of northern Sumatra embraced Islam and established the first Islamic kingdom in the Indonesian archipelago, it paved the path for rulers in other parts of Sumatra and Java to follow suit. The tombstone of the first Islamic ruler, Sultan Malik Al-Saleh of Samudra, dated 1297 had been perused by Ibn Batutta, the Moroccan traveller, who on his way to China in 1341 had stopped at Samudra and became a royal guest of the then ruler. Marco Polo, who visited Perlak earlier in 1292, had also referred to the existence of Samudra as an Islamic state. The projection based on available information suggests that Samudra ruler was under the impact of Sufism. Such observations, however are opposed by a section of the intellectuals who argue that Islam came to Indonesia through Muslim traders from Persia and Gujarat. There are some who say that Arab missionaries (Egypt, Hejaz or Hadramut) had introduced Islam in Indonesia.

Whatever may be the reality, nobody can refute the impact of Sufism on art and culture, namely the *Wayang*, myths and folklores, poems and songs, the Islamic calendar, ceremonies and festivals, etc. Sufi saints understood that the

Javanese were very fond of art. So they inserted Islamic teachings in the stories of Ramayana and Mahabharata to be played in *Wayang*. They created new myths, stories, poems and songs, which had local names and local languages but Islamic teachings. A Sufi saint, Walisongo, led the Sufi movement in the 15th century and became very popular in Java. His strategy of adopting local stories, local heroes and myths were followed by the Sufi saints in other parts of the archipelago. Thus, a proper atmosphere was created, and the people started accepting Islam without any holy war or bloodshed. Here it is important to remember that the different islands and regions in Indonesia had different traditions, culture and myths and when they accepted Islam, they did not reject them. As a result, Islam did not remain a monolithic force as in many other parts of the world. There are thus different types of Islamic peoples spread all over Indonesia. For instance, Islamic people in Aceh are much more different than their counterparts in Jakarta. They are so different in their lifestyle and temperament that they are demanding a separate nationhood.

Threats to the System

Indonesia is faced with numerous problems of different types, but here an attempt is made to point out outstanding political problems. The archipelagic concept as enunciated by the founding fathers is losing its importance, and the *Pancasila* doctrine, especially its third principle "Unity of Indonesia" has been endangered. The separatist movement in Aceh and Irian Jaya are too serious to be ignored. East Timor, which had been annexed after a military action in 1975, has already become an independent state in 1999 and separatists in Aceh and Irian Jaya articulate similar demands.

Aceh, situated at the northernmost region of Sumatra, has a distinct culture and history. Its 4.5 million population has been strong a supporter of Darul Islam movement and views the authority of central government un-Islamic. This is because Javanese, who are Abangans, dominate the government. The people of Aceh have been struggling for its own identity and separate nationhood because the government of Indonesia has not been sensitive to their grievances. The government gave them autonomy in religious and educational affairs after a long struggle in 1959 but it was withdrawn without any rhyme or reason. Though it is rich in iron, oil, gas and coal, it is not given any share in the benefits. At the same time, the government has supported migration and transmigration of population to that area which has been disliked. The people in Aceh have opposed the presence of new migrants and they have been agitating against it. The continuing conflicts over economic and demographic issues have fuelled separatist movement. In 1976, Hasan Di Tiro established Gerakan Aceh Merdeka (Free Aceh Movement) and subsequently declared independence. However, this movement was suppressed and Tiro fled to Sweden. It was from Sweden that he announced the formation of Aceh government in exile. The unrest mounted enormously in Aceh in 1989 when National Liberation Front Aceh Sumatra (NLFAS) was established. They mounted onslaughts on the government forces and Amnesty International claimed that two thousand people were killed during 1989–93. The casualty number has been increasing every year.

Similar is the situation in Irian Jaya, where *Organisasi Papua Merdeka* (OPM), also known as Free Papua Independence Movement leads separatist movement. There has been a lot of bloodshed in that province also and cases of human rights violations are reported. Irian Jaya is rich in timber, gold and silver. Indonesia is trying to exploit the natural resources of the area, but the indigenous people are resisting it. They have not yet been fully integrated with the national mainstream as their outlook and cultures are different. They have not accepted their integration so far and they display much in common with the people of Papua New Guinea. It is a fact the Dani, Asmat and other ethnic groups of the province are Melanesian stock and they are entirely different in their customs and traditions compared to Javanese Malays. Some of the tribal groups have procured weapons to kill transmigrants and foreigners. The army, on the other hand, has been vindictive while assuring law and order.

The separatist tendencies in both Aceh and Irian Jaya have religious dimension. As far as Aceh is concerned, it is a Muslim dominated area. They believe that the government of Indonesia is under the control of the Javanese, and a Javanese cannot be a true Muslim. The Javanese leaders regarding the nationalism of Acehnese as well have reciprocated such a feeling. There has been persecution of the leaders in Aceh and mass graves have been found. Some of the dissident leaders have left their homeland to seek asylum elsewhere. Their participation in the government has been nominal and guerrilla warfare continues. On the other hand, Irian Jaya has eighty-three per cent Christian population. The Church is the main centre of social congregation. They know that the province had not been handed over to Indonesia along with other provinces by the Dutch Colonial masters because of ethnic and religious grounds. Their projection is that given the situation in which they are, their identity is bound to be lost forever in Indonesian state.

Both Aceh and Irian Jaya advocate their case for autonomy or independence on economic ground as well. Free Aceh Movement leaders claim that they contribute to seventeen per cent of Indonesia's oil and gas export earnings, but they are used for their suppression and not for their development. On the other hand, OPM leaders find that their forest wealth and gold reserves cannot be properly used by the central government as the latter are temperamentally exploitative and colonial in nature. They think that protection of their forest is necessary for their identity, customs, traditions and way of life.

The socio-economic factor is the root cause of trouble in Ambon also which is the capital city of Maluku. History says that majority of the pro-Dutch elements and militias inhabited in that area, especially on the eve of independence. They had struggled against their integration with the Indonesian Republic and had fought for their independence.

Ambon, known as Amboina in the historical past, has a number of people with the Dutch descent. There are some people of Portuguese origin. On the other hand, there are some Chinese traders who have prospered in business and trade. Although the government statistics claim that 55.8 per cent are Muslims, 38.2 per cent are Protestants and 5.3 per cent are Catholics, but this is the figure of Maluku province in general. A study of social life in Ambon presents a different picture. The Chinese and Christians are relatively better off economically than their Muslim counterparts.

There have been violent clashes between the Muslims and Christian communities especially after Indonesia was gripped by the economic crisis (1997–98). Hundreds of peoples have lost their lives. Militant groups have emerged to protect the lives of their people and communal virus has engulfed the area. Islamic outfits such as Islam Defender's Forum have given a call for jihad and such a call is appropriately reciprocated. It is believed that the government was lackadaisical in their attitudes about the happenings in the area in the post-1998 period and did not act swiftly to stop rioting.

The development in Aceh, Irian Jaya, and Ambon clearly suggest that the concept of *Bhineka Tunggal Eka* (Unity in Diversity) is endangered. We find that anti-Chinese riots have taken place in Jakarta also on one pretext or the other.

The Chinese, who have traditionally been involved in business and trade, and who have prospered economically are made victims of looting, arson, rape, riots and humiliation since 1998. Anti-Chinese riots have been taking place and the worst affected areas are Medan, Titipatan, Solo and Samarinda. The hooligans involved in rioting argue that the Chinese are responsible for spiraling price rise and the economic crisis. In February 1998, the riots in Medan were serious enough to compel some ethnic Chinese to leave their houses. Many Chinese owned shops had been torched and dozens of buildings damaged at Kendari in Sulawesi. The looting of Chinese stores and shops have been occurring off and on since then.[6]

Earlier religion came in the path of Megawati Sukarnoputri's candidature as president of Indonesia. Though she was a popular leader and daughter of the Father of the Nation, her credentials to uphold Muslim values were questioned because of her genealogy. When her candidature for presidency was considered, there were lots of debates that her mother and grandmother were Hindus and therefore her Muslim heritage was diluted. The military supported Golkar Party made allegations that Megawati secretly prayed at a Hindu temple in Bali. Another criticism was that she had chosen a majority of non-Muslim candidates for her party, and if appointed the president her conduct would be identical. Finally, since she was a woman, she could not be appointed the Head of the State of a Muslim-dominated country. All these opinions prevailed in the deliberations of the MPR. However, they were quietly forgotten when all the political parties joined together to dethrone Wahid.

Needless to say religion is assuming centre, stage, and the use of Islam is increasing in the struggle for power. *Nahdlatul Ulama* (*NU*), Muhammadiah and Syarikat Islam (SI) feel that they would lose their popular support if they ignore the importance of Islam in socio-economic life.

Another debatable issue is the role of the Armed Forces in the politics of the country. Their intrusion in administration and politics had been legitimated with the acceptance of *dwifungsi* (dual functions).[7] Under the stewardship of Suharto, *dwifungsi* principle became operational and serving and retired army officers took a wide variety of posts, from that of a cabinet minister down to the village head. They assumed a major role in the economy as the managers of the Dutch enterprises, which had been nationalised in 1957. They also took major part in the administrative system. The increasing importance of *dwifungsi* resulted in making democratic institutions subservient to army rule. Political parties, pressure groups, media and information channels had limited freedom to express their viewpoints. The working of the intelligence network to monitor the activities of the civilian population was outrageous.

Indonesia is also known for corruption in high places. Former President Suharto supported his children to develop business connections, based on privileged access to government contracts, licenses and subsidies. Hutomo Putra Mandala (Tommy) had obtained exclusive rights for the purchase of cloves from farmers. He extracted benefits from monopolies over flour and tin plates. He also got the coveted post to produce the Indonesian car (Pt Timor Putra Nasional) and establish Sempati Air. Suharto's daughter, Siti Prabowo, had got the share in a $10 billion project for linking Malaysia and Indonesia over the Malacca Straits. Likewise, his two other sons, Bambang and Sigit Harjojudanto had greatly benefited in business matters because of their genealogy, and the President knew it. The *Economist* had reported that the members of the Suharto clan could walk into any state bank and demand a loan at favourable terms. The government always awarded the juicy contracts to the Suharto family in the areas of power generation, telecommunications and toll-roads.[8]

Corruption and cronyism had become an important part of his administration and effected the socio-economic life. The political and economic situation had deteriorated because most of the monitoring agencies — the legislature and judiciary — had been turned subservient to the executive. The political parties were either banned or if they survived had to observe a code of conduct favourable to the armed forces. *Pancasila* had been declared a national ideology, and the government was responsible for formulation of ideas and interpretation of the *Pancasila*.[9] The meaning of *Pancasila* had been stretched to prescribing a society modelled on the traditional family in which parental authority was respected and in which individual interest was subordinate to the community. The government came forward with some laws under its framework, like *Pancasila* labour relations, which implied that there could be no conflict of interest between workers and management and that the strikes were inherently anti-social.

Political reform has been on the agenda of the government in the post-Suharto era. They have decided to lift control over the political parties and thus a multi-party system has emerged. All parties were given financial aid from the government, the amount depending on the number of votes received in the elections.[10] They also reduced the number of appointed members with MPR and DPR from thousand to seven hundred, and increased their powers in rule-making. For instance, although the MPR was declared supreme power through Article 1 of the 1945 Constitution, vested with three important tasks, namely, approving the constitution, deciding the guidelines of state policy, and election of the president and vice president, its authorities had been eroded. MPR indeed had abdicated all its responsibilities except ritually appointing the president after five years. Now there is a growing demand that it should play an active role in decision-making. The most important aspect of the reform process is that they have decided to restore Article 28 of the 1945 Constitution in letter and spirits, which guarantees the right of "free assembly and association, of expression of opinion, orally or in writing", to the Indonesian citizens.

Human rights

The issues concerning human rights of Indonesian people have assumed importance as human rights is an important element of civilised society. In accordance with the Universal Declaration of Human Rights, the ideal law of free human beings, enjoying freedom from fear and want can only be achieved if the conditions are created whereby every one may enjoy his economic, social and cultural rights, as well as civil and political rights. The removal of poverty is essential in order to promote human rights. Indonesia adopted development programmes for its impoverished population in 1967, when Suharto signed the documents of declaration of world leaders on population. In view of this policy, national family planning programmes were supported and the schemes proved successful in limiting the increase of population. Total fertility rate came down to fifty per cent as desired by the government and Indonesian expertise was appreciated in most of the neighbouring countries.

However, the policy, which proved controversial was transmigration of the people from densely populated areas to less populated zones. Java and Bali inhabit sixty-five per cent of Indonesian population. Java alone has a hundred million people. This island however occupies only 6.8 per cent of the total land of the country. Sumatra, which is comparatively bigger in size, has forty-one million, Sulawesi thirteen million, Nusatenggara 11.5 million, Maluku 11.9 million and Kalimantan has eleven million population.[11] It is known that only nine hundred and ninety-two out of 17,508 islands are mainly populated zones, though Haryati Soebadio says that five thousand islands are inhabited.[12] Indonesia endeavoured to diversify its population from densely populated areas to new zones. Between 1960 and 1973, they transmigrated people from Java to other islands. Initially, 17,116 families were settled in Irian Jaya and 8,155 in Maluku but a number of people were also transmigrated to Katimantan, East Timor and Aceh.[13] Joan Hardejono says that the number of transmigration were 49,772 in 1979–80, 108,081 in 1980–81, 123,846 in 1981–82, 167,477 in 1982–83 and 86,298 in 1983–84.[14] As the government supported it, transmigration continued. Yet, it has not resolved the problem of population density in Java. As job opportunities are available mostly in Java, poor and impoverished people continued to come to Java, and the problem remains the same.

Some opposition groups argued that the alien population was arbitrarily introduced to change the demographic complexion and that this was an intrusion in their human rights. The indigenous people in Irian Jaya, Maluku, who have significant number of Christians were unhappy that their distinct identity would be diluted in due course if the transmigrants was not stopped. They alleged that Javanese migrants were arrogant, and had a sense of superiority. They assumed that the unwanted people thrust upon them had been sent to colonise the entire area. Worse, the new migrants generally searched jobs in oil exploration, mining and forestry department, which the local people projected as being contrary to their interests. They argued that ultimately the new transmigrants would deprive them of their wealth and resources.[15]

Besides human rights, the issue of environment has assumed importance in Indonesia in the past few years. The increasing denudation of forests and logging have led to environmental problems. The smoky haze resulting from the forest fire in Sumatra and Borneo in 1997 engulfed a large part of Southeast Asia for months. The fire had reached Malaysia, Brunei, Singapore and Australia as well. The smoky haze generated a number of health problems and disrupted tourism and transport system. A forest fire at Sumatra in March this year caught Malaysia and Singapore as well. The neighbouring countries are alarmed of the recurring forest fire in Indonesia. The environmental problems are serious and can be resolved only with the support of the ASEAN, the APEC and the UN.

To maintain territorial integrity of Indonesia, the problems of Irian Jaya, Aceh and Ambon need to be resolved but solutions to their grievances are not in sight. It is feared that the demand of the dissidents for a referendum on the pattern in East Timor, would lead to secession. The succession of even one province would encourage fragmentation of the Indonesian republic resulting in political instability in the region. The Indonesian legislature (DPR) might be ready to discuss autonomy proposals. For instance, DPR representatives are suggesting that Aceh might be allowed to decree radical Islamic Laws in place of *Pancasila*. It may be apportioned up to seventy-five per cent of the revenues on account of its oil, besides the right to generate other sources of revenues.[16] Similarly Irian Jaya, which is the largest and remotest province of Indonesia, can think about autonomy. The DPR might discuss apportioning the share of that province in the profits due to mining of gold, logging of timber, etc. The question of introducing Christian laws would also arise.

References

1 *Indonesia* (1997) An official Handbook, Jakarta Department of Information, Republic of Indonesia, pp. 37–40.

2 The Composition and the Status of the MPR, DPR and Regional House of Representatives, Jakarta, Department of Information, Republic of Indonesia, 1996, pp. 9–10.

3 *Ibid*, pp. 19–20.

4 *Indonesia Handbook*, Jakarta, Department of Information, 1989, p. 196.

[5] *Indonesia,* Information Section, Embassy of the Republic of Indonesia, New Delhi, 1995, p. 64.

[6] *The Times of India,* New Delhi, 20 February, 1998.

[7] General Edi Sudradjat, "The Dual Function of the Indonesian Armed Forces", *Indonesia,* New Delhi, Embassy of the Republic of Indonesia, 1995, p. 32, and also see Nugroho Notosusanto, *The National Struggle and the Armed Forces in Indonesia,* Jakarta, Department of Defence and Security, 1975.

[8] "Indonesia: Dear Daddy", *The Economist,* 13–19 December, 1997, p. 61.

[9] "*Pancasila,* the State Philosophy", *Indonesia*: An official Handbook, Jakarta, Department of Information, 1997, p. 41.

[10] "Political Reform", *Image of Indonesia,* Jakarta, July 1998, p. 3.

[11] Juwono Sudarsono, "The Challenges to Indonesia's Unity", *Indonesia: 50 years,* Embassy of the Republic of Indonesia, New Delhi, 1995, p. 51.

[12] Haryati Soebadio, ed. *Dynamics of Indonesian History,* Amsterdam, North Holland Publishing Company, 1978, preface.

[13] Soewartoyo, "Internal Migration between Java — Bali and Eastern Indonesia', *Indonesia Quarterly,* Vol. 24, No. 3, 1996, p. 310.

[14] Joan Hardjono, "Transmigration: Looking to the Future", *Bulletin of Indonesian Economic Studies,* Vol. 22, No. 2, August 1986, p..29.

[15] Michael Richardson, "Making Irian Jaya Pay its way", *Far Eastern Economic Review,* 13 June, 1975, p. 15.

[16] Harsja W. Bachtiar, *The Indonesia Nation: Some Problems of Integration and Disintegration,* Singapore ISEAS, 1976, pp. 29–30.

5

Trouble Spots — East Timor, Aceh, Ambon and Irian Jaya

V. Jayanth

Gen. Suharto, who assumed power in 1965–66 after crushing a Communist-inspired coup under the orders of Indonesia's first president, Sukarno, declared himself the President and established in 1967 what he called a 'New Order Government'. For a full thirty-two years, he ruled with an iron hand. Even as his family members — sons and daughters — garnered all the wealth and riches by creating their own monopolies and controlling the country's trade and industrial empire, Suharto also helped to build a new economy. The country enjoyed stability on the political front, a hallowed peace enforced by the Armed forces (then known as ABRI) and continued prosperity. The economy maintained a growth of seven to eight per cent of GDP in the 1990s, till the regional crisis blew up. So, there was a relative calm and all round tolerance in the country, despite the undermining tensions.

All through his three decades in office, Gen. Suharto did face the same problems that his successors did and are still doing. It was only his way of handling and suppressing the uprising that made a difference.

With the might of the ABRI behind him and his son-in-law, Maj. Gen. Prabowo in charge of the special forces, the Suharto regime managed to crush dissent and flaunt its economic power of a two hundred million nation to silence the international community.

The East Timor issue has been burning bright and long ever since his forces invaded the former Portuguese territory in 1975 and annexed it. A rubber seal parliament legalised the annexation and announced East Timor as the 27th province of Indonesia. However, the United Nations and the international community did not accept or recognise the annexation, though the so-called champions of democracy in the West, remained silent. It was only on the human rights front that Jakarta and the Suharto regime faced any pinpricks. Yet, they brushed aside all the international criticism on this score and went ahead with their agenda.

Every year, as an annual ritual, a group of East Timorese stormed one or two of the Western Embassies in Jakarta and sought political asylum. This way, the individuals got their freedom and the East Timor issue remained alive.

The basic Java-Sumatra divide runs deep and strong across Indonesia, and there are several burning problems that need to be sorted out; at least four major 'Trouble spots' are now crying for solution. They are East Timor, Aceh, Ambon and Irian Jaya.

Basically, they may be different manifestations of the same problem, but they have all reached various stages of 'explosion'. The East Timor issue has burst out in the open and the international community, through the aegis of the UN was forced to intervene and restore order. A transition is now taking place and a UN sponsored peace-keeping force is maintaining calm in this troubled island. At least it is nearer a solution.

Aceh has moved to the centre-stage right now. An underground freedom movement has been active there since the 1960s, but when Gen. Suharto established himself in power, he wiped out all dissent. To this day, there are complaints of genocide, massacre and suppression of political rights in this highly sensitive island. A religious or communal divide has taken shape in Ambon because of the Christian-Muslim divide.

Mass graves have been unearthed after Wahid took over the reigns and for the first time in its history, Indonesia is witnessing a proper inquiry by a human rights panel into these brutal killings. There is hope that at least some of the military leaders and soldiers responsible for the massacre will be brought to book after this trial.

It is Irian Jaya which is still waiting to explode. Even if there have been frequent skirmishes and clashes between the local tribals and army units stationed there, not much is heard about the problems because of the limited access to the island.

The Suharto regime gave away the mineral wealth in Irian Jaya and the mining rights of gold as well, to influential local and foreign companies. This resulted in frequent clashes between the local population and the 'intruders', with the military invariably backing the companies. The extent of damage to the environment and the killings of innocent tribals in the island have still not been fully assessed. It is only when the whole picture emerges that the Indonesian authorities and the international community will wake up to the realities.

East Timor

From the time the Portuguese left this territory in 1975, the trouble began. East Timor was known to be an oil-rich land and the countries near the territory were naturally interested. Indonesia was the immediate neighbour, which had a huge stake in this territory. Its southern neighbour was Australia.

Unfortunately, Portugal vacated its eastern colony without making any alternative arrangement in place and without any transition of power to a local administration. There was a political and administrative vacuum. Jakarta found this an inviting proposition and Gen. Suharto, now well entrenched in power, ordered his troops to enter into East Timor.

There was a nascent independence movement growing up in East Timor, but it was certainly not equipped to take on the might of the Indonesian armed forces. It was therefore a cakewalk for the troops and the former Portuguese colony was annexed. The Indonesian parliament swiftly declared East Timor as the country's 27th province and it was all over as far as Jakarta was concerned.

However, the United Nations did not recognise the annexation and Portugal also lodged a strong protest. Under the UN auspices, a tripartite group consisting of the Foreign Ministers of Portugal and Indonesia, besides the UN's representative was set up to negotiate a mutually acceptable solution.

So long as Gen. Suharto was in power, there was no scope for a solution. He and his government would never accept anything other than the recognition of East Timor as part of

Indonesia. At best, they were willing to consider some degree of autonomy.

The peculiarity of East Timor was that it was predominantly a Christian majority area, where the Roman Catholic Church held sway. Without getting overtly involved in the crossfire between the pro-independence militia and the government in Jakarta, the Church played the role of a liaison to minimise the clashes and contain the violence.

Besides running the administration from the provincial capital of Dili, Jakarta stationed thousands of its troops in East Timor to keep the armed insurgents under check. Some trappings of development did take place, but the people refused to accept the writ of Jakarta. For fear of violence and military atrocities, they suffered in silence.

The 1991 massacre in Dili, unleashed by the Indonesian troops, may well have been the turning point in the history of East Timor. The forces gunned down more than a hundred innocent East Timorese as they staged a major protest against the rule by Jakarta.

The *Falintil* will be remembered as the major force, which worked for the ultimate independence of East Timor. During the late 1970s and the 1980s, its guerillas were pushed back by the Indonesian troops and reduced to a bare minimum of a couple of hundred cadres.

However, in the 1990s, *Falintil* grew and developed under a new military leadership and blossomed into a sophisticated freedom movement which began to work in international fora for securing independence for East Timor.

The greatest recognition for East Timor came in 1996, when Dili's Archbishop, Rev. Carlos Belo, and the exiled leader of *Falintil*, Ramos Horta, who was based in Sydney, were decorated with the Nobel Peace Prize for the year. That infuriated Jakarta and provided a new fillip to the independence movement. There has been no looking back since.

If not for the East Asian economic crisis, independence could not have come so soon for East Timor. The political and social upheaval in the archipelago brought the Suharto administration to a standstill. Protests by youths and unrest finally led to the collapse of the government and the resignation of Suharto on 21 May, 1998.

The vice president, B.J. Habibie, was sworn in as the new president of what was recognised to be a transition government. The technocrat-turned politician lacked credibility and a mandate to rule. So he promised elections under a new and liberal political framework, as soon as possible. Yet, this took over a year.

General elections in June 1999 threw up a hung parliament, with the main opposition Democratic Party (Struggle) or the PDI-P of Ms. Megawati Sukarnoputri, garnering thirty-four per cent of popular vote. Still, her own allies did not want to make her the president, raising both the sex card and suspicions over her Islamic identity, despite her being the daughter of founding president, Sukarno.

Even as Habibie planned to try his luck in the game of numbers for the presidential election in October 1999, he promised the UN to hold a 'popular consultation'—an euphemism for a referendum—in East Timor.

However, the unfortunate thing in that territory was the fostering of pro-Jakarta militia by the armed forces. These groups, which received the patronage and arms from the Indonesian troops, went on a rampage time and again, intimidating the East Timorese people and posing a serious threat to a free and fair ballot.

So the UN mission for East Timor postponed the ballot and finally held it on 31 August, 1999. An overwhelming majority, 78.5 per cent, voted for independence from Indonesia. An amazing 98.6 per cent of the registered voters exercised their choice, despite the reign of terror. The vote itself was a big victory for democracy and the UN mission.

Unfortunately, the problem did not end there. Within a week of the vote, to coincide with the formal announcement of the results by the UN Secretary General, Kofi Annan, the pro-Jakarta militia went berserk. From 4 September onwards, the militia, backed up by the Indonesian army, unleashed an unprecedented carnage in East Timor. Hundreds were slaughtered and thousands sought refuge in neighbouring areas. West Timor became home to thousands of refugees and reports suggested that the militia did not spare even them.

After several warnings from the UN and the international community, Jakarta finally agreed to let in multinational forces, led by Australia and insisted on a phased withdrawal of the Indonesian troops from East Timor. Only then sanity prevailed and the rule of law was restored in the territory.

Credit must be given to President Wahid, for acceding to the demand for an impartial inquiry into the brutal massacres in East Timor and the unearthing of mass graves. It is hoped that this human rights inquiry will pin the responsibility for the tragic events in September and bring to book the guilty. Gen. Wiranto, who was the armed forces chief at that time and subsequently named the Minister for Political and Security Affairs, by Wahid, was forced to resign from the cabinet, pending the inquiry.

Despite all these unfortunate developments, the evolution of an independent East Timor is well on course.

Xanana Gusmao, who was initially the chief of *Falintil*, and was detained for nearly eight years by the Suharto regime, was finally released ahead of the ballot and became the President of the National Council for Timorese Resistance (CNRT).

Adopting a statesmanlike attitude, Gusmao and his friends in exile returned to Dili and took charge of the massive rehabilitation programme with UN assistance. In a press conference soon after the ballot, he said, "The international community's commitment to peacekeepers is the only way to end the genocide in East Timor".

The UN and the international community responded positively, and today a massive UN mission is assisting CNRT in rebuilding East Timor and preparing for its independent rule. The process of transition is bound to be challenging.

In an interview soon after the ballot, East Timor's *de facto* Foreign Minister, Jose Ramos Horta, outlined CNRT's plans: "Beyond addressing this emergency situation, we are working on a strategic development plan and we are looking to set up a provisional Government. We have some very good people of the younger generation who have tremendous credibility and professional expertise. I find it laughable that the Indonesians keep telling us East Timor cannot manage itself without Indonesia."[1]

That will be the real challenge. East Timor must rise from the ashes and rebuild itself. The international community and liberation movements around the world will closely watch it, because it becomes the best example of a territory achieving independence through democratic means.

The international community has a duty to provide all the help it can to assist East Timor and CNRT in institution-building, human resource development and nurturing a democratic framework for its future. The new leadership in Dili must rise above petty politics and stick to its assurances and objectives. The pro-Jakarta militia must be reformed and made to accept the new realities — or else, they should leave East Timor.

In a recently written article,[2] Gusmao and representatives of international agencies working in East Timor, noted: "The UN Transitional Administration and international agencies operate in East Timor under clearly defined responsibilities. These include maintaining border security and ensuring public order; assisting in the reconstruction of shattered infrastructure; providing the basics of food, health and education; and helping to create a new administration and institutions to get the economy back on its feet and the democratic process under way".

The developments in East Timor will be the focus of international attention over the next few years. The UN peacekeepers will have to withdraw at some time and the local people must be trained in security, policing and administration before that. As late as 5 September, on the eve of the UN's millennium summit, its mission in West Timor was attacked. The militia beat three UN personnel to death. This must end. East Timor is now a model for the world, but also a trend in Indonesia. Other islands and neglected provinces are now demanding independence or the right to self-determination. The UN must make a success of this experiment.

Aceh

Solving the problem in Ambon could well be the major challenge of the Wahid presidency. In his characteristic and hasty manner, Wahid assured the Acehnese that they too would be granted the favour of a referendum, like East Timor, in deciding their future. That has opened a Pandora's box and the Indonesian military leaders are up in arms against what they describe as "inexperienced and un-thinking assurances" coming from the President. Under pressure, Wahid is now trying to assuage the people of Aceh.

As political analyst and former presidential adviser, Ms. Dewi Fortuna Anwar explained to me (in a conversation): "Aceh can live without Indonesia, but Indonesia cannot live without Aceh". This is both politically and economically true. The province of Aceh accounted for seventeen per cent of Indonesia's $ 11.8 billion oil and gas export earnings in 1997. Moreover, it is a Muslim dominated area and if they want to secede from Indonesia, it could send wrong signals and spark the disintegration of the archipelago. As a result of the military operations and atrocities since the 1960s and 1970s, the Acehnese feel so alienated from Indonesia, and its political leadership that it may be difficult to convince them to stick on with the republic.

Thousands of Acehnese fled the province, taking refuge in Malaysia, Singapore and Thailand. Many of them, detained in Malaysian prisons, created riots in 1997 and 1998, so that the authorities deported them back to Aceh.

The rebel Free Aceh Movement, known as GAM, has been campaigning for freedom, and Indonesian Army officers confess that if the movement decided to take on the military in a do-or-die battle, nothing could stop them. Even the Acehnese women could take up arms against the military to avenge the killing of a father, husband, brother or son. That is the story of army atrocity in Aceh.

As in East Timor, many mass graves have been discovered in this province and the Wahid administration has launched several initiatives to atone for the past excesses. The President appointed an Acehnese as his Human Rights minister (a new portfolio in a new era) and another as the deputy armed forces chief. All troops, not based in the province, especially the special task forces, were withdrawn. Four ministers were sent on a 'hearing mission', to listen to all the grievances and Wahid himself visited Aceh and addressed meetings.

Only a negotiated, political settlement can bring peace to Aceh and prevent its secession. For that, Jakarta will have to talk to various factions of GAM to find an acceptable solution. In the GAM, there are hard-liners, based in Sweden; moderates who stay in both Sweden and Malaysia and the military wing, whose locations and leaders remain a mystery.

The hardcore elements will not settle for anything less than freedom and leaders like Hasan di Tiro continue to work for that objective, trying to win diplomatic support. The moderates may be willing to negotiate with Jakarta and perhaps settle for an autonomous framework within a federal Indonesia. The military wing terrorises the people in Aceh and accuses the other groups of having links with authorities in Jakarta. It is therefore a confused scenario. Who can speak Jakarta to and clinch a deal to douse the flames in Aceh?

Fortunately, for Indonesia, the international community may be fatigued with independence and liberation after East Timor. There is international realisation that any more secession from Indonesia can spell disaster. If a Muslim-dominated province wants to break away from Indonesia, it can have repercussions for Thailand and the Philippines, which are already experiencing [3] similar problems.

How Wahid handles the Aceh problem and the kind of solution that he can find to satisfy all sections of the people will decide the future of the Republic of Indonesia. It has national and regional repercussions. His policy of "accommodation and negotiation" may pay off. In a step forward, Jakarta has signed an agreement with GAM to serve as a ceasefire. Joint committees are to be set up to deal with humanitarian problems and to evolve security modalities to halt the military operations.[4]

Ambon — The Moluccas or Spice Islands

This is a peculiar crisis too. It is a city divided along communal lines—Muslims occupy one end of town and Christians the other. There is a line of partition, as it was, a no man's land, which acts as a buffer zone. For decades, the two communities lived in peaceful co-existence. However, the economic crisis and the attack on the ethnic Chinese, who were mostly Christian, in other islands of the archipelago, in 1997–98, created tensions in Ambon too.

Not only Ambon, but also some other parts of the Malukus (a chain of islands) have witnessed deep divisions and the worst communal riots during the past couple of years. Hundreds of Muslims and Christians have been killed and the islands have also witnessed a clash between the local police (who are often Christian) and the armed forces (basically Muslim).

Most of Ambon was in flames in one of the riots or the other, and the famous Silo church in the centre of the city, today remains a symbol of the deep divisions, with a charred facade. The Maluku islands have a 740,000 strong Protestant population. One community accuses the other of trying to 'Christianise' the area or 'Islamise' the island.

When Muslims in Ambon were killed in the clashes, it sparked countrywide protests and riots. Fundamentalist groups like the Islam Defenders Forum want jihadis in

Amber to save the Muslims and accuse the government and the armed forces of adopting 'double standards' when it comes to investigating human rights violations in Amber.

Many refugee camps had come up in the islands to provide food, shelter and protection to people of both communities, fleeing the scenes of violence. Nursing their wounds and bringing the two communities back to the path of peaceful co-existence may be a real challenge to the authorities.

An estimated 300,000 people in the islands are said to have been displaced in the continuing riots. There were frequent reprisals and the arrival of 'jihadis' from other parts of Indonesia to support the local Muslim population, things went out of control in June and July 2000.

Television footage released by the Associated Press on clashes in July clearly showed the Indonesian military providing cover to the Muslim militants during an attack on a Christian neighbourhood. Reports from Ambon indicated that the militants used M-16 and SS-1 rifles, normally available only with the Indonesian troops. An armoured personnel carrier was also used as a shield for these fighters.

The former Defence Minister, Juwono Sudarsono was quoted as saying "some or even many members of the army have become a major cause of the clashes" and urged the Army leadership to fire the 'rogue soldiers'.

With the pressure from within and the international community mounting on Jakarta, the president, Wahid acknowledged that his government would consider seeking limited international help to contain the religious strife. After declaring a state of emergency in the province, he said, "If the outcome is still not satisfactory when we have done our best, we may ask for help in the form of equipment and logistics". However, he ruled out the involvement of foreign troops or peacekeepers, as requested by the Church.[5]

Unless the government is able to quell these clashes and restore normalcy in the Moluccas in a matter of weeks or months, it is quite possible that international pressure would mount on the government to take some necessary steps.

It is time for the Indonesian Army to realise the seriousness of the situation and protect whatever is left of its credibility.

Irian Jaya

Thanks to its isolation and limited access, the problems in this province did not reach the climax or receive the kind of attention that the others have done. However, that does not mean that it is less serious. The crisis in Irian Jaya has now blown the whistle and come out in the open.

It is essentially a clash among the local tribes, unused to and unwilling to taste the fruits of modern development or civilisation, a hardened military which wants to exploit the mineral wealth of the region and foreign investors who have sunk huge funds to tap the gold and other deposits in the area. With the army trying to protect the investors and foreigners, a guerilla war is on in Irian Jaya. People from all the three sides are falling prey to this clash of interests. The tribals, one generation of whom still live in the Stone Age, have developed their own breed of deadly weapons and take on the might of the army. They make it a point to target immigrants from other islands and the foreigners as well, for exploiting their land. An American multinational company, which won mining rights and operates a port in this province, is at the heart of this crisis.

It has become another major crisis. A congress of West Papuan leaders recently came up with a "declaration of independence". The problems may be similar to the troubled province of Aceh, but there is also the tribal question and the perceived atrocities of foreign investors—Freeport McMoran Copper and Gold Inc.

West Papua remained under Dutch rule till 1963, when its sovereignty was transferred to Indonesia and this ratified in a controversial UN approved referendum six years later.

However, at the recent congress over five hundred West Papuan community leaders met at the provincial capital of Jayapura and adopted the independence declaration. Irian Jaya, which President Wahid has agreed to rename West Papua, has a population of 1.8 million. However, only half of them are indigenous Papuans. The rest are migrants from other parts of Indonesia. The indigenous people are complaining against exploitation and atrocities and may well take the East Timorese example seriously.

Before the Irian Jaya problem goes out of hand, it is up to the Wahid administration to initiate a dialogue with the Papuans and find a compromise. If the rights and culture of the tribals need to be protected, that must be done. If some undue concessions or favours have been shown to the foreign investors, they must be reviewed. The military excesses have to be stopped.

What is needed in Irian Jaya is an acceptable compromise between the middle-aged past and civilisation of the indigenous people and the 'invasion' of foreign culture and investors that can upset the uneasy balance. There is also a need to maintain the bio-diversity of this province. The influx of both Muslim and Christian migrants from Java and Eastern Indonesia has to be contained.

The best solution will therefore be to depute a team of experts to study the entire province, its pattern of settlement, its mineral and forest wealth, and then come up with a comprehensive, integration plan for its development. Any such plan will mean the full involvement of the local tribes and their leadership in the decision-making process. Development cannot be 'thrust' on them. They have to be gradually sensitised and educated to decide on their future, without losing their individual or cultural identity.

Sulawesi

A more recent trouble spot is Sulawesi, which has never seen communal strife before. There have been repeated instances of communal killings and clashes. The Far Eastern Economic Review, in its 6 July (2000) issue reported an outbreak of "religious blood-letting in the Central Sulawesi coastal town of Poso". This was considered to be a symptom of the disease that is spreading in Indonesia—renewed fears that the Moluccan disease may spread to other islands as well.

"In areas of the sprawling island of Sulawesi, where people describe gun attacks and black magic in the same breath, the roots of the conflict are elusive. The violence in Poso district, which has a population of about 300,000 is usually described as having three chapters: December 1998 marked the beginning of the drunken brawls; April saw Muslims burn down three hundred Christian homes; in May, the Christians retaliated', the Review reported, commenting "local political elites have used the communal strife as a means of galvanising support drawn on religious lines".

Unfortunately, the strife in the safe haven of Sulawesi has spread. After Poso, Gorontalo and Ternate have witnessed riots and clashes. Many of them are predominantly

Christian town or habitations. As a result, Menado, in the north of Sulawesi has become a sanctuary for thousands of Christian refugees, fleeing many eastern Indonesian islands. President Wahid recently attended a 'peace ceremony' in Poso, to heal the communal wounds. However, the problem is that the atmosphere is so charged that at the drop of a hat, the spread of rumours or circulation of anonymous circulars, the lid blows off.

Challenges and the solutions

On the whole, it is a daunting challenge for President Wahid, who does not enjoy very good health. While striving to revive and rebuild the economy, he and his government will have to fight all these problems and prevent another upheaval or chaos.

His main problem may still be the armed forces. Though both the people and the international community may not countenance a military coup in Indonesia, Wahid may be treading on its toes all too often. In solving these burning issues, he will have to rake up the past misdeeds and mishandling by the armed forces, on whom he must also depend for maintaining the integrity of the archipelago.

There are reports, every now and then, of a plot by some senior military commanders, who have an axe to grind. The ailing President cannot afford to antagonise all of them. He must certainly make amends for the past and act to protect human rights, but that does not mean he can alienate the armed forces. No leader or government in Jakarta can afford to survive without the cooperation of the military, which has enjoyed unimpeded power for too long.

In the course of constitutional reforms, the powers of the armed forces are already being curtailed. They had both political and social roles, in addition to ensuring the security of the country. It calls for diplomatic skill and political sagacity to see through this period of transition and reconstruction.

Wahid will have the full support of his neighbours and the international community to deal with these problems. His vice-president, Ms. Megawati Sukarnoputri, enjoys considerable popularity, even if she is equally inexperienced in administration. After a stormy session of the People's Consultative Assembly, which ended in August, the President has reconstituted his cabinet and handed over day-to-day administrative power to his deputy. Together, they must strive to understand the complexities of these problems, realise the aspirations of the people and come up with acceptable and satisfactory solutions to each of them.

Unfortunately, the patience of parliament and the Indonesians seems to be running out. Having censured him already, the disgruntled lot of parliamentarians may be waiting for an opportunity to remove Wahid from office and install a more pliable leader who will take them back to the days of political patronage. With his predecessor, Suharto, now made to stand trial for his misdeeds, there could be more trouble for the President.

What is protecting Wahid is the lack of a credible alternative and the growing international support for his leadership. Before his critics and the pro-independence movements in Aceh, Irian Jaya and the Church in Ambon could internationalise their problem, Wahid has taken it up in bilateral and multilateral forum to enlist their support for his phased reforms.

There are no standard formula or solutions each of these areas faces different problems, calling for different solutions.

The next year or two may turn out to be very critical for Wahid and Indonesia. It is only if Indonesia overcomes these challenges that the rest of Southeast Asia, or ASEAN, can fully recover from its recent crisis and economic turmoil. There is so much at stake in Indonesia. The silver lining in all this is the international support for Wahid. The international community has woken up to the fears of 'Balkanization', and political leaders across the spectrum are now united in defending the territorial integrity of the archipelago. The President needs all the support he can muster at home and abroad to maintain peace in the midst of the wrenching transition to democracy.

References

1. *Asiaweek*, 24 September, 1999.
2. *International Herald Tribune*, 26 April, 2000.
3. *The Hindu*, 14 May, 2000.
4. *The Hindu*, 14 May, 2000.
5. *International Herald Tribune*, 18 July, 2000.

6
Islam And Political Movements In Indonesia

Dilip Chandra

The Dutch colonial rulers of Indonesia were always fully aware and alive to the potentials of Islam as a political force, especially as a rallying point against their rule and had endeavoured to contain it. The studies of Dutch Islamologists like C. Snouck Hurgronje (which were based on his first-hand knowledge) had emphasised the latent potentials of Islam.

The rather sudden departure of the Dutch from the scene in 1942, however, brought about some major changes in the Indonesian political scene. The Japanese, who replaced the Dutch, sought to use Islam to mobilise the masses to bolster their own strength. This policy, in fact, laid the foundations of Islamic political movements in Indonesia, which gathered momentum in the years to come. Although Islamic organisations like the *Muhammadiyah* (comprising mainly of urban 'modernist' Muslims) and the *Nahdlatul Ulama*

(Organisation of Islamic religious teachers called *Kiyais*, based mainly in rural East and Central Java) had existed since long, they had not been politically articulate. This articulation came with the founding of the *Majlis Syuro Muslimin Indonesia or Masyumi*, which actually was founded during the Japanese rule as a Consultative Body for Indonesian Muslims. The leadership of this important Islamic organisation was mainly from among the followers of *Muhammadiyah*, and this organisation was a precursor of the post-war or post-independence *Masyumi* political party which became the chief protagonist of an Islam state in newly independent Indonesia.

Their struggle was mainly in the nature of a conflict between the 'secular' ideology of *Pancasila* (Five Pillars) championed by Sukarno and the secular nationalists on one hand and the Islamic state protagonists on the other, who believed that Islam should be the state ideology, and that the Muslims should be obliged to follow the Islamic Law. This was the genesis of the debate over *Pancasila* versus Islam, which became intense shortly after Indonesia proclaimed independence on 17 August, 1947.

The debate on *Pancasila* versus Islam is therefore, as old as the Republic of Indonesia itself. It started in 1945, when the Japanese Military government set up the Preparatory Body For Indonesian Independence with the objective of handing over power to the Indonesian in the wake of the Japanese defeat in the Pacific War.

The controversy mainly centred on the Djakarta Charter (Piagam Jakarta), which contained the words "With the obligation for the Muslims to follow the *Sharia* (Islamic Law)".[1] The largest Muslim political organisation of this period, the *Masyumi*, argued that this Charter ought to be treated as the preamble to the 1945 Constitution commonly known as UUD'45, and the obligation for the Muslim community be endorsed. The debate continued for the next fifteen years, both inside and outside the parliament, and this issue became the major point of contention in the debates of the *Dewan Konstituante,* or Constituent Assembly, set up by Sukarno to draw up a new constitution for the Republic. While the *Masyumi* and some of its supporters vehemently argued in favour of an Islamic state where Muslims would be obliged to follow the *Sharia* (their main arguments being the overwhelming majority of Muslim population in the country and Islam having played the major role as the rallying point in anti-colonial struggle), the nationalist Secular and Christian parties vociferously rejected their demands on the ground that all other ethnic and religious groups had played an equally important role in the struggle for independence and a secular basis of state would satisfy the demands of all sections of society. Three long years of debate failed to resolve this issue and eventually Sukarno disbanded the Assembly and later adopted the UUD"5 as the Constitution for the Republic. The First *Sila* or Pillar of the *Pancasila* was modified to 'Belief in One and Only Almighty God' which, it was explained, would also take care of the obligation of the Muslims. This period also marked the introduction of 'Guided Democracy' by Sukarno where the Communists came to play a more dominant role and the *Masyumi* found itself marginalised.[2]

These and several other developments at the centre led to (what has come to be known as) the *PRRI/PERMESTA* rebellion in the outer islands, specially Sumatra and Sulawesi in 1958, which was also joined by some top leaders of the *Masyumi* like Mohammad Natsir, Syafruddin Prawiranegra, etc. The rebellions were however effectively put down by the Army and the *Masyumi* was banned in August 1960. The issue resurfaced a decade later in 1968 when it was indirectly raised in the *MPRS (Majlis Perwakilan Rakyat Sementara)* session by one of its chairmen, General A. H. Nasution. He defended demands of the Muslim groups in the session that Jakarta Charter be given legal status.[3] The military government for reasons not difficult to find rejected the demand. The Army had been suspicious of Islamic extremist movements, especially since the days of *Darul Islam/Tentera Islam* in Indonesia in the early 1950s who had sought to establish an Islamic state through rebellion. Bitter armed clashes had taken place between the two sides over the years.[4] The memories of the *PRRI* also were still fresh in the minds of the Armed Forces, and this became evident when President Suharto summarily rejected the demands for the resurrection of the banned *Masyumi* under the leadership of even some of its erstwhile 'moderate' leaders like Mohammad Roem.[5]

The new rulers turned to *Pancasila* again which was found to be a convenient weapon to counter and curb all other political ideologies, especially Islam. *The Army made Pancasila into an article of faith,* an opposition to it was increasingly regarded as an act of disloyalty to the State and the UUD'45 which was in force. On the other hand, it was reiterated by Suharto that the *Sila* (Pillar) of 'Belief in one and only Almighty God', as explained in the *Pasal 29, ayat1* of UUD'45, allowed every citizen, including Muslims, to carry out worship according to their own religion. Suharto argued that since this First Pillar guided all the other Pillars, it guaranteed development and fertile growth of religious life, while at the same time, taught religious tolerance.[6]

While this *Pancasilisation* sought to remove ideology based politics, the depoliticisation process initiated by the government, soon after assumption of power, was meant to bring the parties under effective control of the government. The process was hastened by events such as severe protests against the Marriage Bill, the *Malari* Affair and increasing political activity in and around university campuses like Bandung Institute of Technology, etc. Emergence of various Islamic splinter groups, at times referred to as *Gerakan Sempalan Belaka* in many parts of Java, as an impact of the Iranian Revolution caused a lot of concern to the government. The 1978 MPR session decided upon what was known as *Ekaprasetia Pancakarsa* guidelines (which came to known as P4) for the implementation of *Pancasila*. It authorised the President, as the Mandatory, along with the MPR or People's Representative Assembly, to implement P4.[7]

This decision, which was preceded by heated debates and walkouts from MPR by certain sections of Islamic parties, formally set into motion the process of implementation of *Asas Tunggal Pancasila* (*Pancasila* as the sole basis) which was finally enacted in 1985. Increasing debates, protests and violence, which culminated in September 1984 in the Tanjung Priok riots, marked the intervening period.[8] This period also witnessed debates and controversies among political parties themselves and also between the national leadership and their branches with regard to acceptance of *Asas Tunggal*.[9]

These debates were more serious in the *Nahdlatul Ulama* or *NU* than any other organisation. In fact, since the decline of the *Masyumi*, it was the *NU*, which was looked upon to channelise the political aspirations of the Islamic community. The political aspirations of this party or religious scholars or *Kiayi* was represented by the *Tanfidziyah* (Executive Body) which, in fact, constituted the link between the organisation (claiming thirty million supporters in rural Java) and the government. The *NU* had been successful in forcing the government to change certain clauses of the controversial Marriage Bill of 1973 and, later with the support of other Islamic parties, in preventing the elevation of the status of various *Aliran Kepercayaans* (Streams of Beliefs) to the status of religions. These lessons were not lost on the government and, through successful manipulations of the PPP (the grouping of political parties with religious basis) leadership, dissensions were created among its constituents. Matters came to a head when many *NU* stalwarts found their names dropped from the list just prior to the General Elections in 1982. A year later, at a meeting of top *Ulamas* of the NU's Legislative Body (*Syuriah*), the *NU* decided upon the acceptance of *Asas Tunggal Pancasila* and upon withdrawing from active politics. They felt that the implementation of *Asas Tunggal* made the ideological struggle of Islam irrelevant, and hence a policy of confrontation with the government lost its rationale. The decisions were formalised at the *NU* national conference in 1984 at Situbondi in East Java. The leadership of the *Tanfidziyah* passed to Abdurrahman Wahid, the present president of Indonesia, popularly known as Gus Dur, who belonged to the new generation, considered to be a generation of intellectuals.[10] The emergence of this new leadership in *NU* also facilitated greater understanding with other Islamic mass organisation, *Muhammadiyah,* which too made adjustments to accept the *Asas Tunggal* in 1985.[11] Both organisations, however, maintained that their Islamic values had not changed with the acceptance of *Asas Tunggal Pancasila.*[12]

A review of these trends, therefore, indicates a decisive shift in the approach of the Islamic parties and organisations towards a greater accommodative and inclusivistic approach in the last decade and a half. The movement which was perhaps singularly responsible for creating this congenial atmosphere was what has come to be known as *Gerakan Pembaharauan Islam* (or Islamic Renewal Movement), one of the main proponents of which is Nur Cholis Majid, fondly called Chak Nur. He best represents the new generation of Islamic intellectual leadership of *Santris* (those coming from the background of religious schools or *Pondork Pesantrens)* with western education as well. Chak Nur is regarded by some as the first Muslim figure to conceptualise the accommodation of Islam to the state policy on Islam in Indonesia.[13] His views, therefore, came to be echoed by a host of other younger Muslim leaders. In 1970, Chak Nur, while stressing the need for renovation and integration of the *Ummat* (Islamic Community) explained that attitude of the people now was 'Islam Yes, Islamic State No'.[14] He stressed the need to separate spiritual life from worldly affairs, and asserted that there was no injunction for the Muslims to create an Islamic state. He cited the Medinah experiment of the prophet as an example of how Islam enjoins Muslims to live in harmony in a non-Islamic pluralistic society. He advocated that the state philosophy of *Pancasila,* which embraced the Quranic concept of Belief in One God was a common platfrom for all.[15] The ideas of Chak Nur are shared by a large number of the present generation of Muslim intellectuals who want to see the interests of the Muslims promoted in various ways other than through political struggle, though they should not all be regarded as his followers. However, they want the Islamic community to prosper through taking active part in every department of public life and benefit from the economic prosperity of the nation.

There is, of course, wide divergence of views on how this should be achieved. Gus Dur, for instance, is in favour of broad-based organisations and cooperation with other secular and democratic forces, rather than Muslim exclusive organisations like the ICMI.

Gus Dur's views have a strong basis because, for one thing, among Muslim intellectuals, there are serious differences with regard to how to promote the interests of the *Ummat*. For instance, leaders like Amien Rais, M. Imaduddin, etc., in the tradition of earlier generation modernist Muslim leaders, look at Islam as a complete ideology. They, therefore, appear to be accommodating to the state's political will, while not necessarily confirming to its ideological view.[16] Then there are leaders like Dawam Rahadjo, who view social action of various non-governmental agencies as the main channels of aspiration of the people. The LSM (*Lembaga Swadaya Masyarakat*) or NGOs have become increasingly important in recent years —particularly since the emasculation of political parties. Gus Dur's elevation to presidency and his alliance with the secular democratic forces in the country, the beginning of which was made by him through the *Forum Demokrasi* in 1991, will, for obvious reasons, be of greater interest now than ever before.

Nevertheless, if this new generation of Muslim leaders, in a way, facilitated the acceptance of *Pancasila* by the *Ummat*, the government itself took various steps to enlist the support of the Muslims by promoting alternatives to Islamic political parties to channelise their aspirations and resolve thorny issues.

In fact, the government plans to garner Muslim support started shortly after the take over by the Army when the Golkar (Golongan Karya or Functional Groups) was formed as a mass organisation. This was prompted by the theory of 'Floating Mass' or large sections of Muslim population which were not represented by any organisation. For instance, we find the Golkar using the GUPPI (*Gabungan Usaha Pembaharuan Pendidikan Islam* or the Federation of Initiatives to Renew Islamic Education), a traditional *Ulama* organisation of Sukabumi in West Java, in its 1971 campaign to muster Muslim votes.[17] The government in 1975 took a more important step when the *Majlis Ulama Indonesia* (MUI) was created to act as a liaison between the *Ulama* and the government officials, and to interpret the government policies. Especially the ones regarded as sensitive by the Muslims, favourably to the masses.[18] The MUI has helped resolve several controversial issues like the *Jilbab*, Halal meat, etc. At times, it has even issued *Fatwas*, (Legal advice in Islamic jurisprudence) that did not conform to the government views,[19] which have helped give it an image of an impartial body. Apart from issuing *Fatwas*, MUI has also brought out a kind of an official history of the Islamic community of Indonesia in September 1991, which has been prepared by well-known Muslim intellectuals including Dr. Taufik Abdullah, Dr. Kuntowjoyo and Dr. Hasan Ambari.[20] Another body, which has played an increasingly important role in this process, is the Department of Religion, which has actively implemented government policies for promoting religious harmony, regulating preaching activities, and removing ignorance through education. The state institutes of Islamic religion or IAIN, which are under this Department, are making significant contribution by fulfilling the need for well-educated trained teachers in different branches of Islamic education. The Army regime also set up bodies like the MDI *(Majlis Dakwah Indonesia)* to gather Muslim votes for its party Golkar in 1977 elections. It is said that MDI membership reached seventeen million by 1990.[21]

Apart from making efforts to muster Muslim votes and interpreting its policies through various Muslim organisations, the government made several significant concessions to the *Ummat* in the wake of *Asas Tunggal Pancasila*. One such step was the passing of the Bill on Religious Courts in 1989, which gave legal base to Islamic courts.[22] The Islamic community regarded it as a major victory. The noted Islamic scholar, Deliar Noer, stated that "one of the institutions of utmost importance in Islam is law or *Shariat*, which is even regarded as Islam itself. Observing how Islamic law is applied in society might help to assess the position of Islam".[23] In this context, the former Religious Affairs Minister, Munawir Sjadzali, observed that Muslim aspirations could be realised even without the Islamic political parties.[24] The 1989 Law on 'System of National Education' could also be viewed in the overall context of integrating Islamic education within the mainstream (except in the case of *Pondok Pesantren*).[25] The *Guidelines of Religious Propagation* (1978) also helped to assuage Muslim concerns against conversion to other religions when it banned proselytisation of people who were already adhering to any one of the five recognised religions.[26]

Islam in post-Soeharto era

In spite of the rise to power for the first time of a Muslim *Kiyai* (religious teacher), Abdurrahman Wahid, predicting the political future of Islam in the strife torn nation is extremely difficult, since Islam is not monolithic even as a social force in Indonesia.[27] For instance, inspite of pronouncements of unity of the *Ummat* by the top leader of the two key organisations, *NU* and *Muhammadiyah*, their differences persist. The recent strident criticism of Gus Dur and demand for him to step down by the *Muhammadiyah* (in connection with what is called the Bullogate affair) reflect the lack of confidence among the *Muhammadiyah* leader and followers in the ability of a *Kiyai* to lead the *Ummat* and the nation. The consequent belligerence of Gus Dur in retorting to such demands (as expressed to a HMI delegation recently) has served only to further undermine the unity of the *Ummat*.[28] As it always happens in Indonesia, subsequently leaders of the two organisations, tried to underplay the whole thing by talking of their unity, and the youth wings of the two went on to stage a 'road show' of popular music in Jakarta jointly as an expression of their solidarity. However, given the personal differences of the leaders of the two bodies and the historical background, it would take a lot more than mere pronouncements of Islamic unity by the two organisations to provide a political leadership, which would be acceptable to the *Ummat*.

Be that as it may, ascendancy of Islam in society and even in politics in Indonesia is likely to continue and gain further ground in the days to come. There are several factors, which could give credence to this supposition. For one thing, many of the western educated Islamic leaders of the new generation have found important places in the government (see appendix I). Secondly, even though Gus Dur may not have made much of an impact on the political scene yet, the very fact of the rise of a *Kiyai* to the highest office is significant. The *NU*, which had vowed to stay away from politics in the mid-eighties, now finds its top leader catapulted to the highest office in the land. Given its massive following and influence in the densely populated provinces of Central and East Java, *NU*, traditionally believed to be the moderate face of political Islam, could well visualise for itself a key role as the moderate civil political alternative in a political scenario which seems to be fast polarising between the two main political actors left in the field, i.e., army and Islam, the secular democrats losing much of their initial advantage after the overthrow of the military regime of Suharto. There are already indications that in a possible scenario of confrontation between the two, the secular democrats/ nationalists and other civilian forces would join hands or rally behind the only civilian alternative, and such an alliance would be easier to form, with the *NU* the moderate section of Islam — in the lead. In this context, the action taken by the government against erring army personnel in Aceh is significant. It has earlier been pointed out that one of the main reasons of Sharyo clipping the wings of political Islam was the army's long standing suspicion of it, specially the fundamentalist variety of Islam in view of years of armed encounters with Islamic extremist groups, like DI/TII, etc. The present government action could well be viewed as efforts to send the right signals to the army. This phenomenon needs to be observed more closely in the days to come.

The societal role of Islam, however, merits greater attention. Over the past one and a half decade, rise of Islamic consciousness among the Muslim inteligensia in Indonesia has been remarkable. This has been fostered to a considerable extent by the availability of quality publications on Islam, books and magazines alike, and a consequent rise in the readership of such literature, especially among the urban *Santris*. Also, the increasing stress on Islamic identity seems to be a direct consequence of the phenomenon of globalisation over the past decade. Scholars visiting Indonesia regularly for the past three decades have observed that the attendance in mosques has grown greatly.[29] The *Khotbah* of the Imams in the mosques after the Friday prayers have traditionally been sermons to make Muslims conscious of their identity, and their religious obligations. During the Suharto regime, when political activity was restricted, many political speeches/sermons with Islamic colour were delivered in certain mosques. One of them in Bandung, the Salaman mosque, in fact became a centre of such activities. The Acehnese have been critical of the previous regime, even at the time when the military was at the height of its power. Hence, mosques and Friday prayers have often provided political articulation to the Islamic community.

However, the phenomenon is not homogeneous in Indonesia. Traditionally, the fundamentalist variety of Islam seems to have been prevalent more in parts of West Java (which saw the rise of Darul Islam movement after independence) North Sumatra, Daerah Istimewa Ache, etc., than in other areas. The Javanese, by and large, have an inherent aversion towards fundamentalist Islam, and hence have always been a fertile ground for other movements. Some scholars have observed recently that Sufism or rather neo-Sufis is making some inroads in this part of the country.[30] It has been suggested that the key features of this neo-Sufism or *Tasawuf positif* as some like to call it, are their stated link with *Sharia* based Islam, pursuit of an inner dimension of religious life distancing itself from the hierarchy, authoritarianism of the conventional *'Tarekats'* (Orders). This new Sufism responds specifically to the conditions of Indonesian liberalism.

In conclusion, it may be reiterated that although the political future of Islam in Indonesia still remains uncertain, its societal role, which started gaining prominence in the eighties, continues to gather strength. As pointed out earlier, the social and religious demands of the *Ummat* can no longer be ignored, the latest example being the demand for closure of the *THMs* or *Tempat Hiburan Malam* — literally nightclubs, during the month of Ramadhan. In fact certain sections have called for an outright ban on them.[31] Similar demands against things that are perceived to be anti-Islamic are likely to be made in the days to come. However, the greatest threat/ challenge to the Islamic leadership may yet come from the fundamentalist sections, that could seriously undermine the already deteriorating law and order situation in the country.

Finally, the creation of ICMI (*Ikatan Cendakiawan Muslimin Se Indonesia)* or the Association of Muslim Intellectuals of Indonesia) in December 1990, under the chairmanship of ex-president, Prof. Habibie, was then regarded as a new landmark in government's efforts towards strengthening relations with the Islamic community. ICMI, which attracted a large number of Muslim luminaries, was created specifically to promote the interests of the Islamic community. The role of this organisation will be watched with interest now since the present president, Gus Dur, has been one of its most vocal critics stating that ICMI supporters are a minority in the Muslim community.

There has been to a major shift in the focus of the Islamic movements and its new leadership who appear to be more pragmatic and prepared to adjust them to the changed situation. This is particularly apparent in the *Santri* middle class who can now be seen in large numbers in many BUMN or state owned enterprises, LSM or NGOs, etc. This devoutly

Muslim but western educated leadership could act as 'pressure group' in the society. They want to see the *Ummat* grow in society and become economically strong.

A new chapter is being written in the struggle of Islam in Indonesia. The Islamic organisations are more inclusivistic now and have a wider area of operations. The increasing *santrinisasi* of the government and bureaucracy testifies to their strength. The Islamic political struggle is no longer for an Islamic state but for an Islamic society where culture and social values of Islam could find full manifestation. This search for a new direction could well become a model for many other Islamic nations.

List of names of some of the Ministries in Gus Dur Cabinet (2000–2004)

Dr. Rizal Ramli	:	Ph.D from Boston, USA
Prof. Dr. Ir. Bunuaram Saragih	:	Ph.D. from N. Carolina, USA
Al Hilal Hamadi	:	Product of ITB, (Banding Institute of Technology)
Dr. Mohd. Mahfood	:	Professor at Universities Islam Indonesia Yogjakarta
Prof. Dr. Yusril Ijhza Mahendra	:	Ph.D. from Egypt, Author of
Alwi Shihab	:	*Islam Inklusif : Menuju Sikap terbuka dalam beragama'* (1998)
Dr. K.A. Muhammad Thol Chah Hasan	:	(Former Head of the Central *Nahdlatul Ulema*) from Pesantren Pondok Tebuireng, Jombang, East Java.
Dr. Achmad Sujudi	:	Studied in Sydney, Australia.
Dr. A. Yahya Muhaimin (Education Minister)	:	Ph.D. from MIT, USA and a former Professor of International Relations at the Gadja Mada University.
Dr. A.S. Hikam	:	Ph.D. from Hawai. A well-known social activist, specialisation in comparative politics; product of Gadja Mada.
Dr. H. Zarkasih Nur	:	Product of IAIN, Jakarta Syarif Hidayatullah (Indonesian institute of Islamic Religion).

References

[1] See Engang Saifuddin Anshari, 1983. Also see Boland, J, 1971, for details of events relating to the debate in *The Struggle of Islam in Modern Indonesia*, The Hague, 1971.

i. Belief in one God Almighty
ii. Humanitarianism
iii. Indonesian national unity
iv. Democracy led by the wisdom of deliberation in representative bodies
v./ Social justice for all

* Sources :*Indoneisa*, Information Section of the Indonesian Embassy, New Delhi, 1997.

[2] Deliar Noer, *Administration of Islam in Indonesia*, Cornell University Monograph, No. 58, Cornell, Ithaca, New York, 1978.

[3] Mohammad Kamal Hassan, *Muslim Intellectual Response to 'New Order' Modernization in Indonesia*, Kuala Lumpur, n.d.

[4] Dijk, C. van, *Rebellion Under the Banner of Islam: The Darul Islam in Indonesia;* The Hague, 1981.

[5] Ward, K. E., *The foundation of the Partai Muslimin Indonesia* (Interim report service, modern Indonesia Projects, Southeast Asia Programme, Cornell University) Ithaca, New York, n.d.

[6] Krissantono, ed., *Pandangan Presiden Suharto tentong Pancasila*, Jakarta, 1976.

[7] Aziz Arnicum, ed., *Lima GBHN*, Sinar Grafika, Jakarta, 1994.

[8] Tapol, *The Indonesian Human Rights Campaign, Indonesia: Muslims on Trial*, April 1987, London.

[9] Zifridaus Adnan Islamic Religion 'Yes'; Islamic (Political) Ideology 'No' in Arief Budiman, ed., *Islam and State in Indonesian State and Civil Society in Indonesia* (Monash Papers on Southeast Asia, No. 22, Monash University) Clayton/Victoria.

[10] Department Penerangan RI and Department Agama RI, Jakarta: UU No. 3/1985 on Parpol and UU No. 8/1985 on Ormas.

[11] Sujarwanto, ed., *Muhammadiyah dan Tantangan Masa Depan: Sebuah Dialog Intelektual*, Yogyakarta, 1990.

[12] Laode Ida, *Anatomi Konflik NU Elit Islam dan Negara*, Jakarta, 1996.

[13] See Zifridaus Adnan, n.9.

[14] See Mohammad Kamal Hassan, n.3.pp. 187–233.

[15] Ibid, 232–33.

[16] See Zifridaus Adnan, n.9, p. 465.

[17] Heru Cahyono, *Peranan Ulama dalam Golkar, 1971–1980,* Jakarta, 1992.

[18] Deliar Noer, n.2.

[19] See *Himpunan Keputusan dan Fatwa Majlis Ulama Indonesia* (MUI Secretarit Mesjid Istiqlal Jakarta) 1995. It is declared SDSB, government sponsored lottery as *Haram* (prohibited according to Islamic law), pp 114–23.

[20] Taufik Abdullah, ed., *Sejarah Ummat Islam Indonesia,* MUI, Jakarta, 1991.

[21] See *Tempo,* 3 March, 1990.

[22] H. Zain Badjebar, 1989.

[23] Deliar Noer, n.2, p. 42.

[24] Mohd. Hisyam 'The Dynamics of the Interaction of Religion and State in Indonesia: the case of the Islamic court. Draft discussion paper for first international conference on *Islam and the 21st Century,* Leiden University, June 1969,

[25] Ludjto, H.A. 'Islamic Education in Indonesia Pre and Post the Law No. 2 year 1989, on the system of national education. Paper presented at the seminar of Islamic studies, INIS, University of Leiden, October, 1996.

[26] Bambang Prawond M., "Which Islam and Which Pancasila? Islam and the State in Indonesia: A Comment" in Arief Budiman, n.9.

[27] Satu P. Limaye, *Islam in Asia* Seminar series, Asia-Pacific Centre for Security studies, Honolulu (Feb. 2000), p. 25.

[28] *Republika* on line. 31.10.200 to 18.11.2000 (Gus Dur challenged them saying, *Kalau tidak Mau ###*)

[29] Mentioned to the authority Prof. B.D. Ghoshal, of JNU, New Delhi, after his recent visit to Indonesia couple of months ago.

[30] Julia Day Howell, 'Indonesia's urban santris; challenging stereotypes of Islamic revival' in *ISIM*, Leiden, Newsletter, 6/00, p. 17.

[31] *Republika* online, dt. 28.11.2000.

7
Hinduism in Modern Indonesia

M. Ramstedt

The international news coverage of the violent clashes between Muslims and Christians, which have increasingly haunted Indonesia since Suharto's demise in May 1998, has obscured the fact that there are also other minority religions threatened by the Islamic resurgence in Indonesia. One of them is Hinduism, which is usually exclusively associated with Bali. It is hardly known that it was only between 1958 and 1961 that the religious leaders of the Balinese unanimously declared the "Balinese religion" to be Hindu, and that Hinduism was then adopted by adherents of other ethnic religions comprising *Agama Budha* (Tengger, East Java), various groups of the Javanese *kebatinan* tradition (Central and East Java), *Aluk To Dolo* (Sa'dan-Toraja, South Sulawesi), *Ada' Mappurondo* (Mamasa-Toraja, South Sulawesi), the *Towani Tolotang* tradition (Bugis, South Sulawesi), *Kaharingan* (Ngaju- and Luangan-Dayak, Central and South Kalimantan), and *Pemena* (Karo-Batak, North Sumatra).

The development of "Indonesian Hinduism" or *Hindu Dharma Indonesia* has in fact been a response to the religious policy of the Indonesian state which has been based on opportune interpretations of the *Pancasila*, the five principles contained in the preamble of the Indonesian Constitution of 1945. Sukarno, the foremost leader of the Indonesian independence movement who then became Indonesia's first president formulated them. The first and highest principle is "Belief in the One and Almighty God" (*Ketuhanan Yang Maha Esa*) which has made Indonesia a religious state, albeit not an Islamic theocracy. It was formulated in such a way that it would hopefully placate the radical Islamic strand within the independence movement, which had wished to see the *Shariat* (Islamic law) being made the basis of the Indonesian Constitution, without alienating the significant Christian segment of the Indonesian people living for the most part in Eastern Indonesia. On the basis of this principle, the Muslim-dominated Indonesian Ministry of Religion formulated a definition of religion (*agama*) that requires a sacred tradition to be monotheistic, universal, and scriptural in order to qualify as "religion". It consequently has not recognised the country's plethora of ethnic religions because they do not match the official definition of *agama*. Instead, they were classified as "currents of belief" (*aliran kepercayaan*) and equated with "primitive animism", parochialism, "superstition", "magic", polytheism, and ancestor worship.[1]

The Balinese eventually succeeded in having their ethnic religion recognised as "Hindu" and "religion", after their religious leaders had reformulated the traditional beliefs and practices along the lines of the official definition of "religion", having taken recourse to monotheistic versions of Indian Reform- or Neo-Hinduism in order to allay accusations of "animism", parochialism, ancestor worship, and "polytheism". When Suharto's purge of Communism increased the necessity to register as a member of an officially recognised religious community, quite a few adherents of the above-mentioned ethnic religions resorted to Hinduism between 1965 and 1980.

The heterogeneous Indonesian Hindu community remained rather fragmented during the period of relative religious tolerance, i.e., between 1965 and 1989. With the onset of the Islamic resurgence at the end of the 1980's, however, pressure that had never quite fully subsided, increased, forcing the Hindu community to bridge its inherent factionalism based on ethnicity, caste, and sect, and to realign itself with the universalist Hindu movement in India. Yet, the increasing orientation towards universalism on the part of the modern Indonesian intellectuals has incited some traditionalists to turn away from Hinduism and to embrace Christianity or Islam.[2]

In order to elucidate the issues that are at stake here, it is necessary to retrace the development of Indonesian Hinduism from its very beginning, starting with the transformation of the Balinese worldview through Dutch colonialism.

The transformation of the traditional Balinese world view through Dutch colonialism

The Dutch conquest of Bali, which was completed between 1846 and 1908, triggered a process of modernisation and religious and ritual transformation that was accompanied by the introduction of the concepts of "modernity", "(world) religion", and "Hinduism" through Dutch colonial administrators, Muslim and Christian missionaries,

European "orientalists", Javanese theosophists, and Indian Hindus.

These concepts contested the sacred cosmology of the Balinese people comprising the "visible" (*sakala*) and "invisible" (*niskala*) world. Traditional religiosity consisted of divergent local orthopraxies that were geared to bring or keep the visible world into correspondence with the principles of the invisible world. Correspondence between *sakala* and the *niskala*-principles activate the positive, constructive or life-giving aspects (*kerta*) of the transcendent, yet immanent cosmic principles, while disruption of this correspondence evoke their negative, destructive or purgative aspects, important agents in the sacred endeavour (*dharma*) to achieve and maintain *kerta* were the divine ancestors (*bhatara*) of the powerful families. Dwelling in the realm of *niskala* and thereby participating in its powers, the *bhatara* could and would give important advice when called upon by their descendants in trance or through the mediation of the Brahmin priest (*purohita*) of the respective family.

These powerful families successfully claimed descent from Majapahit noblemen and priests. Hence, they were linked through their ancestors to the historical origin of the Balinese cosmology as well as to the spiritual source of the cosmic powers itself. The East-Javanese empire of Majapahit was the last and most powerful of the Indianised states in the archipelago. It was also the last empire in a series of three East Javanese polities that had created a distinctly Old-Javanese culture, blending various elements of Indian influence (from Mahayana- and Vajrayana-Buddhism as well as from various Shaiva-and Vaishnava-sects) with the local "animist" culture. The rich literature created in these polities was still influenced by Sanskrit sources but written in the

Old-Javanese vernacular, an Austronesian language with a high percentage of loan words from Sanskrit. Bali had twice temporarily been a satellite of Majapahit's predecessors, the kingdoms of Kediri and Singasari. During the 14th century, the hey-day of Majapahit, Bali was permanently conquered until Majapahit itself was vanquished under the onslaught of the two North Javanese sultanates of Demak and Japara around 1530.

While Java was slowly Islamised, giving birth to a syncretic culture which blended core elements of the Majapahitan culture with Sufism, many noblemen and priests unwilling to convert to Islam found refuge in Bali. According to Balinese historical sources, these East Javanese noblemen and priests became the ancestors of the three upper *warna (triwangsa)* or "castes" of the traditional Balinese society, i.e., the *brahmana, satria*, and *wesia,* constituting the cultural and political elite of the traditional Balinese state (*nagara*). Successfully defending the island against encroaching Islam, this elite came to regard itself as the sole heir of Majapahit. The East Javanese empire became the golden past, the sacred point of origin as well as the sacred source of power of everything "Balinese". Hence, worship of the Majapahitan ancestors became the predominant ritual practice in pre-colonial Bali, and hardly anybody ever mentioned India.[3]

When the Dutch colonial administration began to dominate the visible world of the Balinese, European "orientalists" became interested in the Balinese notions of the invisible world. They, however, did not investigate these notions in their own right but were either inclined to regard them as a blurred mirror of ancient India or as survivals of an Old-Indonesian cultural layer which had been distorted by the Indianised culture of the "despotic" Balinese elite. Both groups of "orientalists" discriminated between "Hindu-Buddhist" and "*adat*" elements within the Balinese tradition. The term *adat* was actually a common denominator for the mostly unwritten local customary law and customary routines of all ethnic groups in the archipelago, which are based on a sacred "animist" cosmology. When it was used in connection with the Balinese tradition, it referred to those elements, which were regarded as being incident to an Old-Indonesian cultural layer.

Those scholars who investigated the Balinese culture as a blurred mirror of ancient India tended to neglect or to denigrate its indigenous or *adat* elements. In order to explain the appearance of Indianised early states in the archipelago, they supposed an Indian invasion and a subsequent conquest of various locations in Sumatra, Java, and East Kalimantan between the 4th and the 9th century. The conquest then resulted in the dissemination of Indian influence in the Western part of the archipelago. This scholarly model is known as the *ksatriya*-theory. With increasing knowledge about the sophisticated, yet idiosyncratic Hindu and Buddhist architecture of ancient Java that showed considerable independence from Indian prototypes, and due to the absence of definite proof of the existence of Indian colonies in the archipelago, scholars began to question the *ksatriya*-theory which had been modelled after the dissemination of Dutch influence in the archipelago. They now considered the possibility of a peaceful dissemination of Indian influence through the agency of Indian merchants. This model has come to be known as the *vaisya*-theory. Van Leur proposed a more sophisticated elaboration of this theory, crediting highly developed chiefdoms or petty kingdoms in the pre-Indianised archipelago with the initiative to establish trade relations with Indian counterparts. They had subsequently invited Indian Brahmins and Buddhist priests to have them upgrade the local administration and provide a new religious legitimacy.[4]

The history of the early Indianisation of the archipelago is still not fully elucidated. It is, however, safe to assume that Indians had settled in various locations but had not necessarily come as conquerors. With the Islamisation of India and Southeast Asia, large-scale contacts between India and the archipelago were severed. Yet economic relations with both northern and southern Indians of various backgrounds continued through the ages.

Once European "orientalists" had discovered traces of ancient Indian culture in Java and Bali, some Indian scholars started to turn their gaze to the Netherlands Indies, too. One of them was Ananda K. Coomaraswamy who fully embraced the *ksatriya*-theory when writing a book on Indian and Indonesian art, which was published in Germany in 1927. The "re-discovery" of Indonesia by Indian scholars coincided with the beginnings of a growing nationalist movement in India. The important role Annie Besant and the Theosophical Society played with regard to the awakening of Hindu nationalism, is well known.[5] The Theosophical Society was also influential in the Netherlands' Indies. The Javanese Mas Djono first introduced theosophy to Bali in 1915. Mas Djono was associated with the *Budi Utomo*-movement which promoted a kind of Javanese nationalism that took a great pride in Java's golden past, i.e., the history and culture of the Hindu-Javanese kingdoms of Mataram (Central Java), Kediri, Singasari, and Majapahit. When Rabindranath Tagore visited Java and Bali in 1927, he greatly inspired many leaders and members of the *Budi Utomo* as well as Balinese intellectuals. By 1915, ideas of Tagore, Gandhi, and Theosophy, the teachings of the Bhagavad Gita, and hence various notions of "Hinduism" had spread among Balinese intellectuals through the *Budi Utomo*-network. Due to its preoccupation with "natural hierarchy", Theosophy was much favoured by conservative members of the Balinese nobility (*triwangsa*). In 1937, the Adnjana Nirmala Lodge was founded. It had sixteen members who were led by I. Gusti Ketut Djelantik, a member of the royal family of Karangasem. Tagore's democratic, universalist, and tolerant notion of Hinduism was very influential among intellectuals who fought for a democratic reform of Balinese society and culture. Many of them were *Sudra* who had acquired formal education at one of the schools established by the Dutch colonial government.[6]

Already from 1917 onwards, Balinese intellectuals had begun to organise themselves in different associations due to the increasing attacks on the religious beliefs and practices of the Balinese on the part of Christian and Muslim missionaries. While some European scholars praised Bali as a storehouse of survivals from ancient India, and theosophists acknowledged its culture as an offspring of the "Aryan invasion", the missionaries claimed that neither were the Balinese religious practices "religion" nor were they "Hindu". That the missionaries found fault with the Balinese ritual system, which largely consisted of ancestor worship, denying it the status of "religion", is not very surprising, given the narrow definition of "religion" or the equivalent "*din*" within Christianity and Islam. More astonishing is, perhaps, their claim that the religious system of the Balinese is not "Hindu". This judgement seemed to echo the position of those European scholars who viewed Balinese culture as essentially being indigenous *adat*, predominantly consisting of survivals of an Old-Indonesian cultural layer which had been distorted by the Indianised culture of the "despotic" Balinese elite. While these scholars — most of whom were Dutch colonial administrators — intended to de-legitimise the traditional Balinese "despots" in favour of the Dutch colonial government, supposedly safeguarding the "original" and "innocent" Balinese culture against "oriental despotism", the missionaries sought to legitimise their attempt at proselytising "animists" or "primitive heathens". Christian missionaries had, by the way, employed the same rhetoric strategy in South India.

Eventually, the missionaries did not succeed in making many proselytes. Totally unsuccessful were the Muslim missionaries of the *Sarekat Islam*, who had come to Bali on the initiative HOS Tjokroaminoto, one of the spiritual mentors of Sukarno.[7] Their failure was probably due to the long-standing anti-Muslim sentiment among the Balinese. After a rather long period of frustration, the Dutch Reformed Church finally made a few converts in 1931, owing to the successful efforts of the Chinese "zendeling" Tsang Kam Foek. Javanese missionaries from the Reformed "Church of East-Javanese Christians" (*Gereja Kristen Jawi Protestan*) succeeded in founding a "Community of Balinese Protestants" (*Pasisikan Kristen Protestan di Bali*) in 1937. Moreover, some Balinese had taken refuge with the Catholic priest, Father J. Kersten.[8]

Despite the relative failure of the missionaries, their attacks on the "Balinese religion" were very disturbing to many Balinese. Furthermore, the socio-cultural changes induced by the Dutch colonial government threatened the local orthopraxies and thus their soteriological goal of keeping *sakala* in correspondence with *niskala*. Both factors stimulated discussions on the essence of Balinese religion and culture or the nature of *agama* and *adat*. These discussions took place in the meetings and publications of various reform organisations that sought to "purify", to foster, and to safeguard the "Balinese religion". All these organisations agreed that "static" elements of Balinese *adat*, which were neither in conformity with the demands of modern times nor in conformity with *agama*, had to be changed. They differed, however, how far they wanted to carry out these reforms. The abolishment or preservation of "caste" privileges was, of course, the issue here. More progressive organisations like *Suita Gama Tirtha* or *Surya Kanta* set out to improve the social status, the economic situation, and the level of education of the common Balinese (*Sudra* or *jaba*), including those of the women. More conservative associations like *Tjatur Wangsa Derya Gama Hindu Bali* or the editors of the newsletter *Bali Adnyana* advocated more temperate measures in order to improve the lot of the Balinese people. They highly recommended "inter-caste" co-operation, while wanting to improve the situation of the *sudra* in accordance with the regulations of *adat*.

Besides, major controversies arose with regard to the actual name of the "Balinese religion". Some would have liked to call it "Shiva-Buddha religion" because of the confluence of Hindu and Buddhist teachings in the Majapahitan tradition, which had been continued in Bali. Others pleaded for "Religion of the Holy Water" (*Agama Tirtha*) because of the importance of holy water (prepared by the Brahmin priests) in every Balinese ritual. A large part of the conservatives argued for "Hindu-Balinese religion" which would emphasise its Balinese — that is to say the *adat* — aspects, while the progressives opted for "Balinese Hindu religion" in order to stress the universal, Hindu character of the "Balinese religion", thus de-emphasising its *adat* aspects. In the discourse of the reform organisations, holding up *adat* regulations meant reinforcing the principles of the traditional social hierarchy, whereas "Hindu" referred to a kind of democratic and modern Hinduism represented by contemporary Indian thinkers like Rabindranath Tagore or Swami Vivekananda. Thus, the indigenous discourse on *adat* and "Hinduism" ran contrary to that of the European "orientalists". Whereas the latter associated *adat* with an egalitarian Old-Indonesian cultural layer which had to be liberated from the despotic Hindu court culture, Balinese intellectuals referred to *adat* as a legitimising force for the preservation of "caste" privileges, alluding to "Hinduism" when trying to tear them down.

The progressive reform organisations began to undermine the religious monopoly of the Balinese Brahmin priests (*pedanda*) by educating common Balinese in the content of the traditional sacred literature. Not only was Balinese literary heritage introduced to a wider circle of educated Balinese, the Indian *Catur Veda*, the *Bhagavad Gita*, and the systematic teachings of the *Sad Darshana*, previously unknown in Bali, were now studied by many.

With the progressing dissemination of the related concepts of "Hinduism" and "(world) religion", people started to feel the necessity to organise their religion along the Judaeo-Christian Muslim notion of "religion". In 1937, the leaders of the reform organisation *Bali Dharma Laksana* instigated the compilation of a "holy book", which was to be carried out by a team of *pedanda*. This book would have to contain the standard doctrines and ritual prescriptions of the Balinese religious system. The project, however, eventually failed due to the fact that the priests found it impossible to decide on a certain standard.[9]

The development of Hinduism under Sukarno

Immediately after World War II, many Indonesian nationalists felt greatly inspired by India's successful struggle for independence. Moreover, India was fervently supporting Indonesia's own fight for independence. When in 1950, the unitary Indonesian nation state had finally obtained international recognition, India's prime minister, Jawaharlal Nehru, was the first foreign head of state to visit free and independent Indonesia. However, in spite of a treaty professing "unalterable friendship" between the two countries, the relationship began to deteriorate when Krishna Menon replaced "the able and amiable" Sir Bengal Rau as leader of the Indian delegation of the Afro-Asia group within the United Nations. One of Indonesia's most distinguished diplomats, the late Ide Anak Agung Gde Agung from the royal Balinese family of Glanyar, attributed Sukarno's growing mistrust against India to Menon's arrogance and impatience in dealing with the other delegates. The situation was aggravated by Nehru's paternalistic behaviour during the Bandung Conference of 1955. When Nehru's claim to the leadership of the non-aligned countries clashed with Sukarno's own aspiration, the foreign policy of the two countries became irreconcilable. Given the violent Indian-Chinese border conflict, the emergence of the so-called Jakarta-Beijing axis did not help to bridge the growing rift. Official relations had deteriorated to a point of no-return when India was supporting Malaysia against Sukarno's "crush Malaysia!" policy, and Indonesia was growing close to Pakistan.[10]

When Bali was integrated into the unitary Indonesian nation state in 1950, the Balinese had still neither succeeded in standardising their traditional religious system or in agreeing on a common name with which to refer to it. Hence, it was classified not as "religion" but as a "current of belief" (*aliran kepercayaan*) by the Indonesian Ministry of Religion. Since the Ministry considered adherents of *aliran kepercayaan* as people "still without religion" (*belum beragama*), it empowered both Muslim and Christian missionaries to bring "religion" to these people. Facing the danger of becoming targets of Muslim and Christian proselytising, many Balinese religious leaders started to look to India as a source of inspiration and guidance.

At the beginning of the 1950's, some Balinese went to India to study at the Shantiniketan Vishva Bharati University, founded by Rabindranath Tagore, the Benares Hindu University, and the International Academy of Indian Culture, established by Raghu Vira, profiting from the good relations between Indonesia and India at that time. Around the same time, the *Arya Samaj* sent Narendra Dev Pandit Shastri to Bali. He became quite influential, took a Balinese wife, and settled permanently in Bali. Other Indian scholars and religious teachers visited the island on short-term trips. Direct and indirect contacts were established with the Gandhi Peace Foundation, the Divine Life Society, and the Ramakrishna Mission. The Balinese founded numerous religious organisations, which ranged from the ultra-conservative *Paruman Par Pandila* to the very progressive *Majelis Hinduisme*.

In 1958, a joint effort of the leaders of several Balinese reform organisations, Pandit Shastri, the Balinese graduates from the above-mentioned Indian universities, and a Dutch "orientalist", Roelof Goris, who had become an Indonesian citizen, succeeded in formulating a new theology for the "Hindu-Balinese religion" both along the lines of Indian "Neo-Hinduism" and in conformity with the definition of "religion" put forward by the Indonesian Ministry of Religion. The new theology was said to root in the Sanskrit *mantra: "Om tat sat ekam eva adityam"* ("Om, thus is the All-Pervading or Infinite, Undivided One"). When referring specifically to the all-pervading, Undivided One, the reformers used a term from the Old-Javanese sacred literature: *Sanghyang Widhi Wasa*. This sacred term or name has actually two readings: (1) "Divine Ruler of the Universe", and (2) "Divine, Absolute Cosmic Law". While the first reading complies with the Judaeo-Christian-Muslim notion of a personal, almighty god, the second reading recalls the term *sananta dharma* used by Indian Hindu fundamentalist to refer to Hinduism as cosmic truth.

While Indian-Indonesian relations were continuously deteriorating, Sukarno officially acknowledged "Hinduism" as "one of the religions adhered to by the Indonesian people" in 1961, after any reference to Bali in the name had been dropped. Three factors facilitated the official recognition: (1) The growing irritation on the part of Sukarno with the separatist *Darul Islam* movement; (2) The fact that many members of his inner circle were deeply influenced by theosophy; and (3) The fact that his mother was Balinese.

Strangely, the newly established *Parisada Dharma Hindu Bali*, sole representative of the Balinese Hindu community modelled after the Indian parishad, did not include Pandit

Shastri. Was the growing alienation between India and Indonesia the cause for his exclusion, or was it the growing jealousy on the part of the Balinese priesthood who did not like to see their authority thwarted by the influence of "foreign", i.e., Indian, rivals? Pandit Shastri was to be further marginalised as time went on. He retained some influence, though, through his book "*Hindu Dharma*", for which he had received an award from the Birla Foundation in India.

In 1962, the *Parisada Dharma Hindu Bali* ordered the construction of a new type of temple. Whereas the traditional Balinese temples accommodate many shrines of different deities and ancestors, this new type of Hindu temple was to house only one shrine, a *padmasana*, dedicated to *Sanghyang Widhi Wasa*. Besides, such a *padmasana* was erected in every traditional temple. There was no need, however, to dismantle all the other shrines, since the different deities and divine ancestors were now defined as being different aspects of the All-Pervading One, likened to the rays of the sun. Likewise, the traditional *warna*-system underwent redefinition, holding that *warna* was originally based on merit and function, and not on birth. Hence, the traditional social hierarchy of the Balinese was officially seen as an aberration. This view did not only result from the new religious ideology. It was also an opportune statement at a time when Communism was on the rise within Indonesian society. Besides, a new daily prayer was introduced, called *tri sandhya*, to be performed three times a day, involving the recitation of the Vedic *Gayatri Mantra* hitherto unknown in Bali

In 1964, two further steps towards universalisation were taken. Firstly, the *Parisada Dharma Hindu Bali* changed its name to *Parisada Hindu Dharma*, thereby dropping the last reference to Bali. This was due to the fact that the Hindu community in Indonesia did not any longer exclusively consist of Balinese Hindus. There were, for instance, the Indonesians of Tamil origin who for the most part lived in and around Medan in North Sumatra. In the late 19th century, many Tamil labourers had immigrated to this area in order to find work on the newly opened plantations (rubber, tobacco, and oil palms). Their descendants retained their religious practices and aligned themselves with the Balinese Hindus soon after Hinduism had been officially recognised by the Indonesian Ministry of Religion. Apart from the Tamil Indonesians, there were also the ethnic Sindhis who had immigrated to Indonesia since the beginning of the 1950s, having lost their homeland during India's partition. Furthermore, some enthusiastic Javanese nationalists had embraced "Hinduism", the supposed religion of their Hindu Javanese ancestors.

Secondly, the *Parisada Hindu Dharma* defined the so-called "five beliefs" (*Panca Sraddha*) as the fundamental doctrines of Hinduism, comprising (1) Belief in *Sanghyang Widhi Wasa*; (2) Belief in *atman*; (3) Belief in *karmaphala*; (4) Belief in *samsara*; and (5) Belief in *moksa*. If we substitute "*Sanghyang Widhi Wasa*" with "*Brahman*", then these *Panca Sraddha* are identical with the frequently described tenets of Indian "Neo-Hinduism". Moreover, a "holy canon" was fixed that was composed of the Indian *Catur Veda*, the Indian Bhagavad Gita, the Indian Upanishad, the Old-Javanese *Sarasamuccaya*, and the Old-Javanese *Sanghyang Yamahayanikan*.[11]

All these steps towards ideological universalisation notwithstanding, the key positions within the *Parisada Hindu Dharma* were exclusively occupied by Balinese Brahmin priests and Hindu intellectuals from the traditional Balinese nobility (*triwangsa*). This was going to cause problems not only among the non-Balinese Hindus, but also among the Balinese themselves.

The development of Hinduism under Suharto

With Suharto's ascent to power after the putsch of 30 September / 1 October, 1965 (GESTAPO) relations between Indonesia and India normalised, even though India lobbied in vain to have South Asia included into ASEAN.[12] The improving relations with India, however, did not result in closer ties between Indonesian and Indian Hindus. This was due to the fact that Suharto's "new order" regime discouraged identification with a transnational religious community, which would inevitably hamper the development of a strong national identity.

Religion was nevertheless promoted as a safeguard against Communism which was purged by the Indonesian military, fervently supported by Muslim organisations such as Ansor. Since atheism was equated with Communism, every Indonesian citizen had to officially register as a member of one of the five acknowledged religious communities (Islam, Protestantism, Catholicism, Hinduism, and Buddhism). Not only were Communists regarded as atheists — people "still without religion", adherents of ethnic religions or *aliran kepercayaan*, were likewise seen as atheists, boosted by the fact that many adherents of Javanese *aliran kepercayaan* had sympathised with Communist ideas. Hence, the advent of the "new order" brought about mass conversion to each of the five "religions".

In the case of Hinduism, the term "conversion" actually only applied to *abangan*[13] Javanese with former Communist leanings who forsook Islam in favour of Hinduism because of the participation of Muslim organisations in the mass killing of Communists.[14] The main reason why Indonesia's

Hindu community experienced a significant rise in numbers, was the fact that adherents of certain ethnic religions demanded the official recognition of their respective traditions as Hindu varieties. They based their claim to Hinduism on traces of Indianisation as well as on similitude to Balinese religious beliefs and practices, hoping to be able to continue their traditions under the umbrella of the supposedly more tolerant Hindu religion. As already mentioned in my introduction, the newly established Directorate for Hindu Affairs within the Indonesian Ministry of Religion assented to their proposition and consequently recognised *Agama Budha* (probably in 1968), *Aluk To Dolo* (in 1968), *Ada' Mappurondo* (in 1968), the *Towani Tolotang* tradition (in 1968), *Pemena* (in 1977), and *Kaharingan* (in 1980) as "Hindu sects" ("*sektu-sekta Hindu*"). Hence, in 1980, the Indonesian Hindu community counted 2, 988,461 members, who made up two per cent of the total Indonesian population of one hundred and forty-six million people.[15]

The official recognition of the above-mentioned ethnic traditions as "Hindu sects" might be rather surprising given the low degree of Indianisation of these ethnic religions and that their similitude to Balinese religious beliefs and practices was based on similarity of *adat*. Yet, there were three factors that facilitated the decision of the Directorate of Hindu Affairs which had of course, to act as agent of the Indonesian government: (1) Sharyo wanted to promote religion as a means to counteract Communism, not in order to encourage political Islam. He, therefore, considered a policy of religious tolerance, implying the equal promotion of all recognised religions, as most conducive to his goals; (2) Recognition of these ethnic religions as "Hindu sects" was likely to strengthen their potential as "cultural capital" for the promotion of tourism which had become a major factor in Suharto's policy of economic development; and (3) Whereas Sukarno had tried to boost the process of Indonesianisation by promoting a modern and homogenous national culture, Suharto regarded "pride in the highlights of the diverse ethnic cultures of Indonesia" as a safeguard against the intrusion of "foreign influence" such as Communism, Western democracy, or Middle Eastern Islam. Consequently, his religious policy was geared to prevent the globalisation of religious identity by tolerating local beliefs and practices, as long as they did not provide avenues for parochialism and ethnic nationalism.

The Indonesian Ministry of Religion exclusively directed the development of religion. Its various departments were instructed to support the priorities of the central government by propagating the singular essence of God, locating the basis of true religion in prophecy and scripture, emphasising the difference between divinely inspired religion (*agama*) and human belief (*aliran kepercayaan*) emphasising the importance of daily prayer, and stressing the central function of religion in the development of the country. In 1968, the Parisada Hindu Dharma had become one of the "functional groups" of Golkar and hence a member of Suharto's ruling party. Mediating between the Directorate of Hindu Affairs and the local Hindu communities, it controlled the formal Hindu education at all private and public institutions, the education of local Hindu priests, the publication of religious literature, and the activities of every non-governmental Hindu organisation in Indonesia. Supporting a process of cultural Indonesianisation rather than religious universalisation, it again changed its name in 1986. Underpinning its national orientation, it now called itself *Parisada Hindu Dharma Indonesia*.[16]

The religious hegemony of the Hindu bureaucracy did, however, not further the unification of the highly fragmented Indonesian Hindu community. The rigid promotion of a greatly rationalised and "semitificated" (Veena Das) interpretation of the religious doctrines on the part of the respective government institutions alienated believers in all local Hindu communities. Disillusioned by the political opportunism of the religious bureaucrats, people either continued to look for genuine religiosity in their respective traditions or resorted to new Hindu sects in order to experience true spirituality. Organisations like Transcendental Meditation, the Hare Krishna Movement, the Satya Sai Baba movement, Ananda Marga, Brahma Kumaris, Osho, or Shri Shri Ravi Shankar increasingly attracted members of the modern urban middle class. Since Balinese Brahmin priests and scholars continued to occupy key positions within the Directorate for Hindu Affairs and the *Parisada Hindu Dharma Indonesia*, educating non-Balinese "Hindus" in the Hindu religion often meant promoting Balinese notions and practices to the disadvantage of non-Balinese local *adat*. The growing resentment against Balinese claims to cultural and religious superiority among non-Balinese "Hindus" prevented them from developing a strong sense of solidarity that would significantly transcend their attachment to their respective local community. This resentment even frequently led to re-conversion to either Christianity or Islam.

The lack of a strong sense of solidarity among the members of the Indonesian Hindu community, which was fragmented along the lines of ethnic identity, social status, education, and sect, proved to be disastrous when Suharto suddenly changed his religious policy at the end of the 1980s. Acknowledging the force of the global Islamic resurgence which had increasingly made itself felt also in Indonesia, he started to court cooperative representatives of Indonesian Islam in order to secure mass support for his regime. This was boosted by the growing friction between Suharto and high-ranking officers in the Indonesian army. Consequently, Suharto, who made his first pilgrimage to Mecca in 1990, took several steps to advance the interests of Islam. For Hinduism, the most serious measure was the sudden cut in financial support on the part of the Indonesian government. Since Hindu institutions could not rely on foreign funding like Christian or Muslim organisations, most Hindu schools and colleges had to be closed down. Similarly, funds were lacking to sponsor local rituals and temples. In addition to the financial discrimination, Muslims started to openly denigrate Hinduism and to harass local Hindu congregations. Discouraged by the rising pressure, many more people converted to Islam or Christianity.

Others, however, were beginning to develop a sense of belonging to a larger, transnational Hindu community, turning to India for inspiration how to live as a Hindu in a modern world. This coincided with an increasing awareness for the economic importance of Asia-Pacific on the part of India, necessitated by the fact that India had lost its main trading partner, the Soviet Union, in 1989, as Christophe Jaffrelot recently pointed out in a conference paper. In 1993, affluent Hindus, mostly from Balinese or Javanese background, started to make short pilgrimages to holy places in India. More and more people went on such pilgrimage trips in the coming years. Since 1995, the Indonesian Council for Cultural Relations has provided ten stipends per annum to students who have mostly been selected from the Indonesian Hindu community. Besides, Indian expatriates working in Indonesia have become generous sponsors of the construction of temples, rituals, and the publication of Hindu literature. These developments enhanced cohesion among the Indonesian Hindus, which was sufficiently strong to provoke massive demonstrations in response to the rising discrimination against Hinduism within Indonesian society.[17]

The development of Hinduism in post-Suharto Indonesia

Pressure on the Hindu community reached a peak after the onset of the financial crisis in the fall of 1997, followed by Suharto's demise in May 1998, and the increasing Islamisation of the Indonesian society under B. J. Habibie's intermediate presidency. The general financial crisis was hardest on the Hindu community that counted 5,987,134 members in 1997, making up three per cent of the total Indonesian population of two hundred million people.[18] Its membership includes a large number of economically, educationally, and geographically marginalised people. Some of them have looked for better opportunities in other religious communities. Moreover, Hindus have increasingly experienced open hostility not only from radical Muslims[19] but also from fundamentalist Christians. Forced conversion to either of the two religion has frequently taken place in hospitals, schools, and other government institutions in Hindu regions outside Bali, despite Abdurrahman Wahid's return to a policy of religious tolerance after he had been elected as the new president of Indonesia in October, 1999. Continuous Muslim immigration to Bali has also alarmed the Hindu Balinese, contributing to the growing radicalisation of the Hindu movement itself. This radicalisation has been accompanied by intensifying relations with Indian Hindu institutions.

In October 2000, the Indian Ambassador to Indonesia, the Governor of Bali, Indian expatriates and Indonesian Hindus of Indian and Balinese origin decided to establish a "Foundation for Balinese-Indian Brotherhood" (*Yayasan Pervaudaraan Bali-India*). In November 2000, the Governor of Bali and a large delegation of Balinese Brahmin priests (*pedanda*) visited India after an invitation had been extended to them by the Indian government. During their stay in India, they also met with His Holiness, the Shankaracharya from Kanchipuram. It is expected that His Holiness will repay their visit some time in 2001. This will then be the first time that a Shankaracarya has left the sacred soil of India to visit a foreign country, thereby acknowledging the sacredness of the "Hindu Island of Bali". Besides, a democratic version of the *Vedic Agnihotra*, influenced by the *Arya Samaj* and primarily disseminated through the agency of the Balinese foundation "*Yayasan Homa Yajna Veda Poshana Ashram*" in Sanur, has become popular among adherents of the new Hindu movements (Hare Krishna, Satya Sai Baba, Ananda Marga, Brahma Kumaris, Osho, and Shri Shri Ravi Shankar, etc.) as well as those Balinese who have come to reject their elaborate ritual tradition because of the immense personal costs (money and time) it requires from those living under the conditions of modernity.[20]

The increasing "Indianisation" or "Neo-Indianisation" of Hinduism in Indonesia has even further alienated traditionalists in Bali, North Sumatra, South Sulawesi, and Central Kalimantan who have felt encouraged by the "Law on Regional Autonomy" recently passed by Abdurrahman Wahid. Non-Balinese traditionalist has even advocated a separation from Hinduism since and the President has recognised *aliran kepercayaan* as "religion" in the first half of 2000. Thus, the development of Hinduism in Indonesia is at the crossroads.

Conclusion

"Hinduism" was introduced in Indonesia as a "continual component of the discourse of modernity" (S.N. Eisenstadt), geared to transform adherents of ethnic religions into modern Indonesian citizens. Its inherent potential for ideological universalisation and social globalisation has, however, been unable to dissolve the friction within the Indonesian Hindu community caused by ethnic nationalism, Balinese dominance, financial plight, ideological fragmentation and outside pressure. Re-traditionalisation will increase with the actual instalment of full regional autonomy, possibly leading to the breakup of the Hindu community. On the other hand, Neo-Hindu nationalism is also likely to increase among modern Indonesian Hindus who have broken with their respective ethnic tradition. Their radicalisation will be accelerated by the probable ascent of radical Islam within Indonesian society. Thus, the simultaneous trends of re-traditionalisation and Neo-Hinduisation are likely to enhance the fragmentation of the Indonesian Hindu community, which will considerably thwart the future development of Hinduism in Indonesia.

Selective Bibliography

AGUNG, Die Anak Agung Gde

ASAD, Talal, 1993: *Genealogies of Religion. Dsicipline and Reasons of Power in Christianity and Islam.* Baltimore et al.: The Johns Hopkins University Press.

ASTITI, Tjokorda Istri Putra, 1995: "Benarkah Bali Berdirl DI Antara Adat Dan Agama?" In: Wiryatnaya, Usadi/ Couteau, Jean (eds.) 1995: *Bali Di Pervimpangan Jalan*. Jilid 2. Denpasar: Nusa Data Indo Budaya; pp. 97–107.

ATKINSON, Jane M., 1983: "Religions in Dialogue: The Construction of an Indonesian Minority Religion". In: *American Ethnologist* 10/4; pp. 684–696.

BAGUS, I. Gusti Ngurah, 1969: *Pertentangan Kasta dalam Bentuk Baru pada Masyarakat Baru*. Denpasar: Universitas Udayana.

BAGUS, I. Gusti Ngurah, 1991: "Bali in the 1950's: The Role of the Pemuda Pejuang in Balinese Political Processes". In: Geertz, Hildred (ed.) 1991: *State and Society in Bali*; pp. 199–212.

BAGUS, I. Gusti Ngurah, 1999: *Renungan Empat Puluh Tahun PHD] untuk Menyejarah*. Denpasar: Forum Penyadaran Dharma.

BAKKER, Frederik L., 1993: The Struggle of the Hindu Balinese Intellectuals. Developments in Modern Hindu Thinking in Independent Indonesia. Amsterdam: VU University Press.

CRIBB, Robert, 1991: *Islam and the Panca Sila*. James Cook University of North Queensland, Centre for Southeast Asian Studies (South East Asian monograph series, no. 28).

DARMAPUTERA, Eka, 1992: *Pancasila. Identitas dan Modernitas. Tinjauan Etis dan Budaya.* Jakarta: Gunung Mulia.

DEPARTEMEN PENDIDIKAN DAN KEBUDAYAAN, 1978: *Sejarah Kebangkitan National Daerah Bali*. Dep. P dan K, Pusat Penelitian Sejarah dan Budaya, Proyek Penelitian dan Pencatatan Kebudayaan Daerah.

FORGE, Anthony, 1980: "Balinese Religion and Indonesian Identity". In: Fox, James/ Garnaut, Ross/ McCawley, Peter/ Mackie, J. A. C. (eds.) 1980: *Indonesia: Australian Perspectives*. Canberra: Research School of Pacific Studies, The Australian National University; pp. 221–233.

FRYKENBERG, Robert Erie, 1989: "The Emergence of Modern 'Hinduism' as a Concept and as an Institution: A Reappraisal with Special Reference to South India". In: Sontheimer, Gunther D./ Kulke, Hermann (eds.) 1989: *Hinduism Reconsidered*. Delhi: Manohar; pp. 29–49.

GEERTZ, Clifford, 1972: Religious Change and Social Order in Suharto's Indonesia". In: 27; pp. 62–84.

GEERTZ, Clifford, (1973), 1993: "Internal Conversion' in Contemporary Bali". In: Geertz, Clifford (1973), 1993: The *Interpretation of cultures*. London: Fontana Press; pp. 170–189.

HOOKER, M. B., 1978: *Adat Law in Modern Indonesia*. Kuala Lumpur et al.: Oxford University Press.

KING, Richard, 1999: *Orientalism and Religion. Postcolonial Theory, India and 'The Mystic East'*. London et al.: Routledge.

LYON, Margaret Louise, 1977: *Politics and Religious Identity. Genesis of a Javanese-Hindu Movement in Rural Central Java*. Berkeley: Dissertation at the University of California.

LYON, Margaret Louise, 1980: "Hindu Revival in Java: Politics and Religious Identity". In: Fox, James / Garnaut, Ross / McCawley, Peter / Mackle, J.A.C. (eds.) 1980: *Indonesia: Australian Perspectives*. Canberra: Research School of Pacific Studies, The Australian National University; pp. 205–220.

MCVEY, Ruth, 1993: *Redesigning the Cosmos, Belief Systems and State Power in Indonesia*. Copenhagen: NIAS Books (NIAS Reports No. 14, revised edition).

NALA, Ngurah / WIRATMADJA, K. Adia, 1993: *Murddha Agama Hindu*. Denpasar: Upada Sastra.

NGURAH, I Gusti Made, 1998: *Buku Pendidikan Agama Hindu Untuk Perguruan Tinggi*. Surabaya: Paramita.

PARISADA HINDU DHARMA, 1978: *Upadeca tentang Alaran-Ajaran Agama Hindu*.

PENDIT, Nyoman S., 1979: Bali Berjuang. Jakarta: Gunung Agung.

PICARD, Michel, 1997: "Cultural Tourism, Nation-Building and Regional Culture: The Making of a Balinese Identity". In: Picard, Michel / Wood, Robert E. (eds.) 1997: *Tourism, Ethnicity and the State in Asian and Pacific Societies*. Honolulu: University of Hawaii Press; pp. 181–214.

RAMSTEDT, Martin, 1998a: *Weltbild, Heilspragmatik und Herrschafislegitimation im vorkolonialen Bali*. Frankfurt a. M. et al.: Peter Lang.

RAMSTEDT, Martin, 1998b: "Negotiating Identities - 'Hinduism' in Modern Indonesia". In: *IIAS Newsletter 17*; 50.

RAMSTEDT, Martin, 1999: "Muslim-Hindu Relations in Contemporary Indonesia". In: *ISIM Newsletter 4*; 14.

RAMSTEDT, Martin, 2000a: 'Relations Between Hindus in Modern Indonesia and India'. In: *IIAS Newsletter* 23 (OCT. 2000); PP.8–9.

RAMSTEDT, Martin, 2000b: 'Two Balinese Hindu Intellectuals - Ibu Gedong Bagus Oka and Prof. I Gusti Ngurah Bagus'. In: *IIAS Newsletter* 23 (Oct. 2000); pp. 12–13.

RAMSTEDT, Martin, 2000c: '>Bali< - kulturelles Kapital im Spiel divergicrender Interessen' ('"Bali" - Cultural Capital Negotiated in Divergent Interests'). In: Hauser-Schdublin, Brigitta/ Riclander, Klaus (eds.): Bali - *Kultur, Tourismus, Umwelt (Bali - Culture, Tourism, Environment)*. Hamburg: Abera; pp. 124–141.

RAMSTEDT, Martin, Forthcoming: "Indonesianisation, Globalisation and Islamisation - Parameters of the Hindu Discourse in Contemporary Indonesia". In: *International Journal for Hindu Studies.*

RUDYANSYAH, Tony, 1986. *Modernization and Religion on Bali. A Cultural-Sociological Study QF the Parisada Hindu Dharma,* Jakarta: Thesis submitted in partial fulfilment of the requirements for the MA-degree in cultural anthropology, Faculty of Postgraduate Studies, University of Indonesia.

SETIA, Putu, 1993: *Kebangkitan Hindu Menyongsong Abad ke-21.* Jakarta: Pustaka Manikgeni.

SMITH, Wilfred Cantwell, 1963: *The Meaning and End of Religion. A new approach to the religious traditions of mankind.* New York: Macmillan.

STIETENCRON, Heinrich V., 1989: "Hinduism: On the Proper Use of a Deceptive Term". In: Sontheimer, Gunther D./ Kulke, Hermann (eds.), 1989: *Hinduism Reconsidered*. Dehli: Manohar; pp. 11–27.

SUPARTHA, Wayan (ed.), 1994: *Memahami Aliran Kepercayaan,* Denpasar: Penerbit BP.

SWELLENGREBEL, J. L., 1948: *Kerk en Tempel op Bali.* s'Gravenhage: N. V. Uitgeverij W. van Hoeve.

TAHER, Tarmizi, 1997: *Aspiring for the Middle Path. Religious Harmony in Indonesia.* Jakarta: Center for the Study of Islam and Society.

TOLLENAERE, Herman A. O. de, 1996: *The Politics of Divine Wisdom. Theosophy and labour, national, and women's movement in Indonesia and South Asia 1875–1947*. Nijmegen: Katholleke Universitelt Nijmegen.

WANDELT, Ingo, 1989: *Der Weg zum Pancasila-Menschen. Die Pancasila-Lehre unter dem P4-Beschlu, 8 des Jahres 1978. Entwicklung und Struktur derIndonesischen Staatslehre*. Frankfurt et al.: Peter Lang.

WARREN, Carol, 1993: *Adat and Dinas. Balinese Communities in the Indonesian State*. Oxford et al.: Oxford University Press.

WIANA, Ketut/SANTERI, Raka, 1993: *Kasta dalam Hindu. Kesalahpahaman Berabadabad*. Denpasar: Yayasan Dharma Naradha.

References

[1] Cf. also e.g. ATKINSON, 1983:687–688; DARMAPUTRA 1002:58; SUPARTHA 1994:76.

[2] Cf. my article 'Indonesianisation, Globalisation, and Islamisation – Parameters of the Hindu Discourse in Modern Indonesia', in: the forthcoming issue of the *International Journal for Hindu Studies*.

[3] Cf. RAMSTEDT, 1998a.

[4] Cf. also RAMSTEDT, 1998a.

[5] Cf. e.g. TOLLENAERE, 1996.

[6] Cf. TOLLENAERE, 1996: 124, 293, 329, 343.

[7] Cf. BAGUS, 1969:2; DEPARTMEN PENDIDIKAN DAN KEBUDAYAAN, 1978:26.

[8] Cf. BAKKER, 1993:38; SWELLENGREBEL, 1948:71, 75–77, 79–84, 89.

[9] Cf. also BAGUS, 1969; BAKKER, 1993:36, 39–45; DEPARTEMEN PENDIDIKAN DAN KEBUDAYAAN, 1978:25–58; FORGE 1980:222–225; PICARD, 1997;189.

[10] Cf. AGUNG, IDE ANAK AGUNG GDE; DUTT.

[11] Cf. also BAGUS, 1991:207; BAGUS, 1999:1–3; BAKKER, 1993:45, 57, 102, 155, 196, 226–238; DARMAPUTERA, 1992:58; FORGE

1980:225–2236; GEERTZ, 1972:77; GEERTZ, 1993; 185–189; NALA/WIRATMADJA, 1993:34; PARISADA HINDU DHARMA, 1978:41–43; PICARD, 1997:193–196, 200.

[12] Cf. e.g. DUTT

[13] *Abangan* Javanese adhere to a Sufi variety of Islam blended with Hindu-Buddhists as well as "animist" elements; cf. e.g. GEERTZ, Clifford 1973 Islam in Java.

[14] Cf. e.g. LYON 1977 and LYON 1980.

[15] Cf. STATISTIK INDONESIA, 1982. Jakarta: Pusat Statistik.

[16] Cf. also BAKKER, 1993:238, 240–241; NALA/ WIRATMADJA 1993:35–36; NGURAH 1998:27–28.

[17] Cf. also RAMSTEDT, 2000c.

[18] Cf. DATA STATISTIK TAHUN, 1997. Jakarta: Departemen Agama RI, Direktorat Jenderal Bimbingan Masyarakat Hindu Dan Buddha; p. 3.

[19] Cf. also RAMSTEDT, 1999.

[20] Cf. also RAMSTEDT, 2000a; RADITYA No. 25 (Augustus), 1999; 18–20, 26–30; RADITYA No. 26 (September), 1999: 4–20.

8

Investment, Banking, Oil & Gas in Indonesia

K. Subramaniam

How does one relate such disparate areas like oil, gas, investment and banking in Indonesia and proceed to deal with its future course of development? It will call for more than heroism to render full justice even to one area, be it banking, investment or oil; and to presume to work out a common link between these areas may be an act of intellectual effrontery. One will not make any such attempt. Rather, one proposes to deal with developments in these areas during the last three decades in a chronological order. While doing so, one may, perhaps, stumble upon a few links connecting these areas. There were years when 'oil and gas' dominated the economy and the Indonesian government sought to treat the sector as the base for development. Then there were international developments affecting oil prices and/or OPEC's quota restrictions and oil revenue became an unreliable horse to hitch the developmental wagon. Later came the focus on 'investment', both domestic and foreign, and efforts to make the economy internationally competitive and outward-oriented. While economic growth was sought to be investment-driven, investment policy was itself driven cyclically in the sense that it became liberal and sought to attract remittances when the balance of payments situation was serious; or turned restrictive when the BOP front was comfortable. It was not realised that there were limits to such policy manipulations in a fast changing world. Alongside rose the banking sector encouraging large inflows of capital for investment, direct or as portfolio, and as loan. There were, no doubt, overlaps between these periods and the demarcation is not watertight. The era of petroleum development led to the formation of national enterprises that were dependent on the government. These enterprises or conglomerates began to have close links with the indigenous Chinese as also with Japanese, Korean and American companies abroad. These links were further strengthened during the years of import substitution. There were indeed under-currents of hostility as between these groups. Hostility was mostly embedded or muted though it could erupt with violence during times of acute economic stress. The conglomerates had cosy relations with the growing banking sector when foreign capital started flowing in large volumes under the liberal financial regime. They could obtain loans for all their projects and operations. With full convertibility on capital account, along with an implicit faith that the exchange rate of Rupiah would remain stable and be pegged to the US dollar, Indonesia had become the darling of foreign investors and was truly included in the list of NIES. In the World Bank's book — *The East Asian Miracle* — Indonesia was listed as one of the high performing economies. That was in the year 1993. Yes, all the indicators seemed to suggest that the chariot would go on full speed. Within the next three years the chariot ran aground. What had gone wrong?

Those economists who wrote *The East Asian Miracle* are either in hiding or are framing econometric models to prove that their assessment was not wrong under *those* conditions. They would refer to the "contagion" which had spread from other areas; to "collusion, cronyism and corruption "prevailing in those countries. Some refer to the failure of governance at the state and corporate levels; to the lack of transparency and accountability. Moreover, there are many who harp on the absence of legal systems that would protect property rights and enforce contracts and the need to build institutions to promote economic growth and welfare. These were the same analysts who related the rapid rates of economic growth in East Asia to Asian *values* and Asian models a few years earlier and wrote learned monographs on them. It is too tempting to be trapped into this mode of analysis. It is not my intention to do this. All the same it may not be fruitful if we dealt with the Indonesian crisis as one of pure foreign exchange, financial or monetary crisis. These elements were predominant no doubt and resulted in a social turmoil and, precipitately, to the fall of an authoritarian regime that held sway for thirty-two years. However, there were more important factors of a historical, social and political nature at work leading to a structure of the civil society and its over arching relationship with the State". Our theme is: given the special civil-society-state structure which emerged in the decolonisation era (post 1950), the regime could withstand shocks whether arising from within, like civil disturbances or the secessionist forces in East Timor,

Aceh or Irian Jaya, or from abroad like balance of payments deficits, exchange rate fluctuations or other financial crises only in the earlier years. Partly, this was because the internal shocks were relatively weak and the state was fierce in stamping them down. The external shocks arising out of BOP or exchange rate issues were also manageable. In the pre-Smithsonian era of fixed par values and low volume capital flows, it was possible for developing countries, particularly those in East Asia which had come, under the security umbrella of the US, to depend on bilateral support or the IMF and by manipulation (depreciation) of exchange rates under the guidance of the IMF. Once the era of deregulation had commenced and capital began to flow in trillions of dollars, it was no longer possible for these countries to keep them under control. The local governments had lost their autonomy in the sense that they *could* not put *through effective* monetary policies to *counter the adverse* situation. Nor could they look to assistance from erstwhile patrons like the US since, in the post-cold war period, the security concerns were less compelling. What we have so far described would hold good generally for all developing countries. Yet, Indonesia had certain other features that led to the destruction of the economy and, with it, the civil society. The question whether it is a 'New Beginning' for Indonesia or not, will depend largely on how the classes and masses are brought under a democratic set-up and how the economy may be restructured or redesigned to serve the expectations of the people. There are no 'quick fixes' and it is going to be a long and tortuous journey.

Evaluation of Indonesian Economy

Now for some history. As Robison described it: "In the decades following Independence, the 1950s and 1960s,

Indonesia's middle class and its bourgeoisie were both minute and without political and economic influence of any real substance. Apart from a small coterie of intellectuals and professionals, the middle class was confined within the sprawling, chaotic and poorly paid bureaucracy. The bourgeoisie was similarly weak and fragmented. After departure of the Dutch trading houses and banks in the late 1950s, here remained only, small- and medium-scale traders and producers. Even the dominant Chinese element produced few figures or enterprises of national significance. Those who did achieve national prominence in the Sukarno period were dependent on access to politically derived rents and proved unable to survive the transition to the new-order government of President Suharto in the mid-1960s. It was the state that became the leading force in investment and corporate ownership."

Ann Booth (2) deals with the historical developments analytically. While the leaders of the Indonesian independence movement were greatly influenced by socialist thought, including its Marxist-Leninist derivatives and the 'rejection of capitalism and espousal of socialism as the preferred pattern of economic organisation has been an almost universal element in Indonesian political thinking since independence', the period from 1950 to 1965 came to be viewed as one of gradual attenuation of government control of the economy, (p.296, ibid.). This was borne out by the fact that in the 1950s and early 1960s there was a gradual decline in the ratios of government expenditure and revenue to GDP. The period was also one of increasing inflation and economic dislocation as the authority of the central government had collapsed and, with it, it's capacity to direct the course of economic events. There were some paradoxes that Ann Booth had noted. Indonesia, as an independent nation, committed to planned economic development along Indian — if not Russian — lines, had failed to increase the share of government expenditure in the national income. Why did they allow the share of GDP and of capital formation to fall even below that achieved by the colonial government three decades earlier? This came about inspite of their drawing up ambitious developmental plans. Though the persistent government deficits during the years between 1950 and 1965 did not exceed seven per cent of GDP, which were not much different from those of early 1930s, they fuelled continual inflation reaching triple digit figures. Why was the effect of budget deficit on monetary stability so different in the immediate post-independent period from the inter-war years? This is attributed to the failure of the revenue policy. While in the early 1950s the ratio of revenue to GDP was higher, the structure of revenues had changed considerably. It was observed that while direct taxes had contracted revenues, trade accounted for over one half of the total government income. What was more, these revenues came from a mixture of 'orthodox' export and import taxes and from the so-called 'inducement certificates' and import surcharges. A study of these certificates and surcharges revealed that 'in effect they amounted to a subsidy to exporters, allowing exporters to convert their exchange earnings at a more favourable rate than the official exchange while imposing a heavy 'exchange tax' on importers. The profits from these exchange dealings were retained by the government.' (p.297, ibid.) This was an early indication of the role of 'external factors' on the Indonesian economy. In later years also we would see the unsettling effect of external factors on which the economy came to be dependent more and more.

When the Korean War boom ended and the exports collapsed and prices slumped in consequence, revenues from export/import trade also fell. There were attempts to control and reform the system. However, the finance ministers lacked the authority to enforce new measures. By the early 1960s the gap widened and largely government borrowing from the central bank, thereby stoking inflation covered the deficit. The government was caught in a vicious spiral of inflation leading to deteriorating revenue performance and which, in turn, lead to larger deficits and. further inflation. The net result was that it was not possible for the government to put through investment programmes or even to maintain the existing infrastructure. This set the backdrop to the coup in September 1965.

The East Asian Miracle describes the above period as one of 'Nationalism and Guided Development (1948–66).' In its assessment, this period of 'growing mismanagement resulted in chaotic economic conditions. Inflation accelerated to 1,000. Exports and foreign exchange reserves dwindled, and debt service exceeded foreign exchange earnings. Economic growth stagnated. By 1965 per capita income was 15 per cent lower than in 1958. Widespread social unrest and violence set the stage for a change in leadership.' (p. 136, ibid.) Though this description may satisfy some economists, it glosses over the hostile conditions which the Sukarno regime had to face. There have been several interpretations of the coup of 1965 and the role the CIA played has also been documented. Internally there were mounting tensions between the very large and active Communist Party on the left and the army together with Muslim groups on the Right. Till such time as Indonesia came under the protective cover of the US in the mid-1960s when the cold war gripped Southeast Asia, there was no assurance of economic support. It is by now known that the US authorities had a hand in engineering the overthrow of the Sukarno regime. The abortive artny coup was the excuse, which enabled Major General Suharto to move in, put down the coup, link it to the Communist Party and assume increasing control of the government. It took two years and the death of several lakhs of people before a semblance of normalcy could be established.

Suharto had the support of the military and, at least in the initial period, a broad coalition of civilians. He vowed to re-establish order and revive the economy. On the economic front he and his advisers initiated a dramatic re-orientation. A stiff stabilisation programme was put in place. This was also accompanied by several measures to open the economy. The economy came under the guidance of the Berkley Mafia and led to the entry of a consortium of creditors which included the IMF, the World Bank, the US and a number of industrial countries extending large-scale financial assistance. It is by now evident that these arrangements were more the result of security alliances with the West in the cold war context. Mansfield has dealt with the relationship between trade and security alliances and economic blocs. (3). The support extended by the US under the aegis of the IMF/Bank to Indonesia in mid-1960s, particularly after the emergence of Suharto, can be better appreciated in that light. Consider again the situation in 1997 when a graver crisis erupted threatening the survival of the economy, the IMF and the US were not so prompt in coming to its rescue. Compare this also with the speed with which they rescued Mexico in 1994 or moved in to help Korea in 1998. The end of the cold war around 1989 and the lower order of Indonesia in the global security framework of the US may possibly be cited as the reason.

Suharto's New Economy

The outward-Oriented New Order era (1967–73) followed next. This was the period when the government embarked on a programme of stabilisation with the advice and support of the IMF. The government moved to restore macro-economic stability and adopted a more favourable stance toward domestic and foreign private investment. Some of the nationalised enterprises were returned to previous owners and a new Foreign Investment Law was enacted providing for a thirty-year guarantee of non-nationalisation. The exchange rate was adjusted through large devaluations. In 1970 there was the move to establish a mechanism for market-driven unified exchange rate. Controls on capital movements were abolished in 1970. Sweeping changes were also introduced in trade and incentive regimes, including abolition of import licensing while the tariff system was not changed. It was estimated that as a result of these measures non-oil exports increased at an annual rate of twenty-six per cent from 1967 to 1973, compared with an annual increase of two per cent during the previous seven years. This IMF programme of stabilisation in Indonesia came to be regarded as one of the most successful in the world (Sutton, 1984). The government was able to reduce the rate of inflation virtually to zero within the space of three years without a rise of unemployment, deteriorating living standards and falling production, which marked IMF stabilisation programmes in many other countries.

The first five year plan (Repelita 1) of the New Order was modest in aims and content. The approach was pragmatic and there was no attempt at grandiose planning. Emphasis was on agriculture, particularly rice production. Government devoted thirty per cent of development budget to agriculture, twenty per cent to rehabilitation, and upgrading of road system to facilitate access to inputs. It was possible for Indonesia to improve rice production substantially and within a decade it was possible for them to dispense with import of rice. There were also other efforts to improve infrastructure like irrigation facilities and construction. This period in retrospect was one of stability and modest achievements. These were also the years prior to the new financial arrangements under the Smithsonian agreement and prior to the emergence of oil and petro-dollars as major actors in the international arena. The relative peace of this period was to be disturbed by the turbulence that would pervade the world markets both in commodities and foreign exchange. That is to say they may lose the autonomy which they had enjoyed hitherto.

Role of oil in Indonesia's Economic Development

Indonesia was a late comer to the oil industry and became a beneficiary of US and Japanese investments. The oil price rise arising out of Vienna and Kuwait agreements of early 1970s and the quadrupling of crude prices in the later years led to efforts to locate newer crude sources. Japan which was totally dependent on oil and whose imports had been significantly tied to Gulf sources found it necessary to locate crude sources closer home. Indonesian and Malaysian sources were strategically located and became reliable sources of crude for Japan. Indonesia became an active member of the OPEC and enjoyed for a long time the benefits flowing from OPEC's control over crude prices and outputs.

However, in the longer run the oil link took its own toll on the economy.

The dramatic jump in oil prices between 1974 and 1980 posed a set of adjustment problems characteristic of economies with booming export sectors. The so-called phenomenon of 'Dutch disease' takes its toll on other sectors, particularly tradable goods, both exports and import substitutes. To begin with, there is this problem of managing large volume revenues which the oil sector generates. If not properly deployed they could give rise to inflationary pressures. It may be possible for a desert kingdom ruled by Sheiks to keep the funds abroad or engage in luxury projects. In a large country like Indonesia crying for investments for development, it would not have been possible to adopt this line. Compared with certain other oil exporting countries, e.g., Nigeria or Mexico, Indonesia used its enhanced revenues well. During the 1970s, about forty per cent of government budget went to infrastructure for the economy. The government also placed strong emphasis on improving education, health services and family planning. As a result of these there was progress in reduction of poverty and improvement in social conditions. Economic growth averaged close to eight per cent through the 1970s and early 1980s due to strong expansion of public and private investment.

There was also the downside to the role oil revenues played. This came up due to the links between the state Oil Company (Pertamina) and the indigenous business class. Even in the earlier years the growth of indigenous enterprises was highly dependent on state-allocated concessions, licenses and credit. Forestry concessions and trade monopolies were the only avenues open to them. In the 1980s the growth of these groups was accelerated by their accessing oil-funded projects as contractors and suppliers (p. 91, ibid.) Pertamina's President Director, Inbu Sutowo, was a person with strong nationalist persuasion and worked for the development of an indigenous capital class. In the early years, several individuals like Aburizal Bakrie, Fahmi Idris, Ponto Sutowo and Siswono Judohusodo were helped with contracts for supply and construction. In the 1980s the role was taken over by the State Secretariat (Sekneg) under the state secretary, Sudharmono. Under the tenets of legislation introduced in 1980, Keppers 10 and 14a, Sekneg was to control the allocation of government contracts for construction and supply and indigenous enterprises secured privileged access to them. The Chinese enterprises were excluded and thus the indigenous enterprises and individuals could score over the Chinese. The Chinese themselves had worked out independently credit arrangements for their enterprises and they could have been helped by the fact that the government lifted control on capital transfers in 1970 (*The East Asian Miracle* described this as Indonesia moving 'ahead by putting cart before the horse', p.238). When deregulation came about in 1986, many of the indigenous business houses had to compete with large Chinese conglomerates and the family groups for contracts. They had to ensure their survival by seeking more and more political support and by becoming members of the Golkar. They were also able to benefit from the govemment's general sensitivity to anti-Chinese and anti-conglomerate sentiments. Banks were instructed to reserve twenty per cent credit for indigenous enterprises. The government put through a linkage programme whereby small indigenous enterprises would make supplies to Chinese conglomerates. These conglomerates had nothing to gain from these linkages but they chose to abide by the programme, more to buy peace and as a measure of goodwill. The years 1989 and 1990 saw an explosion in investment outlays on industrial and infrastructure projects. It is estimated that by 1991 the total investment was around US$78 billion. Much of this was provided by indebted state banks and was also to be rescheduled when the debt crisis broke out. No wonder these years of oil revenue-based investments created close links between the government and enterprises and also resulted in the rise of the 'family' and its involvement in many projects. One may trace the roots of government patronage or cronyism to this period, not that it was not present earlier.

The honeymoon with oil boom could not last long. The year 1982 was the turning point. Though the oil prices held at 1981 levels, Indonesia had to adopt the OPEC mandated production cuts and petroleum exports and revenues declined in absolute and relative terms. The BOP deficit rose sharply and there was the problem of resource constraint, particularly for the public sector. The government had to choose between a retreat from the liberal policy and introduce the regime of controls prevailing before 1965 or to encourage export production by supporting non-oil sectors. During the years 1982 to 1985 it favoured a regulatory or restrictive regime and applied import substitution measures. There were several new initiatives in monetary, fiscal and exchange rate policy. Rupiah was devalued in March 1983 and several deregulatory measures were taken in the financial sector (see later section). It was by 1985 that the government worked on the introduction of an export-oriented regime. The tariff system was rationalised and ad valorem rates were reduced from two hundred and twenty-five to sixty per cent. Customs duty procedures were simplified. This benefited inter-island transfers. There were also reforms in the financial sectors. It is the assessment of some that during the period from 1983 to 1990 much progress was made in terms of the goal of making the economy more internationally competitive and less reliant on exports of oil and gas (Ann Booth, p.301).

There are other interpretations also. They draw attention to the phenomenon that after the massacre of 1966, the military commanders started many enterprises of their own but decided to take the help of Chinese businessmen to build up their firms and fortunes. One of the biggest — if not the biggest — business empires was built by up by Suharto, his family, and their friends. Military commanders and trusts (*yayasans*) in the name of legally recognised political parties controlled or held shares in enterprises spread across the archipelago. The state enterprises, including state banks, had serving or retired army officers as chairmen or managing directors. These banks were given a monopoly of business, since, till the 1980s, new private banks or branches of private banks were forbidden. So the business-finance-industry network meant military-elite family-finance industry network and it was impossible to disentangle the knots. This interlocking nature of the elite-industry Indonesia polity accounted for the support given to Suharto (A.K. Bagchi, EPW, p.1033 and Robison, 1986). Moreover, when the crisis broke, the system had become unsustainable. This would have serious repercussions for the rebuilding of democratic structure in the country; it would also create roadblocks in dealing with the debt hang of enterprises and Indonesian banks. These linkages continue to create insurmountable problems now when the Indonesian authorities are grappling with issues governing restructuring of banks, their liabilities, as also in dealing with bankrupt enterprises. It was not merely that the Suharto regime internalised the economic activities within the network, it also did not provide any space for political dissidence (for an analysis of the 'Dynamics of Indonesian Democratisation', see Olle Tornquist, EPW, 29 April , 2000, p. 1559–1575).

In our view it was not only the state-societal structure that had become skewed, but the economic structure had also become unbalanced. Notwithstanding the panegyrics indulged in by the IMF/World Bank, the long-term sustainability of the economy had come under attack. As an UNCTAD Discussion Paper (UNCTAD D.P. No.137, June 1998, Rajah Rasiah) had analysed, the second-tier Southeast Asian newly industrialising economics (Indonesia, Malaysia and Thailand) experienced rapid growth and structural change. Manufacturing became the prime export propellant from the second half of the 1980s. Sustained growth helped support some strong macro-economic fundamentals. Their rate of growth and their low reliance on industrial policy led to several interpretations of their success and as models for other developing countries. Neo-classical economists (Fund/Bank variety until the eruption of the crisis in East Asia in 1997) attributed the success to the liberal policy regimes. There were others following the "flying geese modeling" and for them this meant an extension of the sweep of the flying squad. These interpretations do not adequately explain the causes of growth and structural changes in these economics and fail to identify the serious flaws inhibiting structural deepening and further growth. As the Discussion Paper summarised, "all these economies failed to lay the institutional foundations for technological deepening, critical to sustain long-term growth. Much of the growth, thus, has come in low-value added industries. Such structural broadening of activities is unlikely to assist long-term growth once factors of production and resources have passed their limits."

FDI in Indonesia

No reliable data are available on investments in India. Two statements (A & B) supplied by BKPM to an Indo-ASEAN Expert Group are enclosed showing the total investments and sectoral distribution. Data from UNCTAD are as under:

1982–87	1988	1989	1990	1991	1992	1993
282	576	682	1,093	1,482	1,774	2,004

($ US Million)

It would be seen from these figures that FDI peaked during the years 1990 to 1994. One problem in handling Indonesian FDI data is that they mix up equity and loan and no meaningful analysis can be made. Yet the broad assessment remains that these investments, though increasing in volume, were in low technology and low value-added items of manufacture and did not strengthen the technological base of the economy.

Paul Krugman in his now famous article on East Asian economies (Foreign Affairs, 1994) doubted the sustainability of rates of growth generally in East Asia since, in his view, the growth was entirely due to capital deepening and not to productivity increases. Indonesia was in the C-category, perhaps in a worse situation.

If we analyse the figures of industrial growth and exports of Indonesia in 1996, we note that out of the total of US$ 49.80 billion exports, only plywood, readymade garments and textiles amounted to US$ 10.2 billion as major items and the rest are either minerals or plantation products. Plywood is a forest-based product. Viewed from any angle, Indonesia's real economy, as distinguished from the financial economy, had been weakened and did not have the strength to sustain persistent or severe shocks. Thus, if its exports collapsed or its imports zoomed for reasons beyond the control of the authorities (Government or Central Bank), the economy would have capsized. As the *Financial Times* observed, the worst ever contraction in GDP took place in 1997 when the crisis erupted.

We have also to add to this, the regional imbalances created under the military rule. Industrialisation has been concentrated in Java and there have been no noticeable developments in many regions and income levels remained low. Even earlier some of these regions were marked by insurgency and violence either due to economic deprivation, neglect or other historical reasons. Regional disparities exacerbated dissidence and insurgency. Only a genuine democratic process tries to ensure a balance in regional development and take special care of depressed areas. Suharto and his coterie had no use for the regions except for military repression. One would have thought the crisis of 1997 would have spared these areas. However, a study undertaken by James Levionsohn, Steven Berry and Jed Friedman (NBER Working Paper No. 7194, June 1999) shows that the notion that the very poor are so poor as to be insulated from international shocks is simply wrong. 'Rather, in the Indonesian case, the very poor appear the most vulnerable.' The World Bank sponsored study ('The Social Impact of the Crisis in Indonesia', Sudarno Sumatò, Anna Wetterberg and Lant Pfitchett, 2000) suggests that urban areas were harder hit by the crisis than rural areas. It also noted that the impact of the crisis was heterogeneous and some urban areas on Java were harder hit. Some of the other islands, particularly large parts of Sumatra, Sulawesi, and Maluku, experienced minimal negative crisis impact. Other areas also showed negative impact, but the team was not clear whether the problems are crisis-related or result from drought and forest fires. It is odd to be told that the World Bank shows greater concern to those poor who have been hit by economic crises and not those who have been poor due to lack of economic development! A case of not all poor being equal! My idea in drawing attention to these studies is to suggest that income disparities are there and these have arisen due to lack of balance in industrialisation. When democratic discussions for a reorganised governmental structure and for new programmes of development are held, the claims of these regional members cannot be ignored. A military regime may ignore their claims for a time. Ultimately even that regime paid a bloody price.

There are some other aspects attached to FDI in Indonesia and these deserve attention. First is that though Indonesia has been adopting a flexible approach to FDI the policy has changed from time to time. It was in 1973 that the Capital Investment Coordinating Board (Badan Koordinasi Pernaman Model) was established. Oil and gas were excluded from its purview and for all others it is a one-stop service. The Batam Industrial Development Authority deals with Batam Island investments. It was in 1994 that by the Presidential Decree No.24/1994 issued on 19 May, 1994, that further liberalisation took place. Except in nine key areas (such as public works, mass media, public drinking water, ports, etc.) foreign investors can have hundred per cent equity. There is a requirement that in cases with hundred per cent foreign equity, a nominal percentage of equity is sold to Indonesians after fifteen years of operation and the two parties could determine the exact proportion. BKPM felt that hundred per cent firms were an increasing proportion of foreign investment approvals. Surprisingly, there is no minimum amount of capital stipulated and the idea was to facilitate smaller units and in consultancy and service activities. There is guarantee against nationalisation of a company's assets and this was there in the 1967 Act also. Non-Indonesians cannot hold land. However, it is possible to circumvent this by adopting legal devices. On paper the legal framework may seem liberal. In reality, however, processing individual proposals was not an easy task. The network of big business, army, 'family', Chinese and other influences rendered the whole scheme opaque and lacking in accountability. It may appear on paper or in form that the government was adopting a selective policy. However, it would be more appropriate to describe the system as one marked by arbitrariness and lack of direction or cohesion.

Though Indonesia was a leading member of the ASEAN, and ASEAN members made noisy statements, the economic strength of their group or what they called 'open regionalism', record showed that during the same years there was no increase in intra-ASEAN trade and the major link of these ASEAN countries was with the US or Japan. As long as the US-Japan trade relations remained calm, these countries faced no major difficulty and it was business as usual. Yet, over time they were caught in the US/Japan trade dispute in the Pacific. In the years before 1990 when the Yen was stronger vis-a-vis the US dollar, the Japanese were able to overcome their difficulties by promoting investments in East Asia. Once the Yen depreciated, it began to have very serious repercussions on the external trade of these countries.

Lack of diversification in the industrial sector and concentration of exports on a few items and over dependence on the US and Japan demand for commodities, electronics in particular, began to have their toll.

In spite of the years of ASEAN's existence from 1967 and claims of promoting regional links by way of trade and/or investments, the intra-regional flows were very small. In a way, ASEAN did not have a common approach or policy when the crisis broke. It was even shrugged off as 'an internal matter'. There was no attempt to go to the rescue of friendly members. There were weak attempts to form an Asian Fund to support the countries under strain. Japan took the initiative but the US summarily vetoed the proposal and the IMF was also opposed to the idea. The US did not want these countries to come under Japanese tutelage; IMF did not want its jurisdiction to be threatened in Asia. Since then there has been no attempt to promote a regional fund. It is only during recent months that the subject has again cropped up.

We may close this section on investment by making a couple of observations of a general nature. It is generally assumed by the advocates of FDI that an openness to FDI would by itself result in technological upgradation, export competitiveness, etc. The relationship between investment and technology is more complex and not fully understood. Much depends on the path taken by the country in the past and the cultural institutions built over the years. These local institutions have their own economic rationale. What are called 'problems of path dependency' have to be faced. These are also problems of technology absorption and the need to evolve new institutions or change the existing ones. In any case these have to emerge from within the society and cannot be set or dictated by external agencies. There are again problems connected with finance and capital formation. The link between 'finance' and 'capital' is not yet adequately understood. Mere infusion of 'finance' does not *ipso facto* create capital or development. Karla Hoff deals with 'underdevelopment traps' in a paper submitted in the last Annual Bank Conference on Development Economics (ABCDE) held at Washington on 10 April, 2000. As he posed it, 'a critical determinant of actions is one of environment, including the behaviour of other agents. Whereas we used to believe that the implication of externalities was that the economy would be slightly distorted, we now understand that the interaction of these distortions may produce very large distortions. He continues, 'in some environments, the entrepreneurial class become entrepreneurs in predation. Development requires a set of complementary changes in the behaviour of agents, which not even the market mechanism can coordinate.' The situation in Indonesia and some other developing countries including India could not have been better analysed. The moral of this story is that development is too serious a matter to be left to economists, particularly to those who work in the IMF and the World Bank. Joseph Stiglitz had made this point in his article in the New Republic. ('The Insider: What I learned at the World Economic Crisis, The *New Republic,* 17 April , 2000).

Crisis of Banking System in Indonesia

Now I would deal with banking. My idea is not deal with all the issues. One would raise some critical issues and relate them to the Indonesian case. Books and articles on the Asian crisis and country studies are flooding the journals and one tends to be blown off his feet. In the industralised countries there is too much of concern of worry about the banking crises in emerging economies. 'The Bank for International Settlements has brought out a number of documents along with proposal for the formulation of new guidelines. Discussions on the elements of the new financial architecture are taking place in many forums. The document given by the Acting Managing Director to the International Monetary and Financial Committee on the Progress in Reforming the IMF and Strengthening the Architecture of the International Financial System on 12 April, 2000, covers all the elements of discussions under various committees or agencies. In many ways these are one-sided exercises where the views of developing countries are not adequately taken or represented. It is not admitted that the crises in the banks of emerging economies have come about due to the wrong policy prescriptions given to them by the same IMF and Bank. They were under pressure to provide capital convertibility and also to deregulate the financial sector. The weakness of the banking system was brought about mainly because the banks and financial institutions were not deep and did not have the strength or the resources to withstand the vicissitudes of exchange rate and interest rate shocks emanating from abroad. As an UNCTAD Discussion Paper (UNCTAD/OSG/DP/ 143, November 1999) explained, the pattern of capital inflows to developing countries had undergone sea change during the years from 1975 to 1998. (ReE Statements C & D). During the period from the end of 1980s through 1997 the cumulative flows were massive, amounting to fifty per cent of GDP in Malaysia and Thailand, over twenty per cent in the Philippines and about ten per cent in Indonesia and Korea. Initially these flows took the form of FDI, but increasingly they took the form of offshore borrowing by banks and non-bank private companies in later years. The challenge these flows posed for macro-economic management was realised. The advisers from the IMF and Bank recommended 'sterilisation' of these inflows. However, sterilisation had the effect of raising the interest rate in the domestic market affecting the growth of indigenous industries. It had also a cost in the sense that foreign exchange so sterilised and acquired by the government or central bank earned a lower interest in the international financial market. This interest differential became a growing fiscal burden. Consider also the directive that fiscal deficits should be contained. In an NBER Paper (Sterilization of the Capital Flow problem in East Asia, 1987–97) done by Shinji Takagi and Esaka of Osaka University, the conclusion reached is '... the policy of sterilization pursued by the monetary authorities of East Asia during the capital inflow episode was effective in fully limiting the growth of Ml or M2, and possibly magnified the risk of capital inflows by keeping the level of interest rate high (hence promoting additional capital flows), by channeling resources to the relatively unsupervised nonbank financial sector, or both.' It is surprising that this unsustainable situation held for some years till the strains on the real sector turned intolerable and very soon the links snapped. It is this unhinging of the real economy from the financial economy that we suggest as the cause of the economic crisis. In her article ('Economic Turmoil in Asia - A Reinterpretation', EPW, 24 July, 1999, p.2071–86) Sunanda Sen provides similar views in a documented manner.

It is not possible to deal with some of the other studies, which have been brought out analysing the causes behind the crisis. There is the view that the crisis was created by the 'contagion' though Indonesia had sound fundamentals.

There is one study explaining 'cross-country variation in the severity of crisis' and relating it to 'three fundamentals: the strength of a country's banking system, its real exchange rate appreciation, and the liquidity of its Central Bank.' It is rather ironical that such conclusions should be drawn without recognising that the weaknesses were themselves brought about by the medicines prescribed to them by the IMF Advisers. A banking system does not grow in a matter of months or years. The western banking system has evolved over a century and the features of the American, English, German, French or Japanese banks continue to be different. It took a decade for the Basel Committee to arrive at capital adequacy guidelines and it was precisely because of the differences in the banking structures. The exchange rate appreciation comes about mainly because of the large capital inflows and the need to sterilise or control them. Central Banks of emerging countries cannot be flushed with resources of the magnitude to handle these inflows. Though the Basel Committee's capital adequacy guidelines were evolved in 1988 after protracted banks in Asia, Indonesia provides an extreme case. The IMF has set the parameters and time limits for achieving these. It seems to me that these issues cannot be resolved soon and may stretch over several years. The endeavour of the IMF seems to safeguard the interests of the Western Banks by creating government guarantees for debts so that these loans could still be shown as 'performing loans' in the books of the banks and within the Basel Accord. Under present economic conditions, it might not be practical for Indonesia to provide such guarantees and go along with these schemes. While they may be giving letters of intent to the IMF, they may doing so more to gain time and for tactical reasons — discussions with the

Japanese authorities over the treatment of real estate in banks'portfolio (which was a special to the Japanese banking system), the hope that the Basel Accord to discipline the banks was not realised. There was no economic rationale sanctity attached to the eight per cent and this norm proved to be an LCD for the western bankers. There is a well-argued view that these capital adequacy guidelines along with deregulation created a situation where banks took excessive risks. (See Harald Benink, 'The search for a cure', The Banker, 1998.)

We would end by relating another view that correlates banking crisis with currency crisis. Prior to the emergence of large volume capital flows and particularly coming from pension funds, etc., it was possible to isolate bank operation domestically from currency crises. With global integration of many banks and with competition among the giants, the whole scene was changing. In an article in American Economic Review titled "The International Transmission of Financial Shocks: The Case of Japan' (September 1997), Joe Peek and Eric Rosengren drew attention to the way Japanese banks operating in the US reacted to domestic shocks in Japan and how they tended to withdraw credit to the companies in the US. In another study (Banking Crises, Currency Crises, and Macro-economic Uncertainty', Victoria Miller, A.E.R., May, 1998) the Argument was that, 'while a banking (currency) crisis may cause a currency (banking) crisis within a country, such transmission mechanism can also operate across international borders.' These were borne out during the Asian crisis and the international banking system, particularly Japanese, American and European banks, are yet to get adjusted to the shocks. We can see the reverberations in the attempts of the IMF advisers to restructure banks in Asia. Indonesia provides an extreme case. The IMF has set parameters and time for achieving these. It seems to me that these issues cannot be resolved soon and stretch over several years. The endeavour of the IMF seems to safeguard the interests of the western bank by creating government guarantees for debts so that these loans could still be shown as "performing loans" in the books of the banks and within the Basel Accord. Under present economic conditions, it might not be practicable for Indonesia to provide such guarantees and go along with these schemes. While they may be giving letters of intent to the IMF, they may be doing so more to gain time and for tactical reasons.

9
Indonesia's Foreign Trade

B. Bhattacharya & Prithwis K. De

Introduction

Favoured by natural resources, Indonesia had experienced almost twenty-five years of sustained economic progress until mid-1997. Rapid economic growth of this country has come about largely because of its emphasis on exports and foreign investment in the early 1990s. However, structural weaknesses had intensified over the years, leaving the economy vulnerable when hit by the regional financial crisis. With the collapse of the Thai bath in July 1997, Southeast Asia, including Indonesia, faced a crisis. Further economic disruption and sharp depreciation of the Rupiah accompanied the political disturbances in May 1998, which culminated in the resignation of President Suharto. Currently, the economies in the region are recovering. The focus of this study is Indonesia's foreign trade and pattern of India-Indonesian trade. From India's view point, Indonesia represents an attractive export market.

'The Economist' (1997) notes that if the 1997 crisis of the Indonesian economy were to deteriorate because of policy mistakes or an external shock, the response might be more, not less liberalisation — a swifter dismantling of monopolies, privatisation of the still bloated state sector, and a freer trade regime and the tackling of the what is blandly termed 'the high cost economy' which refers to the plethora of fees, levies, licenses and bribes the bureaucracy exacts from business.

The external orientation of Indonesia can be seen from the percentage shares of exports and imports in GDP. The shares both for exports-GDP and imports-GDP have increased in the years 1997 and 1998 (Table 1). This might by because of the economic crisis that led to negative growth rate of GDP in those two years.

Table 1

Indonesia's share (%) of exports and imports in GDP

Year	Export/GDP	Imports/GDP
1994	23.40	18.70
1995	22.69	20.60
1996	22.41	19.31
1997	24.90	19.91
1998	56.45	30.32

Source: World Development Report

Table 2 shows selected economic indicators for the period from 1996–97 to 1999–2000. The estimated rate of growth of GDP is negative in 1998–99 and the projected dollar in 1996–97 to the estimated figure of about 35 billion-dollar in 1998–99. The capital account is negative in all the years except 1996–97. The direct investment is less than US$ 1 billion both for 1998–99 and 1999–2000. Indonesia's exchange rate fell to Rp/US$ 10200 in 1997–98 from Rp/US$ 2403 in 1996–97.

Table 2
Indonesia: Selected Economic Indicators, 1995–97 to 1999–2000

	1999–97	1997–98	1998–99 (Est)	1999–2000 (Proj)
Real GDP Growth (% change)	8.2	2.0	-16	-2 to 1
CPI Inflation (end-period) (% change)	5.3	39.1	45	10 to 13
CPI Inflation (period average) (% change)	5.2	12.9	66	15 to 20
Current Account Balance ($ billion)	-8.1	-1.7	5.5	3.4
Current Account Balance (in % of GDP) ($ billion)	-3.4	-0.9	4.8	2.0
Trade Balance ($ billion)	1.2	8.8	17.2	17.4
Exports ($ billion)	52.0	56.2	52.2	54.5
Imports ($ billion)	50.9	47.4	34.9	37.1
Capital Account ($ billion)	14.1	-11.6	-3.0	-1.4
Direct Investment ($ billion)	6.5	1.8	0.9	0.5
Exchange Rate (Rp/US$, end-period)	2403	10200	8700	-

Sources: Indian Trade Journal, January 2000.
Note: Year refers to fiscal year

Indonesia's total exports in 1994 were US$ 40053 million. It increased to US$ 48848 million in 1998. Exports during the period from 1994 to 1998 were the highest (US$ 53444 million) in 1997. Imports on the other hand, were US$ 27337 million in 1998 while in 1994 it was US$ 31983 million. Imports were the highest (US$ 42928 million) in 1996. Indonesia enjoyed favourable balance of payment during the period from 1994 to 1998 (Table 12-A & 13-A).

Indonesia's exports in August 1999 rose by 8.62 per cent to US$ 4.60 billion. The better export performance was largely due to higher oil prices. With this the total exports for the period January-August 1999, reached US$ 30.52 billion, an 18.18 per cent drop over the same period last year. As regards imports, the figure in August 1999 was $ 2.01 billion slightly higher than $ 2.0 billion in July 1999. The cumulative import figure for the January-August 1999, was US$ 15.56 billion — a decline of 13.23 per cent over the same period in 1998 (Indian Trade Commissioner's Report on Indonesia, October 1999).

In the first ten months of 1999 exports fell overall by 3.5 per cent in dollar terms, but with imports declining more rapidly than exports (by 12.6 per cent in January–October), the merchandise trade surplus continued to rise (by 7.5 per cent). A 15.3 per cent increase in the value of oil and gas exports helped to offset a 7.1 per cent decline in non-oil and gas exports. The continuing decline in imports in October (of 16.1 per cent year on year and 4.7 per cent month on month) and the weak showing of non-oil and gas exports suggest that the recovery of manufacturing is still weak. In the first eight months of 1999 there were signs of a revival in exports to some Asian destinations as sales to Japan rose modestly in value terms (by 4.4 per cent) and those to South Korea shot up by 18.5 per cent. However, this may simply reflect the fact that oil and gas prices were rising in both countries which are major importers of Indonesian oil and/ or gas (EIU, 4th Quarter, 1999).

The recent available data, covering the first half of 1999, reveals a slightly healthier balance-of-payments position than the previous year period. The current account surplus was up by nearly forty per cent, not because of an improvement in the trade position, but because of a 24.1 per cent fall in the deficit on the invisible account.

Table 3 reflects the present encouraging state of the Indonesian economy. The economic growth for the year 2001 will be 6.1 per cent (forecast), which is better than those for Malaysia and Philippines, from a growth rate of -13.2 per cent in 1998.

Table 3
Recent Economic Indicators of Indonesia, Malaysia and Philippines

		Indonesia	Malaysia	Philippines
Economic Growth (%)	1998 Actual	-13.2	-7.5	-0.5
	1999 Estimate	0.1	5.4	3.2
	2000 Forecast	3.5	6.7	4.0
	2001 Forecast	6.1	5.7	5.0
International Reserves ($ billion)		26.45 (Dec. 1999)	32.18 (Jan. 2000)	13.23 (Dec. 1999)
Export ($ billion)	Latest 3 months (Nov–Jan)	13.17	22.97	8.73
Import ($ billion)	Latest 3 months (Nov–Jan)	6.26	18.05	7.66
Current Account ($ billion)	Latest 3 months	-1.56 (Apr–Jun)	3.73 (Apr–Jun)	0.48 (Oct–Dec)

Source: Far Eastern Economic Review, 6 April, 2000.

India-Indonesia Trade

In 1998, India accounted for 2.24 per cent of Indonesia's total imports from the world and 1.53 per cent of its total exports to the world whereas Indonesia accounted for 1.7 per cent of India's total imports from the world and 1.5 per cent of its total exports to the world.

An attempt has been made to analyse whether the level of exports from India to Indonesia and imports from Indonesia to India are above or below the normal level to be expected from the levels of global trade of India and Indonesia. It has been done by estimating the export intensity index and import intensity index (Kojima, 1967).[1]

If the value of the index, (export or import) is hundred, it indicates that the level of bilateral trade (export or import) is consistent with the share of the partner countries in the global trade. (If the index value is more than hundred, it means that the level of bilateral trade (export or import) is more than what can be justified by the levels of global trade of the partner countries. For index values of less than

Table 4
India-Indonesia Trade Relation — Export Intensity Index

(Values are in US$ Million)	Symbol	1993	1994	1995	1996	1997	1998
India's total export to the world	XI	20259	24196	30537	32325	33248	36739
India's total import from the world	MI	21100	24845	34484	36055	39080	43458
India's total export to Indonesia	-Xji	200	253	501	569	596	543
Total imports of Indonesia from	mi	283281	31992	408071	42959	42728	291851
Total world imports	Mg	3785700	4318800	5151500	5383900	5758700	5611200
Export intensity of India's trade	xji	131.19	140.34	205.73	219.13	239.96	281.96

Source: Direction of Trade Statistics Yearbook, International Monetary Fund.

Note: 1) xji=[(Xji/Xj)1(Mi/(Mg-Mj))]*100
2) Values are DOTS world total

Table 5
India-Indonesia Trade Relation — Import Intensity Index

(Values are in US$ Million)	Symbol	1993	1994	1995	1996	1997	1998
India's total export to the world	XI	20259	24196	30537	32325	33248	36739
India's total import from the world	MI	21100	24845	34484	36055	39080	43458
India's total import from Indonesia	mji	88	283	384	578	703	740
Total exports of Indonesia to the world	xi	36823	40037	449481	49873	53435	54341
Total world exports	Xg	3713300	4246000	5068400	5279700	5622800	54746001
Import intensity of India's trade	mji	41.83	120.11	124.81	168.67	188.17	170.40

Source: Direction of Trade Statistics Yearbook, International Monetary Fund.

Note: 1) mji=[(Mji/Mj)1(Xi1(Xg-Xj))]*100
2) Values are DOTS world total

hundred, the opposite conclusion holds. The estimated results have been presented in Tables 4 and 5 which provide the complete data on export and import intensity indices.

The export and import indices are higher than hundred. It implies that India enjoys a level of exports and imports to/from Indonesia, which are more than what can be expected from their global trade levels.

The growth rates of India's export/import to/from Indonesia, the rest of the world and the world are given in Table 6 and 7, respectively. It is evident from the data that the export growth rates to Indonesia are higher than the world in all the years except the year 1998. This may be because of the crisis that Indonesia experienced in that year. However, regarding imports no conclusion can be reached about the relative growth rates. Out of the five years under observation, the growth rates to Indonesia were higher in three years and lower in two years compared to the growth rates to the world.

Indo-Indonesia bilateral trade in 1994–95 was Rs. 1883.64 crore and reached Rs. 4210.45 crore in 1998–99. India faced unfavourable balance of trade of Rs. 139.82 crore during 1994–95 with exports at Rs. 871.91 crore and imports at Rs. 1011.73 crore. Similarly, in 1998–99 exports were Rs. 785.55 crore and imports were Rs. 3424.90 crore resulting in a trade deficit of Rs. 2639.35 crore. India enjoyed favourable balance of trade (Rs. 673.52 crore) only during the year 1995–96.

Table 8 shows the recent Indian exports and imports to and from Indonesia. India's import from Indonesia for the period 1999 (January to July) is more than the India's exports to Indonesia for the same period. India's import from Indonesia experiences a positive growth rate whereas India's export to Indonesia witnesses a negative growth rate for the period 1999 (January to July).

Table 6

India-Indonesia Trade Relation — Growth Rates of Exports (%)

(Values are in US$ Million)	Value 1993	1994	1995	1996	1997	1998
India's total export to the world	20259	24196	30537	32325	33248	36739
India's total export to Indonesia	200	253	501	569	596	543
India's total export to the rest of the world	20059	239431	30036	31756	326521	3619
		Growth rate (%)				
India's total export to the world		19.43	26.21	5.86	2.86	10.50
India's total export to Indonesia		26.50	98.02	13.57	4.75	-8.89
India's total export to the rest of the world		19.36	25.451	5.73	2.82	10.85

Source: Direction of Trade Statistics Yearbook, International Monetary Fund.

Note: 1) Year refers to the calendar year
2) Values are DOTS world total

Table 7

India-Indonesia Trade Relation — Growth Rates of Import (%)

(Values are in US$ Million)	Value 1993	1994	1995	1996	1997	1998
India's total import from the world	21100	24845	34484	36055	39080	43458
India's total import from Indonesia	88	283	384	578	703	740
India's total import from the rest of the world	21012	24562	34100	354771	38377	4271 q
		Growth rate (%)				
India's total import from the world		17.75	38.80	4.56	8.39	11.20
India's total import from Indonesia		221.59	35.69	50.52	21.63	5.26
India's total import from the rest of the world		16.90	38.8		8.171	11.31

Source: Same as Table-6

Note: Same as Table-6

Table 8
India's Exports and Imports to/from Indonesia in 1999
(US$ Million)

	February	March	April	May	June	July	Jan-July	Jan-July (Growth Rate %)
Exports	25.05	22.36	29.7	29.61	17.43	21.16	177.62	-8.35
Imports	68.05	62.16	76.28	74.06	55.51	76.24	451.39	18.81

Source: Indian Trade Commissioner's Report on Indonesia
Note: Growth rates refer to the corresponding period last year.

India's major export/import items to/from Indonesia are given in Table 9 and 10, respectively. According to the figures of 1998–99, important items of India's exports to Indonesia included oil meals, primary and semi-finished iron and steel; machinery and instruments; manufactures of metals; inorganic/organic/agro-chemicals; dyes intermediates & coal tar chemicals; cotton yarn fabrics made-up, etc.; drugs, pharmaceuticals & fine chemicals, groundnuts; and manmade yarn fabrics made-up, etc. The items, which have registered increase over 1997–98, are only manufactures of metals, and manmade yarn fabrics made-up, etc. So far as the composition of India's imports from Indonesia is concerned, the main items during 1998–99 were vegetable oils (edible); other commodities; coal, coke & briquettes; metal ferrous ores & metal scrap; petroleum crude & products; organic chemicals; textile yarn fabrics, made-up articles; wood & wood products; artificial resins, plastic materials, etc.; and pulp & waste paper. The items, which have registered significant growth over the year 1997–98, include vegetable oils (edible); metal ferrous ores & metal scrap, and wood and wood products.

Table 9
India's Major Exports to Indonesia

(US$ Million) Commodities	1996–97 Value	1997–98 Value Value	Growth (%)	1998–99	Growth (%)
Oil meals	136.68	108.14	-20.88	51.44	-52.43
Primary & semi-finished iron & steel	49.42	45.51	-7.91	17.25	-62.10
Machinery & instruments	35.21	31.51	-10.51	13.00	-58.74
Manufactures of metals	7.95	9.45	18.87	10.90	15.34
Inorganic/organic/agro-chemicals	20.401	14.82	-27.35	10.63	-28.27
Dyes intermediates & coal tar chemicals	17.68	12.83	-27.43	10.04	-21.75
Cotton yarn fabrics made-up, etc.	11.68	15.58	33.39	9.08	-41.72
Drugs, pharmaceuticals & fine chemicals	9.44	9.76	3.39	8.46	-13.32
Groundnuts	51.57	44.24	-14.21	6.94	-84.31
Manmade yarn fabrics made-up	4.91	3.55	-27.70	5.61	58.03

Source: Trades, CMIE Trade Database
Note: Growth over preceding year

Table 10
India's Major Imports from Indonesia

(US$ Million) Commodities	1996–97 Value	1997–98 Value	Growth	1998–99 Value	Growth
Vegetable oils (edible)	129.77	6.03	-95.35	284.53	4618.57
Other commodities	75.27	76.71	1.91	102.8	34.01
Coal, coke & briquettes	36,491	76.43	109.45	70.59	-7.64
Metaliferrous ores & metal scrap	10.3	17.1	66.02	42.07	146.02
Petroleum crude & products	114.8	112.64	-1.88	37,121	-67.05
Organic chemicals	70.06	44.75	-36.13	37,081	-17.14
Textile yarn fabrics, made-up articles	23.16	143.42	519.26	24.15	-83.16
Wood & wood products	3.71	6.03	62.53	23.72	-293.37
Artificial resins, plastic materials, etc.	27.64	17.99	-34.91	22.17	23.24
Pulp & waste paper	21.58	315.09	1360.10	20.52	-93.49

Source: same as Table 9
Note: same as Table 9

ASEAN Free Trade Area

The agreement on the Common Effective Preferential Tariff (CEPI) Scheme for the ASEAN Free Trade Area (AFTA) was signed in Singapore on 28 January, 1992. CEPT is an agreed effective tariff, preferential to ASEAN, to be applied to goods originating from ASEAN Member States, and which have been identified for inclusion in the CEPT Scheme in accordance with Articles 2(5) and 3 (Website: htt:// www.aseansec.org).

Noting the economic turbulence in the past year, the AFFA Council viewed that AFTA would enhance economic integration and strengthen resilience towards such external volatility. Increased trade interaction would help to overcome the negative impact of unprecedented currency devaluation of ASEAN countries. The Council also noted that AFTA would create the appropriate impetus for economies to eliminate any inherent weaknesses, consolidate, readjust and strengthen economic fundamentals to improve economic competitiveness and engineer and export-led recovery.

To build up business and investor confidence, the ASEAN leaders agreed in December 1998 to further accelerate the implementation of the ASEAN Free Trade Area. The six original members (Brunei Darussalam, Indonesia, Malaysia, Philippines, Singapore and Thailand) will advance the implementation of AFTA by one year from the year 2003 to 2002. The acceleration will be accomplished in stages. Individually each country will commit to achieve a minimum of eighty-five per cent of the Inclusion List with tariffs of zero to five per cent by the year 2000. Thereafter, this will be increased to minimum of ninety per cent of the Inclusion List in the zero to five per cent tariff range by the year 2001. By 2002, all of items in the Inclusion List will have tariffs of zero to five per cent with some flexibility. Member countries also agreed to deepen, as soon as possible, tariff reduction to zero per cent and accelerate the transfer of products which are currently not included in the tariff reduction scheme in the Inclusion List.

Now the question is what could be the possible impact on India's export to Indonesia of the above development.

The impact of the ASEAN Free Trade on Indonesia's imports from India has also been looked into. Impact of AFTA tariff reduction of ASEAN countries on India's export to those countries will primarily depend upon two factors. First, the extent of tariff reduction on a particular commodity. Second, import structure of Indonesia is a crucial determinant: if a particular commodity is simultaneously imported by Indonesia from India and other ASEAN countries, the impact will be positive. On the other hand, if import structure of Indonesia from India and other ASEAN countries is totally dissimilar, the impact of AFTA tariff will be zero. Even if the import structure of Indonesia from India and other ASEAN countries are broadly similar, the extent of the impact depends on the cost of the product and the exchange rate of India and other ASEAN countries. However, for analysing the impact of tariff reduction, the *usual ceterisparibus assumption* has been made.

ASEAN Trade

Intra-ASEAN exports growth (over the previous year) has come down to minus-twenty nine per cent in 1998 from about twenty-five per cent in 1995 (Table 11-A & B). This might be because of the crisis experienced by these countries in that period. Total ASEAN (original five countries — Singapore, Malaysia, Thailand, Indonesia, Philippines) exports growth also has come down to minus-twenty three per cent in 1998 over 1997 from US$ 340475 million in 1997 to US$ 261552 million in 1998, whilst intra-ASEAN exports has come down from US$ 78966 million US$ 56010 million. Excluding intra-ASEAN trade, ASEAN's (original five) total exports has come down to US$ 205542 million in 1998 from US$ 261509 million in 1997, representing a minus-twenty one per cent decline. The ASEAN's (original five) outward orientation is reflected in the higher rate of growth of exports of extra-ASEAN compared to intra-ASEAN after 1996, although intra-ASEAN trade plays a role in enhancing ASEAN's export competitiveness. In intra-ASEAN exports, countries experiencing positive growth rates are Philippines (11.28 per cent) and Indonesia (2.43 per cent) in 1998. As a result of the economic weakness in the region, the export slowdown has been felt more strongly in intra-ASEAN trade.

However, ASEAN (original five) imports have fallen even further in 1997 and 1998. Intra-ASEAN imports growth (over the previous year) has also come down to minus-twenty eight per cent in 1998 from twenty-two per cent in 1995 (Table 12-A & B). Total ASEAN (original five countries — Singapore, Malaysia, Thailand, Indonesia, and Philippines) imports growth has also decreased to minus-thirty eight per cent in 1998 over 1997. In absolute terms the value of total ASEAN (original five) imports is highest (US$ 359191 million) in 1996 and lowest value (US$ 218395 million) is achieved in 1998. Intra-ASEAN imports have reached a lowest level of US$ 45948 million in 1998 from the highest level of US$ 63944 million in 1997. ASEAN's (big five) total import from extra-ASEAN region has come down to US$ 172447 million in 1998 from US$ 289654 million in 1997, representing a fall of minus-forty per cent 1996 onwards, the growth rates of intra-ASEAN imports are higher than the same for extra-ASEAN imports. In intra-ASEAN imports, only Thailand has experienced a negative growth of imports (-16.75 per cent) in 1997 whereas in 1998, Singapore, Malaysia, Indonesia and Philippines have witnessed a negative growth (the data for Thailand in 1998 is not available).

Therefore, both exports and imports of ASEAN (original five) have fallen significantly in 1998, reflecting the major contractions of these economies in that period.

Table 11-A
ASEAN Export for 1994–1998

(US $ million)

Country	Intra-ASEAN					Extra-ASEAN Value					Total-ASEAN				
	1994	1995	1996	1997	1998	1994	1995	1996	1997	1998	1994	1995	1996	1997	1998
Singapore	28237	34695	3533,d	33574	25547	68588	83568	89676	91414	84358	96825	118263	125008	124988	109905
Malaysia	16136	20098	22015	21640	17532	42707	53680	56296	57089	55771	58843	73778	78315	78729	73303
Thailand	8211	11205	11011	11424	na	36942	45140	44667	46662	na	45153	56345	55678	58086	na
Indonesia	5901	6334	754,c	8897	9113	34152	39084	42266	44547	39735	40053	45418	49815	53444	48848
Philippines 1	137A	2314	296-1	3430	3817	11930	14860	17575	21798	25679	13302	17174	20542	2522@	29496
Above Five 1	598571	7464	78878	78966	56010	194318	236332	260481	261509	205542	264175	310978	329369	340475	261652

Source: PC-TAS CD-ROM; UN

Note: Here ASEAN includes Singapore, Malaysia, Thailand, Philippines, Indonesia, Vietnam and Burnei Dar.

Table 11-B
ASEAN Export Growth for 1994–1998

Country	Intra-ASEAN				Extra-ASEAN Growth Rate (%)				Total-ASEAN			
	1995	1996	1997	1998	1995	1996	1997	1998	1995	1996	1997	1998
Singapore	22.87	1.84	-4.98	-23.91	21.84	7.31	1.94	-7.72	22.14	5.70	-0.02	-12.07
Malaysia	24.55	9.56	-1.72	-18.98	25.69	4.87	1.41	-2.31	25.38	6.15	0.53	-6.89
Thailand	36.46	-1.73	3.75	na	22.19	-1.05	4.47	na	24.79	-1.18	4.32	na
Indonesia	7.34	19.18	17.86	2.43	14.44	8.14	5.40	-10.80	13.39	9.68	7.28	-8.60
Philippines	68.66	28.22	15.60	11.28	24.56	18.2	24.03	17.80	29.11	19.61	22.81	16.92
Above Five	24.71	5.67	0.11	-29.07	21.62	5.99	4.40	-21.40	22.35	5.91	3.38	-23.18

Note: Same as Table 11-A.

Table 12-A
ASEAN Imports for 1994–1998

(US $ million)

Country	Intra-ASEAN					Extra-ASEAN					Total-ASEAN Value				
	1994	1995	1996	1997	1998	1994	1995	1996	1997	1998	1994	1995	1996	1997	1998
Singapore	23154	27464	28930	29411	23582	79515	97039	102410	103031	78150	102669	124503	131340	132442	101732
Malaysia	11282	13466	15445	16082	13154	47804	63580	62460	62352	44643	59086	77046	77905	78434	57797
Thailand	7112	8980	9404	7829	na	47325	61801	62912	54633	na	54437	70781	72316	62462	na
Indonesia	3006	4110	5088	5393	449-i	28977	36519	37840	36287	22840	31983	40629	42928	41680	27337
Philippines	2617	335	4250	5229	471 E	20121	25128	30451	33352	26814	22738	28487	34701	38581	31530
Above Five	47171	57379	63117	63944	4594E	223743	284067	296074	289654	172447	270914	341446	359191	353598	218395

Note: Same as Table 11-A.

Table 12–B
ASEAN Import Growth for 1994-1998

Country	Intra-ASEAN				Extra-ASEAN Growth Rate (%)				Total-ASEAN			
	1995	1996	1997	1998	1995	1996	1997	1998	1995	1996	1997	1998
Singapore	18.61	5.34	1.66	-19.82	22.04	5.53	0.61	-24.15	21.27	5.49	0.84	-23.19
Malaysia	19.36	14.70	4.12	-18.21	33.00	-1.76	-0.17	-28.40	30.40	1.11	0.68	-26.31
Thailand	26.27	4.72	-16.75	na	30.59	1.80	-13.16	na	30.02	2.17	-13.63	na
Indonesia	36.73	23.80	5.99	-16.61	26.01	3.62	-4.10	-37.06	27.03	5.66	-2.91	-34.41
Philippines	28.35	26.53	23.04	-9.81	24.88	21.18	9.3	-19.60	25.28	21.81	11.18	-18.28
Above Five	21.64	10.00	1.31	-28.14	6.96	4.23	-2.17	-40.46	26.03	5.20	-1.56	-38.24

Note: Same as Table 11-A

As a result of regional agreements, competitor countries gain preferential access and Indian exporters suffer a loss in exports — actual and potential. ASEAN Free Trade Area (AFTA) is one such regional agreement. As a result of AFTA, the Indian exporters may face problems in exporting their products. India and Indonesia are competitors in exporting some of their products to the ASEAN. Table-13 shows that the growth rates of India's exports to the ASEAN (except Indonesia) are lower than the growth rates of Indonesia's exports to the ASEAN after 1995. This might be because of the fact that the ASEAN countries have started reducing the tariff rates following the agreements of AFTA.

Table 13
India and Indonesia: Exports to ASEAN

(US $ million)

	Value					Growth (%)			
	1994	1995	1996	1997	1998	1995	1996	1997	1998
India's Export to the ASEAN (except Indonesia)	1621	2028	2260	1972	1576	25.11	11.44	-12.74	-20.08
Indonesia's Export to the ASEAN	5901	6334	7549	8897	9113	7.34	19.18	17.86	2.43

Source: PC-TAS CD-ROM, UN; and DOTS 11
Note: Here ASEAN includes Singapore, Malaysia, Thailand, Philippines, Indonesia, Vietnam and Brunei Dar.

The value and growth of Indonesia's imports from India and ASEAN are given in Table 14. The growth rates of Indonesia's imports from India though negative in the years 1997 and 1998, are higher than the growth rates of Indonesia's imports from the ASEAN in three years out of four years. As a result of the AFTA agreement, some of India's export items that are imported both from India and ASEAN by Indonesia might be affected. We have also attempted here to find out what are those commodities that might get affected.

According to the analysis from ASEAN Secretariat a total of 85.2 per cent of all products would already be at zero to five per cent tariff rates by the year 2000, representing approximately 88.1 per cent of total intra-ASEAN (only ASEAN-6, excluding Laos, Myanmar and Vietnam) imports. There are three hundred and ninety-four items, at SITC four-digit level, which accounts for about fifty-four per cent of India's export to Indonesia in 1998 that are going to be affected because of AFTA. Out of these three hundred and ninety-four products we have chosen fifty-five products (about fourteen per cent) on the basis of Indonesia's share of imports from India and ASEAN which are going to be affected most. The basis of selections is that where Indonesia's share of import from India is higher than the same from the ASEAN in 1998. These items are given in Annex-1. There are five items — other cereal flours (SITC Code-0471); oil-cake, oilseed residue (SITC Code-0813); groundnuts (peanuts) (SITC Code-2221); sesame (sesamum) seeds (SITC Code-2225); and cotton sewing thread (SITC Code-6512) — whose share is more than fifty per cent.

Table 14
Indonesia: Imports from India and ASEAN

(US $ million)

	Value					Growth (%)			
	1994	1995	1996	1997	1998	1995	1996	1997	1998
Indonesia's import from India	318	476	866	703	612	49.69	81.93	-18.82	-12.94
Indonesia's import from the ASEAN	3006	4110	5088	5393	4497	36.73	23.80	5.99	-16.61

Source: PC-TAS CD-ROM, UN; and DOTS
Note: Here ASEAN includes Singapore, Malaysia, Thailand, Philippines, Indonesia, Vietnam and Brunei Dar.

A summary statement of India's tariff disadvantage and trade coverage thereof is given in Table 15.

Investment

According to the data released by the Indonesian Investment Coordinating Board, India's approved investment in Indonesia till March 1999 was merely US$ 748.9 million, constituting just 0.34 per cent of the total approved FDI. The actual amount, of Indian FDI in Indonesia currently stands at around US$ 200–300 million. Indonesia's FDI in India was US$ 115.32 million till December 1998, just 0.22 of the total FDI entering India. According to the Ministry of Commerce Annual Report 1999–2000, out of the total nine hundred and twelve active joint ventures of India dispersed over ninety-one countries, twenty are in Indonesia.

Conclusion

Indonesia's objective for the Indian market is how to increase Indonesia's exports. Most of the Indonesian products sold to India are raw materials and intermediate goods. Indonesia would like to diversify their export basket and include manufactures. If counter-trade mechanism is implemented, it could really prove immensely beneficial. It should also involve exchange of products with projects. Indonesia should strengthen their economic cooperation bilaterally and multilaterally to eliminate the negative factors of globalisation such as unfair treatment to the developing countries and unjustified trade.

The AFTA council reaffirmed those efficient and comprehensive networks of transport services among and between ASEAN member countries are of utmost importance to the fulfilment of AFTA's objectives.

Some people find analogy between the crisis of Mexico and Indonesia. However, Stiglitz (2000) notes that Mexico recovered because of a surge of exports to the US, which

Table 15
India's Relative Tariff Disadvantage

HS Code	Sector	Indonesia's Tariff Rate MFN 1997	Indonesia's Tariff Rate CEPT 2002	India's Relative Tariff Disadvantage	Indonesia's Import from India 1997 (1000 USD)	Relative Distribution of Tariff Disadvantage: Range	Relative Distribution of Tariff Disadvantage: value 1000 USD	Relative Distribution of Tariff Disadvantage: Per cent
01-05	Live Animal	15.6	4.44	11.16	375	0-5	203774	29.54
06-14	Vegetable Products	9.3	4.29	5.01	103828	5-10	157989	22.90
15	Fats & Oils	6.9	4.63	2.27	7 07	10-15	6823	0.96
16-24	Prepared Foodstuffs	26.9	4.89	22.01	220856	15-20	96641	14.01
25-27	Mineral Products	4.4	2.861	1.54	22898	20-25	224887	32.60
28-38	Chemicals	5.4	3.24	2.16	72814			
39-40	Plastics	15.8	4.24	11.56	2737			
41-43	Hides & Leathers	10.6	2.82	7.78	1604			
44-46	Wood & Wood Articles	9.5	4.3	5.2	51			
47-49	Pulp & Paper	9	4.641	4.36	226			
50-63	Textiles & Apparel	21.1	4.92	16.18	95141			
64-67	Footwear	21.2	4.95	16.25	1500			
68-70	Cements & Ceramics	9.6	4.51	5.09	10195			
71	Gems	12.4	3.77	8.63	21			
72-83	Base Metals	8.9	4.31	4.6	107129			
84-85	Machinery	9	3.92	5.08	41249			
86-89	Vehicles	24.8	2.13	22.67	4031			
90-92	Optical Instruments	11.15	4.26	6.89	983			
93	Arms	12.6	N/a	N/a	0			
94-96	Miscellaneous	20	5.021	14.98	511			
97-98	Antiques	14	4.621	9.38	58			

Source: ASEAN Website; and TRAINS CD-ROM, UN

Notes: CEPT implies Common Effective Preferential Tariff
MFN implies Most Favoured Nation Average Tariff
N/a implies not available.

took off due to the US economic boom, and because of NAFTA. By contrast, Indonesia's main trading partner was Japan, which was then, and still remains, mired in the doldrums. Furthermore, Indonesia was far more politically and socially explosive than Mexico, with a much deeper history of ethnic strife.

According to Hanke (2000) the shock wreaked havoc on the countries that allowed their currencies to depreciate the most by adopting the IMF's pernicious economic ideas and Indonesia's crisis was lingered by the IMF and US.

Half of the businesses in Indonesia were in virtual bankruptcy or close to it, and, as a result, the country could not even take advantage of the export opportunities that the lower exchange rate provided.

References

Direction of Trade Statistics Yearbook, (Various issues), International Monetary Fund.

The Economist (1997): "Survey Indonesia", 26 July.

EIU Country Report (1999): Indonesia, 4th Quarter, The Economic Intelligence Unit, and UK.

Kojima, K., (1967): "Trade Arrangements Among Industrial Countries: Effects on Japan", in B. Balassa, ed., *Studies in Trade Liberalisation*, (Baltimore, John Hopkins Press, 1967), pp. 177–216.

Far Eastern Economic Review, 6 April, 2000.

Hanke, S.H., (2000): "Asian's Currency Crisis, A Postmortem", *The Asian Wall Street Journal*.

India Trade Journal (2000): "Focus on International Trade—Indonesia", 26 January.

Ministry of Commerce, Government of India, Annual Report (1999–2000).

PC-TAS CD-ROM, UN.

Stiglitz, 3 (2000): "What I learned At the World Economic Crisis", The Insider, *The New* Republic Online (http: www.tnr.com).

Indian Trade Commissioner's Report on Indonesia (various issues).

Website: http://www.aseansec.org.

World Development Report (various issues), World Bank.

Trades, CMIE Trade Database, Mumbai.

TRAINS CD-ROM, UN.

Annex-1
Indonesia's Import Share from ASEAN and India for 1994–1998

Code	ITC Items	Country	Share 1994	1995	1996	1997	1998
0361	Crustaceans, frozen	ASEAN	16.69	26.25	9.94	20.37	31.08
		INDIA	0.00	1.33	8.18	24.56	38.61
0363	Molluscs	ASEAN	2.07	4.29	0.6	0.81	3.09
		INDIA	0.00	0.00	1.22	7.44	9.66
0471	Other cereal flours	ASEAN	0	59.47	21.16	26.14	14.85
		INDIA	0.00	0.00	0.00	0.00	70.36
0751	Pepper, dry, crushed, ground	ASEAN	1	1.51	1.71	59.95	10.10
		INDIA	3.72	6.99	55.99	10.71	20.96
0752	Spices, ex. pepper, pimento	ASEAN	18.78	37.37	16.32	3.83	10.54
		INDIA	2.82	3.62	3.53	36.52	15.67
0813	Oil-cake, oilseed residue	ASEAN	0.25	0.43	0.63	1.6	4.06
		INDIA	61.53	50.97	44.51	54.60	55.00
2221	Groundnuts (peanuts)	ASEAN	49.78	42.34	40.17	12.9	10.01
		INDIA	13.91	15.16	38.14	83.48	72.23
2225	Sesame (sesamum) seeds	ASEAN	26.92	13.68	0.38	2.8	0
		INDIA	0.00	48.75	74.60	83.99	60.32
2516	Chem, wood pulp, sulphite	ASEAN	2.02	0	0.88	0	0
		INDIA	0.00	0.00	0.00	0.00	0.19
2631	Cotton, not carded, combed	ASEAN	0.52	0.41	0.47	0.62	0.55
		INDIA	2.72	0.03	4.24	9.61	0.64
2641	Jute, textl. bast fibr.raw	ASEAN	12.42	0	0	4.45	0
		INDIA	0.00	20.00	0.00	0.00	1.99
2731	Building, dimension stone	ASEAN	1.15	1.61	0.81	1.5	1.7
		INDIA	22.60	13.03	21.31	26.04	32.64
2783	Sodium chloride, etc.	ASEAN	0.03	0.14	0.57	0.58	0.9
		INDIA	2.65	2.34	0.00	3.98	4.29
2852	Alumina (aluminium oxide)	ASEAN	0.04	0.06	0.14	0.06	0.19
		INDIA	0.01	0.00	10.53	13.95	19.49
2919	Oth.animal materials	ASEAN	1.11	28.44	1.78	4.16	5.17
		INDIA	0.00	0.01	2.41	2.94	21.28
2922	Natural gums,resins, etc.	ASEAN	4.57	0.71	0.68	1.66	6.7
		INDIA	60.93	58.42	78.97	58.87	44.08
4311	Fat, oil, animal, veg.prod.	ASEAN	2.68	2.34	1.8	2.54	3.93
		INDIA	0.00	0.00	9.35	8.10	11.26
5114	Sulph. etc. derv.hydrocarb	ASEAN	0.58	4.09	4.07	4.15	1.03
		INDIA	13.67	8.71	13.16	8.34	8.42
5145	Amine-function compounds	ASEAN	4.08	3.75	4.38	7.37	5.14
		INDIA	6.71	4.83	6.43	4.58	6.94
5146	Oxygen-funct.amino-comp.	ASEAN	10.42	7.68	7.77	18.96	10.06
		INDIA	6.12	8.22	14.60	11.11	29.79
5147	Carboxyamide-func.compds	ASEAN	1.12	1.64	1.35	1.93	3.18
		INDIA	1.78	0.89	4.68	6.56	3.45
5154	Organo-sulphur compounds	ASEAN	1.26	1.19	1.08	4.97	5.85
		INDIA	3.33	5.19	7.78	7.88	19.00

5158	Sulphonamides	ASEAN	0	0.02	0.57	0	0.23
		INDIA	11.81	10.66	13.27	4.60	11.58
5163	Estrs, inorganic acid, etc	ASEAN	0.78	0.22	2.21	2.02	4.3
		INDIA	0.80	2.91	3.68	8.43	10.26
5251	Radio-active chemicals	ASEAN	0	1.3	2.01	0.13	6.54
		INDIA	0.00	0.20	0.20	0.00	8.93
5312	Synth.bdghteners, lakes	ASEAN	1.63	1.67	1.49	2.8	0.98
		INDIA	6.08	5.47	3.67	1.71	1.13
5322	Dyes, tanning extract, etc	ASEAN	6.07	1.88	0.08	5.61	4.87
		INDIA	4.20	1.10	3.80	4.90	4.90
5323	Synthetic tanning substs	ASEAN	2.1	15.99	13.45	15.54	4.95
		INDIA	1.06	1.51	4.44	6.16	5.22
5414	Veg.alkaloids	ASEAN	0.26	1.33	1.62	0.52	0.09
		INDIA	0.66	0.19	1.19	0.82	0.96
5419	Pharm goods, exc.medcmnts	ASEAN	3.33	6.29	2.78	3.07	0.75
		INDIA	0.73	0.23	0.23	0.59	0.88
5911	Insecticides, retail sale	ASEAN	6.96	9.38	1.11	0.56	0.21
		INDIA	1.94	1.60	1.65	1.03	2.01
6116	Goat or kid skin leather	ASEAN	3.03	4.06	1.04	7.9	2.64
		INDIA	26.25	37.27	45.14	17.38	27.21
6129	Oth.leather articles nes	ASEAN	0.95	2.2	2.84	1.45	0.17
		INDIA	0.00	0.00	0.00	0.70	2.01
5512	Cotton sewing thread	ASEAN	0	25.86	0.33	0	0.25
		INDIA	23.60	0.00	22.77	1.20	51.77
5513	Cotton yarn, excl. thread	ASEAN	5.14	5.69	0.47	0.27	0.11
		INDIA	3.60	2.60	11.15	31.08	26.69
6524	Oth85%+cottn.fabric200g+	ASEAN	3.17	3.34	2.15	1.03	0.65
		INDIA	0.77	1.37	1.46	0.90	1.74
6542	Fabric85%+wool, fine hair	ASEAN	0	0	1.01	1.49	1.69
		INDIA	0.00	0.00	1.74	5.68	5.42
6543	Fabric, wool, fine.hairnes	ASEAN	0	0.26	12.25	1.08	0.79
		INDIA	0.05	1.36	2.12	1.12	1.18
6563	Gimped	ASEAN	0.27	0.36	0.12	1.31	1.65
		INDIA	0.44	1.82	0.37	0.54	2.78
6581	Sacks, bags, txti.material	ASEAN	7.96	25.21	0.66	3.6	4.41
		INDIA	0.00	0.00	1.13	1.89	18.53
6613	Building stone, workd, etc	ASEAN	14.56	5.43	10.75	3.23	2.27
		INDIA	11.99	26.64	16.41	5.69	9.63
6651	Containers, of glass	ASEAN	7.76	4.43	5.68	2.73	3.22
		INDIA	1.21	2.56	22.52	49.66	7.84
6726	Semi-finish.iron, steel	ASEAN	0	0.32	0	0.54	1.77
		INDIA	6.24	8.53	2.45	3.50	7.56
6727	Semi-fin.iron, etc.25%+c	ASEAN	5.88	0.18	0	0	0
		INDIA	5.86	0.00	0.00	5.73	7.36
6731	Flat, hot-roled.prod.iron	ASEAN	1.38	2.76	0	1.38	2.76
		INDIA	0.74	12.86	0	0.74	12.86
6732	Flat, hot-roled, prod.iron	ASEAN	2.93	1.22	3.06	5.77	4.28
		INDIA	0.00	0.06	4.05	3.29	5.36
6762	Bar, rod iron, sti.hot-fd	ASEAN	1.43	2.07	4.51	2.66	1.49
		INDIA	0.22	0.34	0.19	5.04	1.79

6851	Lead, and alloy, unwrght.	ASEAN	4.26	5.33	0.89	0.22	0.97
		INDIA	0.00	0.05	0.34	0.00	1.12
7311	Mach.tools, metal removal	ASEAN	16.4	4.05	2.52	7.84	0.32
		INDIA	0.00	0.55	1.43	0.06	1.23
7372	Mti-rolling mills, roled	ASEAN	2.26	0.82	5.44	0.83	0.32
		INDIA	1.09	1.06	8.08	0.22	0.53
7511	Typewritrs, wd-proc machs	ASEAN	1.65	13.65	2.62	4.56	0.88
		INDIA	5.71	4.43	6.30	4.36	10.17
7732	Electrc.insulating equip	ASEAN	5.79	8.64	5.98	7.18	4.49
		INDIA	0.12	0.10	3.78	2.79	4.53
8823	Photo film roll unexposd	ASEAN	2.7	2.85	2.3	1.46	0.97
		INDIA	0.01	0.32	0.00	0.00	2.44
8991	Carved, moulded goods	ASEAN	1.81	1.8	2.87	2.64	0.59
		INDIA	0.05	0.00	0.00	2.00	1.50
8999	Manufactured goods	ASEAN	0.47	10.72	7.48	20.57	5.99
		INDIA	8.99	13.90	17.10	18.94	41.37

Source: Derived form PC-TAS, UN

1 The formulae for estimation of indices are:

Export Intensity Index:

Export intensity of j's trade with i is Xji=[(Xji/Xj)/(Mi/(Mg-Mj))] x 100

Here Xji = Exports of country j to country i.
Xj = Global exports of country j.
Mi = Global imports of country i.
Mg = Total global imports.
Mj = Global imports of country j.

Import Intensity Index:

Import intensity of j's trade with i is mji [(Mji/Mj)/(Xi/(Xg-Xj))] x 100

Here Mji = Imports of country j from country i.
Mj Global imports of country j.
Xi Global exports of countryi.
Xg Total global exports.
Xj Global exports of country j.

10

The Indonesian Armed Forces and Politics

B. Raman

Composition before President Wahid took over

The annual report on global military expenditures during 1998 submitted to the Appropriations Committees of the two Houses of the US Congress on 19 February, 1999, by the US State Department indicated the composition of the Armed Forces of the Republic of Indonesia (ABRI — Angkatan Bersenjata Republic Indonesia) as follows:

Army	216,000
Air Force	27,000
Navy	26,000
Marines	12,000
Police	170,000
Total	**451,000**

The report estimated the official military budget (based on a share of the state revenue and excluding revenue from military-run commercial enterprises) during the financial year 1998–99 at US$ 1 billion, which in terms of the pre-1997 economic crisis buying power, would come to US$ 700 million. This amount of US$ 1 billion amounted to 1.3 per cent in the case of Pakistan.

It commented as follows on the official military spending: "Prior to the financial crisis, officially published Indonesian defence spending, including police expenditure, had been falling in relation to GDP, from a peak level of three per cent in 1981 to levels of about 1.5 per cent in the 1990s. Defence spending had experienced similar decline in relation to overall government outlay. Real growth in the military budget from 1988 to 1997 paralleled the steady expansion of the Indonesian economy during that period."

Authentic estimates of the unofficial defence expenditure, not reflected in the state budget, which is incurred out of the revenue from the military-run commercial enterprises, are not available. There are various tentative guesstimates, claiming that, before 1997, the unofficial expenditure amounted to about four to seven times the official expenditure.

On 1 April, 1999, the Police (POLRI), which was incorporated into the armed forces by the then president, Sukarno in 1964, was separated and made into an autonomous department, no longer under the control of the Chief of the Armed Forces, but still under the supervision of the Defence Minister. After the separation of the Police, the ABRI was re-named as the Indonesian National Armed Forces (TNI—*Tentara Nasional Indonesia*).

Organisational structure

The army is divided into the central and territorial forces. Of the 216,000 personnel in the army, about thirty-five thousand constitute the central forces and the remaining the territorial forces. The central forces are divided into the Army Strategic Command (KOSTRAD), with two light infantry divisions and supporting arms, and the Special Forces Command (KOPASSUS), divided into four operational groups.

The remaining troops have been distributed into ten territorial commands (KODAM), proposed to be increased to seventeen, covering the entire archipelago with its twenty-seven provinces and three hundred and twenty-seven districts. While the KOSTRAD and the KOPASSUS are largely Javanese dominated, the KODAMs have a large percentage of the sons of the soil recruited within the jurisdiction of each KODAM.

The Navy consists of the Western Fleet based in Jakarta and the Eastern Fleet in Surabaya. The jurisdiction of the Western Fleet covers the approaches to the South China Sea and the Malacca and Sunda Straits. The Eastern Fleet is responsible for guarding the approaches to the Pacific Ocean, the Lombok/Macassar Straits and other eastern Straits.

The Air Force has about twenty squadrons, six of them fighter squadrons, meant for the protection of Java.

A pre-1997 twenty five-year plan for the revamping of the armed forces, with the total strength of the army to be increased to 330,000 had to be shelved due to the economic crisis. The plans for the acquisition of new equipment, including five German submarines to supplement the existing two aging ones, were also put off. The only new programme, which has been retained, is the acquisition of an additional squadron of Hawk multi-purpose planes, bringing the total to forty for providing air cover to the approaches to the South China Sea and the Natuna gas fields from a new base at Pontianak in West Kalimantan, which will act in coordination with the existing squadron based at Pekan Baru in Sumatra.

Apart from the shelved plans to augment the submarine strength, other deferred acquisition programmes related to the purchase of Russian fighters and helicopters, production of French artillery under licence in Indonesia, and the locally-ordered (from the IPTN, the indigenous aircraft manufacturers) transport and maritime patrol planes and helicopters.

Before 1965, under Sukarno, the erstwhile USSR was the most important source of military supplies. After 1965, most of the acquisitions came from France, the US, the UK, Germany and the Netherlands. At the same time, to promote self-reliance and reduce the dependence on overseas supplies, the Suharto regime under Dr. B.J. Habibie, the Technology Minister, who later succeeded Mr. Suharto as the interim president in 1998, embarked upon a policy of developing the capability for producing military equipment, including aircraft and helicopters for the Air Force. This programme has not made much progress. Hence, the TNI is still largely dependent upon the external sources for maintaining even its current level of operational capability, but the post-1997 period does not have the funds required for this purpose.

Even before 1997, Suharto had, in an apparent fit of anger, cancelled plans to purchase from the US at reduced rates, the F-16s manufactured for Pakistan before the imposition of sanctions against it under the Pressler Amendment in 1990 following opposition to the deal in the US Congress due to the alleged human rights violations by the members of ABRI in East Timor and elsewhere. He also discontinued Jakarta's participation in the International Military Education Training Programme (IMET) of the Pentagon.

Since then, the only significant external military collaboration (outside the ASEAN), which Jakarta still has, is with the UK in respect of the purchase of Hawk aircraft and with Australia, with which it signed an Agreement on Maintaining Security (AMS) in December 1995, against the Chinese intrusions into the Mischief Reef and other islands/reefs in the South China Sea claimed by the Philippines.

Under the AMS, Australia had been spending annually about US$ 7 million on training the Indonesian military personnel in Indonesia as well as in Australia, low-level joint exercises, exchanges of visits and reportedly also on some material and logistic support, the details of which are not available.

Tasks and threat perceptions

Under Sukarno, the Indonesian armed forces exhibited extra-territorial ambitions and tendencies. Reference could be made in this regard to the period of *Konfrontasi* with Malaysia, the description of the Indian Ocean as the Indonesian Ocean and Jakarta's reported interest in some of the islands of the Andaman & Nicobar group. There was even speculation of Jakarta's interest in acquiring a military nuclear capability.

However, under Suharto, the Indonesian armed forces became almost totally inward looking, with the priorities assigned to the following tasks:

(a) Protection of internal stability and security against the two main sources of threat, the communists and the religious and ethnic separatist groups, as identified by the military. Communism as a continuing threat to internal security is no longer highlighted, but the armed forces are still nervous over the possibility of a resurgence of communism by taking advantage of the widespread popular dissatisfaction caused by the economic crisis and of what the military perceives as the weakening of state authority due to too rapid political liberalisation.

(b) Surveillance over Indonesia's vast Exclusive Economic Zone (EEZ) and archipelagic waters.

(c) Protection of its immense natural resources, on and offshore, from illegal exploitation about China still remains.

Doctrine, concepts and mindset

To understand the *"dwifungsi"* (dual function) role of the armed forces, one has to keep in view certain doctrines, concepts and arguments, which have figured from time to time in debates inside and outside the military. These could be summarised as follows:

(i) *National Perspective:* The military is the only state institution capable of viewing problems from a national perspective. Politicians and others tend to view them from personal or partisan angles. Gen. Sudirman, the first Commander of the Indonesian army, said in 1947: "The governments may change every day; the army remains the same."

(ii) *National resilience:* To keep an archipelagic state like Indonesia with its different religious and ethnic groups united and stable, political, social and economic harmony is essential. The military is better placed than other institutions to promote such harmony.

(iii) *The doctrine of total people's defence:* Keeping in view the archipelagic nature of the state and the present strength and composition of the armed forces, the military would not be able to counter an external aggression only through conventional means. The response has to be a mix of conventional and guerilla fighting. To be able to mobilise the people in different regions to participate in such guerilla fighting, a close association of the military with the people during peacetime is required. This would be possible only if the military is actively involved in administration and community management in the provinces. The concept of the military remaining within barracks during peacetime does not apply to Indonesia — particularly to the provinces and districts.

(iv) *Better managerial capability:* Being in the military's perception, the most well-trained, well-managed and well-motivated institution of the state is the military which has personnel with better managerial capability than the civilian bureaucracy to manage industrial and other business enterprises, particularly in key sectors of the economy such as oil and gas, mining, etc.

(v) *Better local knowledge:* Military officers, being posted for long periods in the provinces and districts, tour widely and interact closely with the people even in remote areas. In contrast, the Jakarta-based civilian bureaucrats rarely travel in the interior and even the members of parliament representing interior districts remain confined to Jakarta and go to their constituencies only during the election campaign. As a result, the military has a better knowledge of the ground conditions all over the country and of the problems of the people than any other section of the administration.

The critics of the military and the advocates for the abolition of the military's dual role put forward the following arguments:

(a) The armed forces were partly to blame for the widespread mismanagement, lack of accountability, cronyism and corruption, which contributed to the economic collapse of 1997.

(b) The blatant violations of human rights in East Timor, Aceh, Ambon and other regional areas and the aggravation of the feelings of alienation of the people in different parts of Indonesia and of social disharmony even in Java were due to the lack of effective political and civilian control over the military.

Origin and evolution of "*Dwifungsi*"

Unlike India and Pakistan, which inherited from the British a hard core of well-trained, well-motivated and experienced civil and military bureaucracy that was further built-up after independence, Indonesia inherited from the Dutch colonial masters no legacy of a well-oiled political, civil and military infrastructure and traditions of apolitical governance. The founding fathers of its independence had to build up, almost from scratch, a military and administrative system through trial and error. This aspect has to be kept in mind while discussing the origin and evolution of "*dwifungsi*".

The other aspect to be noted is the role played by the founding core of the officer class of the military in the freedom struggle against the Dutch after the defeat of the Japanese. They got used to a role in political and administrative policy-making in association with the political leaders of the independence struggle and insisted on retaining this role even after final independence.

The Japanese Army surrendered on 16 August, 1945. Two days later, Sukarno and Mohammad Hatta proclaimed the independence of Indonesia and the setting-up of a Republic. The Dutch refused to recognise it and attempted to re-assert their control over the territory. Sukarno and Hatta proclaimed the formation of the new Republic's army on 5 October, 1945, consisting of Indonesians who had served in the pre-world war Dutch colonial army and the Japanese occupation forces and political activists close to Sukarno and Hatta as well as to the communists. The Japanese-trained Gen. Sudirman took over as its Commander.

The new army waged a guerilla war against the Dutch. In 1948, clashes broke out between troops loyal to Sukarno and Hatta and those sympathetic to the communists. The former defeated the latter. In December 1948, the Dutch arrested Sukarno and Hatta. Thereafter, the new Indonesian army took over the responsibility for the administration of the areas liberated from Dutch control and for the political guidance of the struggle against the Dutch, who finally agreed to recognise Indonesian independence the next year.

The history books taught in the military training institutions overplay the role of the military officers in putting an end to the Dutch rule and underplay that of the political leaders.

Attempts by the parliament of the new Republic to make the military subservient to political and civilian control led to a demonstration by a group of army officers headed by Dutch-trained A.H. Nasution outside the presidential palace on 17 October, 1952, in protest against civilian meddling in the internal affairs of the military. Sukarno rejected their demand for dissolution of the parliament and the Nasution failed.

However, the two spells of martial law — the first between 1957 and 1963 to deal with separatist movements and the second in 1964 to deal with the conflict with Malaysia — saw Sukarno conceding gradually the military's demand for an active role in political and economic decision-making. In 1957, Gen. Nasution, the Chief of Staff of the army, formulated the view that professionalisation of the military did not mean its total apoliticisation. He called for a middle way for Indonesia between the total apoliticisation of the military as in Western democracies and its total involvement in politics as in certain Latin American dictatorships. This formulation became the basis of the concept of "*dwifungsi*".

The same year, after the failure of the members of parliament to form a coalition government, Sukarno, with the support of Gen. Nasution, proclaimed a return to the 1945 Constitution, which had a provision for appointing functional groups in the parliament. The military was declared as a functional group and given parliamentary representation. Thus was born the "*dwifungsi*" concept, which under Mr. Suharto, was put on the statute book in 1982.

The policy of large-scale nationalisation of plantation, oil, mining and trading companies introduced in 1957 saw an increase in the military's role in economic management too, with many military officers being appointed to head the new public sector companies.

Between 1965 and 1998, Indonesia passed through two kinds of dictatorships. For about twenty years, it was the dictatorship of the military as an institution, with Sharyo acting as its guiding spirit. From the middle 1980s onwards, there was a gradual transformation of this into the personal dictatorship of Sharyo, as an individual with a civilian facade, ruling with the help of a mix of military loyalists, civilian technocrats and businessmen close to the armed forces.

The first phase saw priority being given to internal security and political stability, and more than half a million people were killed and an equal number imprisoned on suspicion of begin communist sympathisers. Among half a million people rounded up, only about a thousand were formally tried before a court of law in a sham judicial process. The rest did not have the benefit of even this sham process and were kept under illegal detention till the late 1970s, when the military regime started releasing them. Even after their release, they were kept under surveillance and debarred from employment in any office or enterprise connected with the government. Their identity cards showed them as former security suspects, thereby creating difficulties in their getting jobs even in private enterprises. They were reduced to third class citizens.

At the height of the militarisation of the administrative structure in 1980, about fifty per cent of the Ministers in the Cabinet, seventy-five per cent of the secretaries-general in the various departments, sixty per cent of the directors-general, eighty-four per cent of the Secretaries and seventy-five per cent of the provincial governors were officers with a military background, most of them serving.

Thus, almost totally militarising the administration, Suharto tried to give the facade of a civilian democracy to his regime. While retaining the title of the Supreme Commander of the Armed Forces, he resigned as the Chief of ABRI, nominating handpicked officers to exercise administrative and operational control over the military.

To serve his dual purpose of strengthening the civilian facade of his regime and, at the same time, retaining a watching brief for the military in the political, economic and social management of the country, he promoted the primacy of the officially-floated Golkar party, which worked under the guidance of the territorial commanders. He strictly regulated the functioning of other political parties allowed to participate in the elections to the People's House of Representatives (*Dewan Perwakilan Rakyat* or the DPR) and the People's Consultative Assembly (Majelis *Permusyawaratan Rakyat* or the MPR), which is the highest constitutional authority and elects the president. He also nominated vice-president, and reserved a certain number of seats for the armed forces and the police in the DPR and MPR under powers entrusted to him by the MPR to nominate up to twenty per cent of the total strength of the DPR.

After a gap of fifteen years, the first elections to the DPR were held in 1971 and Sharyo was unanimously elected as the president of the country and his nominee as the vice-president. Under the pretext of simplifying the party system, Suharto allowed only three parties to function — the Golkar, which was formed by merging the various functional groups; the People's Development Party (PPP), formed by the merger of four Muslim political parties; and the Indonesian Democratic Party (PDI), formed by the merger of five nationalist (followers of Sukarno) and Christian parties.

As initially constituted, the Golkar party had three components — the military, the civil servants and the civilians. The military officers, serving as well as retired, formed the most powerful component at the national and regional levels. Sharyo designated himself as the Chief Supervisor, with powers to suspend or dismiss the central executive board.

The critics of "*dwifungsi*" used to sarcastically refer to the Golkar as the political wing of the ABRI. In the face of their criticism, the 1978 Congress of the Golkar decided that while both serving and retired military and civil officers could become members, only retired officers could hold party positions. The critics, thereupon, started ridiculing it as the retired Generals' party. Despite this, the party, with the support of the administration, managed to secure over sixty per cent of the vote in every general election.

Finding no political space for themselves under the carefully-controlled party system, critics of the military and "*dwifungsi*" started floating non-governmental organisations (NGOs), ostensibly to take up social issues such as workers' welfare, women's welfare, environmental issues, etc., but really to articulate their dissatisfaction with the lack of democracy and accountability under the Suharto regime. The country saw a mushrooming of about seven thousand NGOs, two thousand eight hundred of them located in Jakarta alone.

In the face of this, Suharto started changing the emphasis from internal security and political stability to people's welfare. To project his dictatorship as welfare-oriented and no longer purely security-oriented, and to further strengthen the civilian facade of the government, Suharto discontinued the practice of appointing a large number of military officers as cabinet ministers. He drastically reduced the percentage of officers with a military background in the various government departments and correspondingly increased the percentage of civilian bureaucrats occupying key positions at the decision-making level. While, thus, diluting the visible role of the military at the national level, he did not do so at the regional level.

Towards the end of the 1980s, there were signs of differences inside the armed forces over the wisdom of continuing with "*dwifungsi*" and over what many secular-minded officers looked upon as Suharto's new tendency to court the new Islamic elements making their appearance in different parts of the country and contesting the primacy of the PPP as the only legally-permitted Muslim party.

Nasution, the original author of the "*dwifungsi*" concept in 1957, was one of the firsts to express the view that the time had come to review it. In the early 1990s, a group of fifty retired military officers and former politicians, who came to be known as the *Petisi* 50 Group, became increasingly vocal in its criticism of the political style of functioning of Suharto.

In 1987-88, differences erupted between Suharto and Gen. Benny Murdani, a Catholic, who was the Chief of the ABRI, after the latter criticised the activities of Suharto's family and allegedly tried to make the armed forces more independent of the president, Gen. Murdani was transferred as Defence Minister, from which post he was removed in 1993.

This was followed by a purge of Murdani loyalists from the armed forces and the Intelligence and Strategic Centre (BIAS) set up by him, which was re-organised and renamed as the Military Intelligence Unit (BIA). The number of Christians in the Cabinet and the DPR was reduced. Amongst the prominent Christians removed from influential positions were Mr. Radius Prawiro, who was the Coordinating Minister for Economy, Finance and Industry, Mr. Adrianus Mooy, who used to be the Central Bank Governor, and Mr. Johannes Sumarlin, who was the Finance Minister.

While, thus, diluting the role of the Christian officers in the civilian and military bureaucracy, Suharto, at the same time, gave a lift to a number of officers who were considered to be *santris* (strict Muslims) as distinguished from the secular-minded *Abangans*. Amongst the *santris* favoured by Suharto during this period were Try Sutrisno, who later became the vice-president in 1993, despite Suharto's preference for Dr. Habibie because of the insistence of *status quoists* in the military, Feisal Tanjung, who became the Chief of the armed forces, and Hartono, who became the Chief of the army staff.

Before the 1992 elections, Suharto performed *haj* for the first time and started calling himself Muhammed Suharto. Earlier, in 1990, he had also encouraged the formation of the Association of Muslim Intellectuals (ICMI) by Dr. Habibie.

While courting the newly-emerging Muslim political elements in order to keep them on his side without letting their emergence affect the *Pancasila* ideology, which stresses belief in one God, a just and civilised humanitarianism, a united Indonesia, democracy guided by wisdom, consultation and representation, and social justice for all Indonesian nationals, he also tried to make some concessions to the critics of "*dwifungsi*" by having Harmoko, a civilian, elected in 1993 as the Golkar chairman, defeating retired General Soesilo Soedarman, who was backed by the *status quoists* in the military. Suharto also reduced the number of seats reserved for military in the two Houses from hundred (twenty per cent of the total strength of the DPR) to seventy-five in 1997. After Suharto's resignation, this was further reduced to thirty-eight (slightly less than eight per cent) in June 1999.

Under Dr. Habibie

Dr. Habibie, who took over as the president after the resignation of Suharto on 21 May, 1998, in the face of unrelenting student demand for his resignation, massive street riots on the issue and deepening economic crisis, stopped exercising the powers of the president relating to appointments, promotions and transfers in the armed forces and let Gen. Wiranto, the Defence Minister and Chief of the TNI, handle this power, thereby once again strengthening the position of the TNI Chief.

However, Dr. Habibie's interim term saw some genuine reforms such as a dilution of the restrictions on the right of other political parties to contest the elections and fixing the tenure of the president and the vice-president to two five-year terms.

In the face of unrelenting demands from the critics for the abolition of *"dwifungsi"*, the military seems inclined to accept the abolition of reservation of seats for the armed forces in the parliament from the year 2004. However, in statements made before his suspension by President Wahid, Gen. Wiranto laid down the following conditions:

No interference by the political leadership in the internal affairs of the armed forces (meaning all powers regarding appointments, promotions and transfers of senior officers would be exercised by the chief of the armed forces).

No interference by the armed forces in the political process.

No attempt to isolate the armed forces from the people (this is interpreted to mean that while the military is reconciled to further dilution and ultimate abolition of its dual function at the national level, it is not yet prepared to accept it at the regional level).

In the June 1999 elections to the DPR, forty-eight parties contested as against only three in the past and parties advocating political reforms defeated the Golkar, with Mrs. Megawati Sukarnoputri's Indonesian Democratic Party

(Struggle) emerging as the largest single party with one hundred and fifty-three seats in a House of five hundred. The final results were as follows:

1.	The Indonesian Democratic Party (Struggle) and its allies	153
2.	The Golkar party and its allies	120
3.	The United Development party (PPP) and its allies (Military-supported Islamic elements)	58
4.	The National Awakening Party of the President Wahid and allies	51
5.	The National Mandate party of Mr. Amien Rais and its allies	41
6.	The Crescent Star party and its allies	13
7.	The Indonesian Unity and Awakening Party and its allies	12
8.	The United People's Sovereignty Party and its allies	11
9.	The Love the Nation Democratic Party and its allies	3
10.	Reserved for the TNI and the police	38

Of these, serial Nos. 1 and 2 are secular-minded parties (two hundred and seventy-three out of a total of five hundred), Serial Nos. 3, 4 and 5 are moderate Islamic parties (one hundred and fifty out of five hundred) and serial Nos. 6 and 8 are Islamic parties of unknown origin and background (twenty-four seats). Nothing much is known about the parties at Serial Nos. 7 and 9 (fifteen seats).

Under President Wahid

Mr. Abdurrahman Wahid, who was elected as the President on 21 October, 1999, had initially not much freedom in choosing his cabinet, having to accept the nominees of the parties which supported him and of Gen. Wiranto, who himself was designated as the Coordinating Minister for Political and Security Affairs.

He devoted the first few months in office to diluting the role of the armed forces in politics at the national level by taking the following action:

(i) For the first time since Djuanda, another civilian, served as the defence minister under Sukarno, President Wahid has appointed Juwono Sudarsono, a civilian, as the Defence Minister. A former Professor of Political Science in the University of Indonesia, he had served as the Environment Minister in the last cabinet of Suharto and as the Education Minister in the cabinet of Dr. Habibie. He had also been the Vice-Chair of the National Defence Institute, a think tank funded by the TNI. Juwono told the press after taking over that he had told the senior military officers "they could no longer collect expensive toys, such as those owned by some outlandishly rich Generals."

(ii) Wahid has sought to reduce the primacy of the army in the TNI by appointing a naval officer (Admiral Widodo Adisutjipto) as the chief of the armed forces (TNI), and air force officers as the Chief of the military intelligence (Air Vice-Marshal Ian Santoso) and as media spokesman (Air Vice-Marshal Graito Usodo) of the TNI. Army officers had traditionally held these posts. President Wahid removed the previous spokesman, Maj. Gen. Sudrajat of the army, following two controversial remarks by him in his media briefings. In one, he said that Wahid would have no right to interfere in the internal affairs of the TNI, while in the other, he said: "Political reconciliation is needed, but this nation will remain anti-Communist."

(iii) He suspended Gen. Wiranto from the cabinet because of the allegations of human rights violations by the TNI in East Timor made by the Indonesian Human Rights Commission.

(iv) He has insisted on exercising his prerogative of making senior appointments, promotions and transfers in the TNI. He is reported to have already shifted about seventy senior officers.

(v) He has started an exercise to ease out the supporters of Gen. Wiranto and other *status quoists* from key positions in the army. He has already reportedly appointed Major Gen. Agus Wirahadukusumah as Commander of the KOSTRAD and Lt. Gen. Djamari Chaniago as the Chief of the General Staff. Both of them were reputed to be the critics of Gen. Wiranto and strong advocates of the abolition of "*dwifungsi*". Strongly criticising the military's involvement in business enterprises, Maj-Gen. Agus has said in an interview: "Who backs and supports the discotheques, brothels and narcotics rings, if not the military or police? An embarrassing fact is that the military has lost the trust of the people."

(vi) He has also reduced the number of military officers in the presidential office from thirty-five to fifteen and imposed restrictions on the type of correspondence that they could see.

(vii) He has indicated that when the government's finances improve, priority would be given to meeting the requirements of the navy. As against this, he is reportedly contemplating a reduction in the strengths of the KOSTRAD and the KOPASSUS.

(viii) He has reportedly removed from the military intelligence the responsibility for the security vetting of government servants. However, it is not yet known to which department he has now entrusted this task.

(ix) At the same time, President Wahid has avoided any action to dilute the military's role in the regions. He seems to be concentrating first on easing out the military from its dual role at the centre.

Reasons for lack of resistance from TNI

Despite periodic reports of unhappiness in the military over his actions and rumours of a possible coup by disgruntled officers, the TNI seems to have accepted his decisions without much resistance, though Gen. Wiranto was initially refusing to quit. President Wahid's success so far in having his decisions enforced, though often in an erratic manner, could be attributed to the following reasons:

(a) Domestic public opinion continues to be strongly against the TNI, and the matter has been made worse by the recommendations of the Indonesian Human Rights Commission for detailed investigation of the responsibility of the army in general and Gen. Wiranto in particular for the human rights violations in East Timor. There have been similar serious allegations against the TNI with regard to its handling of the dissident movements in other regions. This has put the TNI totally on the defensive and Mr. Wahid has skillfully taken advantage of this.

(b) Wahid's actions are getting external support from the US and the European Union (EU) countries. During a visit to Jakarta, Mr. Richard Holbrooke, the US Permanent Representative to the UN in New York, said on 14 January, in an indirect reference to reports of a conflict between. Wahid and Gen. Wiranto: "What we are watching is a great drama, a struggle between the forces of democracy and reform and the forces of backward looking corruption and militarism." Subsequently, he reportedly told American journalists that he had his statement cleared by the Indonesian political leadership before issuing it. His blunt warning against a return to militarism in Indonesia went home loud and clear to the TNI leadership.

(c) The Indonesian economy is not yet out of the woods though its GDP has for the first time since the 1997 collapse recorded a minuscule positive growth rate of 0.2 per cent. The problem of outstanding corporate debt (over US$ 70 billion) is yet to be sorted out. The economy may take another nose-dive if the IMF suspends its assistance because of any military coup. The TNI and its individual senior officers have been badly affected by the economic crisis, and they do not want to provoke another crisis by their unwise actions.

The unusually tough stand taken by the US President, Mr. Bill Clinton, against the military regime of Gen. Pervez Musharraf in Pakistan on the question of return to democracy is partly motivated by fears of any leniency towards the Pakistani regime on this issue being misread by the TNI leadership, thereby encouraging them to move against the elected government of Wahid. Similarly, Washington is likely to be concerned that if the IMF assistance to Pakistan is resumed despite the coup, fears of a discontinuance of the IMF assistance to Jakarta may no longer act as a disincentive to the *status quoists* in the TNI.

Prospects for the future

Would Wahid be able to tame the TNI and keep it confined to its professional tasks? The answer to this would depend on the following factors:

(a) Though he has recovered from his stroke of last year, his vision has been badly impaired and his health seems to be delicate. In the event of any unfortunate incapacitation, the military may not be prepared to accept from Megawati what it is prepared to accept from Wahid, thereby leading to a clash between the political leadership and the military.

(b) For how long does Wahid's reputation for his personal integrity last? Consequent to his visual impairment, he is dependent on his children and brothers and other trusted aides for scrutinising his official correspondence and recommending action. He depends more on oral than on written communications for decision-making. His dependence on them for carrying out his responsibilities has already triggered off rumours of nepotism and cronyism and interference with the due process of the law against bank loan defaulters close to his family. Such rumours and perception could corrode his reputation, thereby depriving him of the moral high ground, which he presently enjoys.

(c) The attitude of the Islamic elements outside Wahid's *Nahdlatul Ulama* organisation which has already been accusing him of a witch-hunt against Muslim military officers. Organisations such as the Defenders of Islam, which have considerable vocal power without much public support, have been projecting the investigations of the Human Rights Commission against Gen. Wiranto and others for the TNI's excesses in East Timor as a conspiracy against Muslim officers by international Christianity.

(d) Wahid has been successful in restoring the economy and controlling the religious and ethnic tensions. If he fails the TNI would be only too tempted to take advantage of it to move against him.

EDITORIAL NOTE:

Since the paper was written in May 2000, a few notable changes have taken place in the profile of the TNI in its attitude towards the civil-military relations, as well as in its relationship with the president. As the country plunges into further political instability, with the killings of the migrant Madurese by the indigenous Dayaks in Kalimantan; Wahid being censured by the parliament leading to a strong possibility of his impeachment; and a culture of violence gripping urban life in Indonesia, the TNI has regained some of its lost ground. Despite an earlier decision to end the military's reserved seats in the parliament by 2004, the last MPR in August 2000 has extended them to 2008. The MPR has also approved a law by which the members of the armed forces cannot be tried for past abuses. The army commanders also rejected Wahid's candidate for the post of the chief-of-staff in the army, Lt. Gen. Agus Wirahadikusuma, a reformist general. Wahid may have laid down the policy direction in Jakarta's dealings with the separatist provinces in Aceh and Irian Jaya, but in its day-to-day implementation the army is now calling the shots, and have intensified their military operations against the rebels. TNI has also rejected any plan on the part of the government to dismantle its territorial structures that allow them to reach to the grassroots of the Indonesian society, and helps its to retain its control over it. It has also been arguing of late that the reduction of its dual functions would depend on the performance of the civilian authority to govern the country. All these, however, do not mean that the army will be able restore its past position. However, the fact remains that it has the disposition to intervene in politics in case the civilians fail to deliver. Ironically it was Gus Dur himself who pushed the TNI back to centre stage. It began early this year when he started toying with the idea of imposing a state of civil emergency to stop the legislature from unseating him. Gus Dur believed that the Constitution empowered him with the status of "supreme commander of the armed forces" that would give him a free hand to do whatever he pleased with the military. This turned out to be his biggest mistake. When he threatened military leaders that they either support his plan to declare a state of emergency or be ready to be replaced by more accommodative generals, it was the last straw for the military leadership and they swore that they could not swallow any more 'humiliation'. The credit for the military's revival must go to army chief of staff, General Endiartono Sutarto. Starting from the end of January this year, he organised meetings among the military top brass to study the political situation in the country. The general feeling among the leadership was a kind of restlessness since they consider themselves as the 'most trusted vanguard of the nation' and the country was at stake. Eventually, it was the corporate interests of the TNI that united the armed forces behind General Sutarto. It was against the united force of TNI that Gus Dur had to deal with when he repeatedly and unsuccessfully tried to get military support for his declaration of a state of emergency.

Hence, there was no doubt that Gus Dur's failure to gain support from the military together with his unsuccessful attempts to secure the police force to back in the plan to impose a state of emergency, was the key to his downfall.

11

Australia-Indonesia Relations and East Timor

G. V. C. Naidu

The year 1999 will go down in history as one of the most momentous as far as Australia is concerned for two reasons: the transition in Indonesia from military dictatorship to democracy and the unexpected emergence of East Timor as an independent country. Both events have profoundly affected Australia, but a major repercussion of the developments in East Timor is the strained relationship with Indonesia even as Jakarta doubts Canberra's sincerity of friendship. The pendulum of Australia-Indonesia relationship has swung from one extreme to another since the World War II bait, the current state of bilateral affairs is probably at its worst ill more than three decades. It is not to suggest that these two will remain as estranged neighbours, but it will take a long time for Indonesia to put the hurt feeling behind. From an Indonesian perspective, it is not simply the question of East Timor severing itself from the country through self-determination, but that it has stoked flames of separatism across several outlying provinces, and put a big question mark on the future of the unity and integrity of Indonesia. Most Indonesians believed, justifiably or otherwise, that Australia played a critical role in the separation of East Timor from their country and continue to harbour doubts about its role in further disintegration of the nation.

Even as Indonesia continues to reel under unprecedented social and economic turmoil, the prospects for closer links between Jakarta and Canberra do not seem to be very bright. The strategic consequences of this development, it may be noted, is not confined just to these two countries, but stretches across the entire Asia Pacific in general and the Southeast Asian region in particular. As it was during World War II, Indonesia's geo-strategic significance to Australia — what Carlyle Thayer calls the "tyranny of geography"[1], continues to be relevant even today as a buffer from possible inroads on a rich and sparsely populated but huge landmass of Australia. Indonesia also emerged as a major conduit for its policy towards ASEAN and Southeast Asia since Suharto's takeover in 1967. Equally importantly, Indonesia, as the largest power of Southeast Asia, has a special role to play in the promotion of peace and stability in the region. Not least are the economic opportunities that a vast market of more than two hundred million people Indonesia offers for trade and investment. Though many Australians may scorn at the idea, it is obvious that Australia needs Indonesia much more than Indonesia needs Australia. Hence, Australia has much greater stakes.

What appeared to be a qualitatively different kind of relationship that had been assiduously built since the late

1960s has come under tremendous pressure because of the East Timor issue, especially the events that followed after the referendum in September 1999. Certain pronouncements and the overall attitude of the conservative government of Prime Minister Howard have once again raked up the Indonesian mistrust of the Aussies. Though currently attention is riveted to the events in East Timor and the problems the peacekeepers are confronted with, from a long-term viewpoint Australia-Indonesia would remain strained and that will cast its shadow over the rest of the region.

This chapter is not just confined to the East Timor problem but also deals with major other issues that have arisen from time to time that shaped the bilateral relations between Australia and Indonesia. While it is not within the purview of the following study to examine in detail the foreign policy priorities of the two countries and the evolution of the bilateral relationship, it concentrates on certain vital issues, such as Indonesia's independence movement, the West Irian issue, Indonesia's *konfrontasi* toward Malaysia, and East Timor. Two important agreements, among others, the Timor Gap Treaty and the Security Agreement, are also discussed? Attempt is made to incorporate both the perspectives of Australia and Indonesia in order to understand the dynamics of bilateral relations between two crucial middle-powers in the Asia Pacific.

Backdrop

Australian involvement in Asian affairs began with the initiation of the cold war and its foreign policy was firmly laid as seen through the prism of cold war environment and politics. Australia's active participation both in the two major wars that the US was involved in, Korea and Vietnam, and a multitude of security-related arrangements that the US and UK started[2] are indicators of the directions and goals of its external policy, particularly in Southeast Asia. Specifically with regard to Indonesia, one has to recognise and always keep in mind the vast differences that exist between Australia and Indonesia in terms of history, culture, language, race, population, and topography. Though both claim to be multicultural, grounded as such in the geographical region of what is called Pacific Rim or Pacific Asia, probably the similarity ends there. Whereas Australian history can be traced back to about two centuries as a white settlement, Indonesian history dates back several millennia. Similarly, the gross asymmetry between Australia and Indonesia cannot also be ignored. Indonesia is a vast archipelago consisting of several thousands of islands teeming with more than two hundred million people, but Australia is primarily one huge landmass with just seventeen million. By any yardstick, Australia is a developed country, while Indonesia is still in a developing stage and the recent financial crisis has pushed it backward by several decades. In 1999, Australia's per capita income was US$ 20,050 in contrast to Indonesia's US$ 580.[3] This vast disparity is bound to create problems and is reflected in the recurrent tensions between these two countries. Nonetheless, Australia cannot but envy the amount of clout and influence Indonesia enjoys in Southeast Asia. Notwithstanding the substantial growth in economic and strategic interaction particularly after the enunciation of Australia's avowed policy of getting engaged in Asia since the mid-1980s, perhaps the bonhomie was primarily confined to political issues for most part of the post-World War II period. Australia has considerably eased its immigration policy allowing a large number of Asians to settle down, but somehow most Australians are unable to overcome the fear of millions of Indonesians swarming their country. The current turmoil in Indonesia would further exacerbate this feeling: hence, the Australian anxiety about Indonesia.

East Timor

The anti-Communist Suharto regime in Indonesia greatly facilitated the establishment of the closest possible political relationship between Canberra and Jakarta till the fall of this regime and the eruption of the East Timor issue. The East Timor problem needs to be examined in a more detailed fashion as this issue is more directly concerned with the current relations between the two countries.

East Timor came under the colonial occupation of the British, the Dutch and the Portuguese, the latter controlling East Timor for more than four centuries after the Netherlands ceded it to Portugal under an agreement. The prolonged Portuguese rule was also responsible for the spread of Christianity. Since East Timor was not decolonised along with others after World War II, it became difficult either to grant dependence to it in the absence of its ability of sustaining that independence, or to ensure that it would not be gobbled up by its giant neighbour later on. However, changes came about within Portugal itself.

Portugal was under dictatorship for about fifty years — Salazar 1926–1968 and Caetano 1968–74 — and its neutrality during World War II put constraints on the Japanese to go slow on the occupation of Portuguese Timor. Even after the end of the war, Portugal did not pay much attention to Timor simply because economic returns were far less than the colonies in Africa. It was only after the left-wing army took over power in Portugal in 1974, through what is called the

Carnation Revolution, that the process of decolonisation was initiated in right earnest. Part of this effort was all attempt to promote democracy in East Timor resulting in the establishment of three political parties: Democratic Union of Timor (UDT), Timorese Social Democratic Association (ASDT),[4] and Timorese Democratic People's Union (APODETI). While the ASDT was the left-leaning radical organisation that advocated total independence, the APODETI promoted integration with Indonesia. In the local elections that were held in early 1975, FRETILIN won fifty-five per cent of the vote and the UDT came a close second. Nearly ninety per cent of the people supported these two parties. While the battle for political supremacy was beginning to rage between FRETILIN and the UDT, the Indonesian military was quietly supporting and encouraging the UDT to stage a coup in August 1975. This was challenged by FRETILIN through an armed struggle and succeeded in establishing its supremacy. In the meantime, the Portuguese were gradually reducing their presence and the last remaining Portuguese, including the governor, secretly left Timor on 27 August, 1975. Thus, neither the hand-over of administration to the locals nor a decolonisation took place.[5] That way East continued to be a colony of the Portuguese because they never gave up power nor were they driven out. In fact FRETILIN repeatedly requested the Portuguese to return to East Timor so that some order would be established and a peaceful transfer of power could take place.

While FRETILIN was winning the civil war, because of its larger following and better arms, and was beginning to take control of the administration, the Indonesian generals were plotting to militarily intervene. Sensing that the Indonesian intervention was imminent, FRETILIN declared independence on 28 November, 1975, as a pre-emptive move. Taking advantage of the politically unstable conditions and chaos (in part created by Indonesia itself), Indonesia created a pretext in the form of the Balibo Declaration (named after a small town in West Timor on East Timor's border but actually penned in Bali), purported to have been issued by those opposed to FRETILIN, which asked the Indonesian government's assistance in East Timor, to embark on an invasion on 7 December, 1975.

The International Context

The Indonesian invasion of East Timor and its incorporation into the Republic of Indonesia in July 1976 has to be seen against the backdrop of domestic as well as global political environment. By the early 1970s, the former Soviet Union had established a military parity with the United States and had begun to actively support the communist movements in the Third World, especially in Africa (Angola, Mozaiilbiqtie and Ethiopia, for instance) with renewed vigour which culminated in the Soviet intervention in Afghanistan thus starting the second round of cold war. By mid-seventies, the three countries of Indochina successfully emerged victorious defeating the Americans under the leadership of communist parties and there had been a resurgence of leftist movements in countries such as the Philippines, Thailand and Malaysia.[6] After the military coup in 1965 deposing president Sukarno, and massacring nearly a million people, General Suharto's credentials as anti-Communist crusader were impeccable as far as the West was concerned. It becomes obvious based on circumstantial evidence that there was Western complicity in what the Indonesians did in East Timor because the FRETILIN-led movement was by and large considered to be leftist.

Indonesia itself would not tolerate the emergence of a radical neighbour on its border, however small it might be.

That the Australians knew of Indonesian plans to invade East Timor was clear when Canberra kept quiet after five Australia-based journalists (two Australians, one New Zealander and two British) were believed to have been murdered while covering Indonesian preparations for an invasion oil 16 October, 1975. Secret official documents of the Australian government, which became available in March 1999, indicate that the prime minister of Australia then, Gough Whitlam, strongly supported Indonesia in two critical meetings with Suharto. The Australian newspaper, *Sydney Morning Herald,* which procured these documents, stated that, "He (Whitlam) affirmed, however that he strongly desired closer and more cordial relations with Indonesia and would ensure that our actions in regard to Portuguese Timor would always be guided by the principle that good relations with Indonesia were of paramount importance to Australia.[7] While reiterating the Australian position that the Timorese would need to determine their future, "the Prime Minister noted in this regard that he was not prepared to accept at face value the claims of the political personalities who have currently emerged in Portuguese Timor. He noted that they were predominantly drawn from the *mestizo* populations; they had their own economic interests to protect and sought to retain their European lifestyle. The Prime Minister implied that they in fact represented a small elite class. It may be that they would be able to win the allegiance of the people of Timor; but their claims were as yet untested. There could be, below the surface, indigenous forces, which could carry the people of Portuguese Timor in directions different from those in which they presently seem to be set."[8]

A scrutiny of the documents related to the talks with President Suharto that went on during Prime Minister Whitlam's visit to Indonesia on 6 September, 1974, reveal that Canberra was amenable to the idea of Indonesia taking over East Timor. The Prime Minister said, "he felt two things were basic to his own thinking on Portuguese Timor. First, he believed that Portuguese Timor should become part of Indonesia. Second, this should happen in accordance with the properly expressed wishes of the people of Portuguese Timor. The Prime Minister emphasised that this was not yet Government policy but that it was likely to become that. The Prime Minister said that he felt very strongly that Australia should not seek, or appear to seek, any special interests in Portuguese Timor. They were people with a different ethnic background, languages and culture. It would be unrealistic and improper if we were to seek some special relationship. At the same time he believed that Portuguese Timor was too small to be independent. It was economically not viable. Independence would be unwelcome to Indonesia. To Australia and to other countries in the region, because an independent Portuguese Timor would inevitably become the focus of attention of others outside the region. The Prime Minister noted that, for the domestic audience in Australia, incorporation into Indonesia should appear to be a natural process arising from the wishes of the people. He recalled adverse public opinion towards Indonesia, which had arisen almost twelve years ago, both in Papua New Guinea and the Australia, in relation to Irian Barat.[9] There was suspicion of Indonesia and its methods in effecting the return of the province. The Prime Minister said that he personally had expressed himself in favour of the return or Irian Barat to Indonesia from the time that he had first entered

Parliament.[10] In response, President Suharto was reported to have emphasised his concern that decolonisation in Portuguese Timor should not upset either Indonesian or regional security... If Portuguese Timor were to become independent, it would give rise to problems. It was not economically viable. It would have to seek the help of another country, but Portuguese Timor would be of interest only because of its political importance. There was a big danger that communist countries — China or the Soviet Union — might gain the opportunity to intervene. This would lead in turn to intervention by the other great powers. Portuguese Timor in that way would become 'a thorn in the eye of Australia and a thorn in Indonesia's back'. Ultimately the Indonesian hoped for the incorporation of Portuguese Timor as being in the best interest of the region, of Indonesia and of Australia. The President shared the belief that this should occur on the basis of the freely expressed wishes of the people of Portuguese Timor."[11]

As if to corroborate the Australian approval of the Indonesian action in East Timor, as soon as these documents came to public notice, Doug Everingham, who served as health minister under Whitlam during 1972–1975, openly apologised to the people of Timor in a letter to the newspaper, *The Australian*, on 24 March, 1999. He said, "I apologise to the East Timorese people. I am ashamed to have belonged to the first of a series of Australian cabinets which failed to protest while our prime minister, unlike the world community, recognised the takeover of East Timor".[12] Fascinatingly, Everingham later confessed that "the reason why successive governments and not just the Whitlam government, have recognised Indonesia and East Timor is to get hold of the oil for big oil companies in the Timor Gap".

As one of the strongest backers of the New Order regime of General Suharto, the role of the US in endorsing the Indonesian plans of an invasion of East Timor is also strongly suspected because of the fact that Indonesia invaded and occupied East Timor a day after US President Ford left Jakarta after a visit to Indonesia. It was most unlikely that Suharto would have undertaken such a move without American implicit support. It may be surmised that, in an atmosphere of resurgent communist activity after the Indo-China victories, any measure that appeared to be anti-Communist, however remote it might have been, would have got Washington's endorsement.

There is also a domestic dimension to the Indonesian invasion of East Timor. Notwithstanding Suharto's ruthlessness, opposition to his rule started building up from the early days within the military, starting from the early 1970s. The division in the military, between those who enjoyed the financial largesse of the military rule and those who were opposed to it, manifested itself in the anti-Chinese riots in Bandung and later more vociferously in the students demonstrations against the visiting Japanese Prime Minister, Kakuei Tanaka in 1974. Better known as *Malari* riots, ostensibly opposed to the growing Japanese ownership of industrial concerns, could not have taken place without the blessings of a section of the army's top brass.[13] This was also the time when the hardliners found favour with the president who believed in taking aggressive steps to consolidate the military's hold. Ali Murtopo and Benny Murdani were among those. It is widely believed that these were the people who convinced a hesitant Suharto to invade East Timor. Muradni had been in-charge of East Timor operations since the time trouble started brewing in East Timor till its incorporation. Despite lingering doubts about possible consequences of the Indonesian action, Suharto went ahead because it served his interests too. He could demonstrate to his mentors in the West that he continued to be a hardliner on anything remotely radical in nature. Second, the East Timor military action not only satisfied growing impatience of younger officers who were beginning to get disillusioned with Suharto's style of functioning, but also to remind his detractors of his intent to use force to suppress opposition.

Probably Suharto never imagined that what he was going to get was much more than he bargained for. For a variety of reasons, the little younger brother of East Timor could never be made an obedient child of a large Indonesian family (as espoused and expected by the military in the Indonesian context) simply because by the yardstick of any trait—language, culture, civilisation, religion, and ethnicity — it was not related to the family. Notwithstanding repeated claims, *Timur Timor* (as it named after its incorporation into Indonesia) continued to boil and a small bank of rebels never allowed themselves to be subdued by the larger and more powerful Indonesian troops. Of course, this was done at an enormous cost – nearly a fifth of that province's population got eliminated in the process.[14] It also remained under international focus even as the UN and most other nations individually, never accepted Indonesia's suzerainty over East Timor. The only conspicuous exception being Australia, which formally recognised Indonesian occupation of East Timor.

Massive deployment of troops did not help Indonesia to subjugate the FALINTIL (the armed wing of pro-independence movement) whose numbers consistently grew despite high toll of casualties in its ranks. The East Timor issue remained alive in the international forums in part because of recurrent incidents of atrocities and wanton killings by the Indonesian army. The Amnesty International brought out a detailed report on widespread human rights violations by the Indonesian army in 1985. It was cited that up to 200,000 East Timorese were killed. The most prominent among the army's actions was the 12 November, 1991, massacre of an unarmed peaceful procession to a cemetery to mark the killing of a guerrilla earlier in the presence of international media. For the first time an official inquiry was conducted by the Indonesian government, which put the death toll at fifty with ninety missing (though by any indication it was far higher) resulting in the removal of two generals and court marshalling of ten soldiers. In 1993, the United Nations Human Rights Commission strongly indicated Indonesia for its human rights violations in East Timor. The end of the cold war and mounting international pressure forced Indonesia to hold high-level talks with exiled resistance leader, Jose Ramos Horta in October 1994. The basic issue had been the question of referendum, which Indonesia was reluctant to hold.

Although Indonesia realised by the mid-1990s that something urgently needed to be done to settle the East Timor issue, it could not for a number of reasons. First, Indonesia had relocated a large number of Indonesian (mostly Javanese) through its transmigration policy who faced an uncertain future if the independence demand was conceded. Second, Indonesia had also pumped in hundreds of millions of dollars toward developmental activities with the intent of blunting the unabated clamour for independence. It would go down the drain if East Timor preferred a separation. Third, in the light of other insurgency movements for independence, especially in Aceh and West Irian, if East Timor was granted independence, these and others too might demand secession from the Indonesian Republic.[15] Finally and most importantly, the reluctance of the army to give up East Timor just because political leaders faced international criticism. From the Indonesian army's viewpoint, they invaded and controlled East Timor at an enormous human and material cost and hence should not be given up. Since the army was the backbone of Suharto, he could not ignore the army's feelings.

Referendum and After

Thus, though it continued to simmer, the East Timor problem could not be settled as long as Suharto was at the helm of affairs. When B.J. Habibie took over the reins after Suharto was forced to quit office in May 1998, he promised to reduce the number of troops in East Timor. However, no one took Habibie, a technologist by training with little mass support, seriously as he was handpicked by Suharto to be his deputy. When he announced in January 1999 that a referendum was possible to decide the future of East Timor in it was a surprise, on the one hand, and it was not so surprising, on the other, because he had to do something to safeguard the presidency which fell totally unexpectedly in his lap. Habibie had his own vested interest in taking the initiative to relent the government's hardline stance because East Timor had become a thorn in the side of Indonesia; external pressure continued to mount; it continued to drain precious resources with no political or economic returns; and, though East Timor had been one issue which was close to the military's heart because of its involvement, the popular unrest that forced Suharto to demit office had put the armed forces on the defensive and hence their reaction would be subdued if a bold initiative was taken on East Timor. In any case, the invasion of East Timor had never been a popular move within Indonesia.[16]

By the time the referendum on self-determination of East Timor was held on 30 August, 1999, the choice before the people was greater autonomy within the union of Indonesia or "eventual separation", a euphemism for independence. The outcome was a foregone conclusion, but what came as a surprise was overwhelming turnout in the first place and 78.5 per cent of the people opting for independence. Instead of recounting the much talked about violence that followed after the result was announced, unleashed by the pro-Indonesia militias, and which was later accepted as highly exaggerated,[17] it may be useful to concentrate on other and more important aspects.

First, the role of the United Nations. Without discounting the stellar role the UN has so far played to reduce conflicts and establish peace across the world, it needs to be kept in mind that right from the day the UN got involved in East Timor, most of the UN observers were biased and partial to Timorese, which means they were politically anti-Indonesia.[18] Moreover, the West-dominated media (particularly the Australian) went overboard to crucify the Indonesians for every act of omission and commission. Unless this tendency is rectified, this will put not only the UN credibility at risk but also set a dangerous precedent for other UN operations elsewhere. It also becomes obvious that even the UN could not make a proper assessment of the ground realities and hurriedly pushed through the referendum.

Second, role of Australia in East Timor. A little known fact is that the Australians fought the Japanese occupation of Southeast Asia during World War II. In the Timor campaign that took place between February 1942 and January 1943, Australian commando forces received invaluable support from Timorese by way of shelter, intelligence about location of Japanese troops and some even fought along side the Australians. Australian historian C. Wray, in his book Timor 1942, summarises the following:

> "The Australians received the willing co-operation of the Timorese people who not only provided the commandos with food, portage and assistance, but also with warnings of Japanese movements. Without this assistance the Australian force would soon have been flushed out and destroyed. The contrast with Dutch Timor [now Indonesia], where the natives refused to assist Allied troops and betrayed them to the Japanese, was significant. The Timorese paid a heavy price for their support of the Australians... hundreds were imprisoned, tortured or killed by the Japanese on suspicions of harbouring Australians. These villages were burned, livestock killed and crops destroyed. While exact calculation of the number of Timorese who died during the years of the Second World War is impossible, it has been estimated that between 40,000 and 70,000 Timorese died... their losses were enormous and the sacrifices suffered and the friendship given by many Timorese during the difficult days of mid to late 1942 were something which the Australians who fought in Timor would never forget."[19]

In 1944, to keep the spirits and resistance up, Australian planes dropped leaflets written in Portuguese in bold letters over East Timor which read: "Your friends will not forget you". However, soon not only was the East Timorese help forgotten, as noted, the Australian government indirectly endorsed the Indonesian plans of invasion.

Whether it was at John Howard's prodding in December 1998 through a letter he sent in December 1998 signaling the reversal of an earlier policy or President Habibie's own personal political compulsion, the referendum has dealt a blow to Australia-Indonesia relations. It is not so much the decision of the East Timorese that enraged the Indonesians but what was considered to be Australia's hypocritical attitude toward the whole issue. Having accepted East Timor as an integral part of Indonesia, Australia's crusade against especially the Indonesian military (now called *Tentara National Indonesia* — TNI) added to Indonesia's suspicions. Not surprisingly an opinion poll revealed that nearly ninety per cent considered Australia "too intrusive" in regard to the East Timor problem."[20] According to an Indonesian scholar: "It is unfortunate that Australia will have to carry this burden in years to come in dealing with Indonesia. Setting the record straight will lessen that burden but will not eliminate it altogether."[21] As Nancy Viviany rightly pointed out, "Australia's strong role in the UN Security Council vote for Interfet and in staffing the peacekeeping force only confirmed its suspicions that Australia had its own agenda and was no longer to be relied on as a friend."[22] While East Timor is a different case, for most Indonesians the nightmare would be the future role of Australia if separatist movements in other parts of the country (these are already strong in Aceh and Irian Jaya) start taking serious dimension. These fears have probably prompted Indonesia to talk in terms of forging a new strategic, political partnership with India, China, and other East Asian countries. Releasing a fifty-seven page policy review, foreign minister Alwi Shihab said: "In particular, a political strategic partnership should be forged with China and India, while at the same time intensifying East Asian regional cooperation."[23] Therefore, East Timor will remain a sensitive issue for a long time and unless Australia exhibits greater sensitivity and understanding toward Indonesia, bilateral relations will remain strained.[24]

The Timor Gap Treaty

Notwithstanding the 1976 UN Security Council resolution, which demanded Indonesia to withdraw from East Timor, Australia first gave *defacto* recognition to Indonesia's sovereignty in the late seventies and a formal *dejure* recognition in August 1985. A major consideration, *inter alia*, that prompted Australia's decision was the petroleum resources that were found in the region. In fact, in 1972 Australia and Indonesia had reached an agreement on oil exploration, and the talks with Portugal to cover the parts under the control of the Portuguese could not materialise. It became convenient for Australia to sign a deal with Indonesia, as it had been friendly. The price for that was recognition of East Timor as part of Indonesia. Thus, in December 1989 Australia signed the Timor Gap Treaty with Indonesia with enabled Australia to undertake undersea oil exploration activities.

The Timor Gap Treaty, officially known as the Treaty Between Australia and the Republic of Indonesia on the Zone of Cooperation in an Area Between the Indonesian Province of East Timor and Northern Australia, was doubtless signed by Australia purely for its economic vested interest (probably at the instance of big oil businesses), but it gave greater legitimacy to Indonesia over East Timor. Supposed to be rich in petroleum resources, this region is strategically very important from an Australian viewpoint. Under the Treaty a

Joint Authority was set up to oversee the exploration for and exploitation of oil resources and a Ministerial Council would meet annually to guide the Joint Authority and was authorised to modify certain terms of the Treaty and approve other agreements related to the Treaty.[25] Much before the referendum, then Indonesian foreign minister Ali Alatas made it clear that if East Timor became independent it could renegotiate the Timor Gap Treaty.[26]

Australia and East Timor's Independence

The change of heart and policy came once Suharto was overthrown. Thus, the overt enthusiasm with which the Australian-led a multinational force to save East Timor from mayhem after the referendum verdict was declared has its roots probably in the guilt-feeling the Australians have nursed for a long time. In the light of the above backdrop, questions have been raised about the sincerity of Australians in undertaking such a peacekeeping effort. From a long-term security point of view, an independent East Timor, which is small, backward and heavily dependent on foreign aid for its survival perhaps serves Australia's interests much more, especially at a time when Australia is striving hard to play the role of a "deputy to the U.S."[27] Contrary to Keating's government, the present administration apparently does not believe that Australia belongs to Asia or in forging a 'special relationship' with Indonesia.[28] However justified the Australian actions may be,[29] many Southeast Asian nations have been uneasy with Australia taking initiatives in such a big way to "save East Timor" because of pronouncements like the above and because of its role and policy toward East Timor.

Australia-Indonesia Security Agreement

Although, Indonesia has unilaterally annulled the Security Agreement with Australia, it is important to examine the circumstances in which it was signed and the motives behind it. This probably had roots in the major exercise Australia took to review its defence policy in the mid-1980s. Professor Paul Dibb, who was entrusted with the task, presented in March 1986 a Report to the Defence Minister, called *Review of Australia's Defence Capabilities*. A slightly modified version of it became the official policy document in the form of White Paper, *The Defence of Australia 1987*.[30] A section of the Dibb Report, which dealt with Indonesia, was kept confidential and this caused considerable consternation in Indonesia. Friendly relations did not remove suspicions about each other. The changed circumstances in the early 1990s provided Australia with a golden opportunity to strike an agreement with Indonesia.

After several months of secret talks, in December 1995 Australia and Indonesia sprung a surprise by announcing that they had reached a security agreement. It acquired added significance because this was the first security agreement Indonesia ever signed since its independence. Nonetheless, it was not as surprising after all when seen against the backdrop of circumstances that prevailed during that time and the kind of strategic relations that these two countries had developed by way of joint exercises and training of military personnel. The end of the cold war and with that the end of all pervasive bipolar security order gave rise to enormous uncertainties, particularly after winding up the largest American bases in the Philippines in 1992.[31] It was not without some basis that concerns were expressed about possible power caucus that might result and the inevitable competition among the regional great powers. China, Japan and India, with their large domestic economic and industrial base coupled with formidable military prowess, were widely considered to be the contenders to fill the void. Perhaps more unnerving was the likely competition among these powers as a consequence of clash of interests. In the absence of any alternative structures or mechanisms to tackle regional security problems, many of the small and medium powers were particularly anxious about peace and stability.

Specifically with regard to Indonesia, the following factors were instrumental in influencing its decision. First, despite a cordial relationship that developed after Suharto ascendance, Jakarta could not completely dispel the feeling of mistrust in Australia. Indonesia probably felt that the most opportune time had arrived to allay fears about Indonesia deeply embedded in the psyche of most Australians as an expansionist and aggressive neighbour. Second, the contest for the resource rich and strategically located islands in the South China Sea had begun to hot up. While Indonesia did not have claims there, Indonesia's ownership of the gas-rich Natuna Island group was undisputed until China released an official map indicating that the Natunas were in Chinese-claimed waters. Third, the then Minister of State, Murdiono's statement soon after signing of the agreement "that 'the two countries have agreed not to interfere in one another's affairs' could also suggest that the Indonesian Government hoped that the Agreement might place an obligation on Australia not to press Indonesia over issues such as East Timor and Irian Jaya".[32] Finally, it was also contended that through the Agreement Indonesia would get closer to the US camp, which, on the one hand, would be reassuring for Indonesia, and it would send right signal to Beijing, on the other.[33]

From an Australian perspective, the security agreement was a major diplomatic triumph in coaxing the largest and most significant power in Southeast Asia, which always shunned any bilateral security arrangement, to come to such an arrangement. Second, notwithstanding the limitations of the Agreement, it would formalise the bilateral strategic links between Australia and Indonesia. Finally, it was a personal victory for Prime Minister Paul Keating who assiduously built a new face for Australia as an Asian power. Keating obviously visualised a larger dimension in his Asia policy which, is vital... "But it is a profound error to see that as the whole story... our interest in Asia has a much broader focus and a much wider purpose. Success in the efforts we make in Asia will affect not just Australia's prosperity but our security..."[34] In this scheme, Indonesia would occupy a crucial place.

Though it has been subjected to various interpretations, with only three major points, the Agreements as such does not provide much other than regular ministerial level consultations "about matters affecting their common security and to develop such cooperation as would benefit their own security and the region." Second, the "parties undertake to consult each other of adverse challenges to either party or to their common security interests and, if appropriate, consider measures which might be taken either individually or jointly and in accordance with the processes of each party." Further, "parties agree to promote-in accordance with the policies and priorities of each-mutually beneficial cooperative activities in the security field in areas to be identified by the two parties."[35]

As Alan Dupont had rightly predicted, "the greater risk to Australia is that rather than being a political circuit breaker, independence for East Timor will actually complicate bilateral relations with Indonesia and post a new set of political, economical and security problems."[36] As the events started unfolding in East Timor after the August referendum, Australia announced the cancellation of a number of bilateral defence activities with Indonesia on 10 September, 1999. Defence Minister John Moore announced that Australia would "review all aspects of Australia's defence relations with Indonesia. In taking this decision, the Government has in mind the need for the Australian Defence Force to be able to continue providing support to the UN operations in East Timor."[37] In response, Indonesia declared the unilateral abrogation of the Security Agreement by claiming that "the attitude and actions of Australia on the question of East Timor have not been helpful in the efforts to maintain bilateral relations with Indonesia on the basis of mutual respect for national sovereignty, sovereign equality and the principle of non-interference in internal affair". Therefore, "Indonesia has decided to abrogate the Agreement between Indonesia and Australia on Maintaining Security which was signed on 18 December, 1995, especially considering the attitude and actions of Australia which are no longer consistent with the spirit and letter of the Agreement".[38] Nonetheless, the Security Agreement was the most important CBM Australia had ever undertaken with Indonesia and to let it wither away would be a great setback in this relationship.

Conclusions

Australia always held its relations with Indonesia as special for a variety of reasons. Probably the most important among them is the strategic dimension, which has been the principal driving force for assigning a unique place for Jakarta in

Canberra's security policy. If the history of bilateral relationship of the last half a century between Australia and Indonesia is any indication, they have no option but to come to terms with each other and restart the process to get the relationship back on track. This is not just political exigency but also strategic necessity despite disparity and asymmetry between the two series of events that affected and shaped the bilateral relationship between the two countries. It was during Suharto's era that Australia-Indonesia relationship flourished and this helped Australia not only to project itself as an Asian Pacific Economic Cooperation (APEC), and an earlier version of the ASEAN Regional Forum (ARF).

Ever since the Indonesia annexation, East Timor has been the most tricky and vexing issue between Australia and Indonesia, for the East Timor issue is quite different from others. Indonesian action in usurping East Timor can never be justified and the UN rightly never recognised that. Nonetheless, Australian role in the acquiescence of Indonesian action for whatever reasons and the extension of a formal recognition to that act smacks of duplicity. At the same time, it was Australia that was at the helm in pressing Jakarta on East Timor when it was most vulnerable. Unlike in the past, the issue of East Timor's separation from Indonesia and Australia's role in that, especially at a time when Indonesia was going through one of the most trying times in its history, will not be forgotten easily in Indonesia. It has generated genuine fears about future of Indonesia remaining as a single political entity. Indonesians have begun to seriously doubt Australian motives and its future policy if other separatist movements started intensifying. A major casualty is the 1995 Security Agreement, which Indonesia unilaterally terminated. This has also cast a long shadow over future Australian involvement in the affairs of the Asia Pacific.

As the events after referendum suggest, Australia and Indonesia will have to work together to ensure a peaceful transition and the survival of East Timor as a nation. Onus probably lies on Canberra in inventing ways to circumvent the misunderstanding over the East Timor issue sooner than later so that the current estrangement is ended and a new modus operandi is evolved in the interest of regional peace and security. As Wiryono Sastrohandoyo, a former Indonesian ambassador in Canberra, has aptly put: "God has made our two countries neighbours, and our economic and security interests link us inextricably. It is the challenge, and grave responsibility, of men and women of goodwill on both sides not to allow the relationship to be damaged further."[39]

References

1 Carlyle Thayer, "Australian Perceptions and Indonesian Reality" (1994), http://coombs.anu.edu.au/CoombsHome.html

2 They were the Colombo Plan (1950), the ANZUS Pact (1951, but Australia formally ratified in 1952), and the South-East Asia Collectively Defence Treaty (1954), which later came to be known as South-East Asia Treaty Organisation (SEATO), and the Five power Defence Arrangement (1971). For a detailed discussion on the background to Australia's participation in these organisations (except FPDA), see Alam Watt, *The Evolution of Australian Foreign Policy, 1938-1965* (London: Cambridge University Press, 1967), pp. 117–163.

3 *World Development Report 2000–2001*, pp. 274–75.

4 ASDT later became Revolutionary Front for Independent East Timor (FRETILIN).

5 This was a pretext the Portuguese used to discount the Indonesian invasion and a moral right to represent the East Timor case in various organisations.

6 Mostly China supported the communist movements in these countries.

7 http://www.pactok.net.au/docs/ct/hforget.html

8 Ibid

9 Irian Barat, before Indonesia took over in 1962, was known as West Irian. It was later renamed as Irian Jaya.

10 http://www.smh.com.au/news/9903/06/features1.html

11 Ibid.

12 http://www.pactok.net.au/docts/ct/ausgwda.html

13 For a comprehensive discussion of the army politics, see Damien Kingsbury, *The Politics of Indonesia* (Mclbournc: Oxford University Press, 1998), pp. 99–126.

14 By most estimates between 150,000 and 200,000 people out of the total population of about 800,000 got killed either due to starvation or in the anti-insurgency operations.

15 In fact, separatist movements intensified in Aceh and West Irian after the referendum in East Timor.

16 It is interesting to note that Megawati Sukarnoputri, currently vice-president and a strong contender for presidency in the future, was probably the only major political personality who had opposed granting independence to East Timor. She obviously had the armed forces in mind whose support was perceived to be indispensable to become the president.

17 The United Nations admitted that it had uncovered no evidence to support allegations that pro-Jakarta militias engaged in mass murder in East Timor. Michel Barton, spokesman for the UN Office for the Coordination of Humanitarian Assistance (OCHA) in Dili stated: "We have heard horrendous stories for which so far there is not a shred of evidence.... There have been murders. There have been terrible things that have happened here. But we do not believe that people in their thousands have been killed and their bodies buried or thrown in the sea. If this had been the case, we would have found evidence of this by now." *International Herald Tribune*, 14 October, 1999.

18 After repeated protests by the Indonesian government, the UN eventually conceded that its observers were not objective in their role and functioning.

19 http://www.pactok.net.au/docs/ct/hforget.html

20 Hadi Soesastro, "Indonesia as Australia's Neighbour", Chris Manning and Peter Van Diermen, *Indonesia in Transition: Social*

Aspects of Reformasi and Crisis (London: ZED Books, 2000), p. 132.

21 Ibid.

22 Nancy Viviani, "The Sharp Deterioration in Relations Between Indonesia and Australia: An Australian Perspective', Ibid., p. 121.

23 http://www.the age.com/au/news/20000129/A52064-2000Jan28.html

24 Jusuf Wanandi suggests three vital areas where Australia can extend tangible help to Indonesia: financial aid, law and jurisprudence and education. Jusuf Wanandi, "it is in our Interest to Ensure Asia's Newest Democracy Thrives", *The Australian*, 16 May, 2000.

25 See part I, II, and III of the Treaty, *Australian Treaty Series No. 9, 1991* (Canberra: Australian Government Publishing Service, 1991).

26 *Indonesian Observer*, 18 February, 1999.

27 *Far Eastern Economic Review*, 7 October, 1999, p. 14. The 1995 Security Treaty, Australia signed with Indonesia was the first casualty. The Australian attitude has also raised strong nationalist sentiments in Indonesia.

28 Cavan Hogue, "Australian Foreign Policy, 1999", *Australian Journal of International Affairs*,Vol. 54, No. 2, July 2000, p. 145.

29 For a detailed description of developments leading to the referendum and the emergence of East Timor as an independent country and Australia's role in that, see Alexander Downer, "East Timor — Looking Back on 1999", *Australian Journal of International Affairs*, Vol. 54, No. 1, April 2000, pp. 5–10.

30 For details, see G.V.C. Naidu "Australian Defence: A New Role in the South pacific", *Strategic Analysis*, July 1987.

31 The former Soviet Union too had vacated its base facilities at Da Nang and Cam Ranh Bay in Vietnam just before the US withdrawal from Clark Air Base and Subic Bay Naval Base in the Philippines.

32 Gary Brown, Frank Frost and Stephen Sherlock, *The Australian-Indonesian Security Agreement; Issues and Implications*, Research paper #25 (Canberra: Department of Parliamentary Library, 1996). Website: http://www.aph.gov.au/library/pubs/rp/1995-96/96ro25.htm.

33 Ibid.

[34] Quoted in Desmond Ball, "Australia's Strategy for Security Engagement in Asia" Coral Bell, ed., *Nation, Region and Context: Studies in Peace and War in Honour of Professor T.B. Millar* (Canberra: Strategic and Defence Studies Centre, The Australian National University, 1995), p. 20.

[35] See the *Agreement*.

[36] Alan Dupont, Indonesia, "Australia and the Problem of East Timor", *Aus-CSCAP Newsletter* No. 8, April 1999.

[37] http://www.minister.defence.gov.au/1999/26499.htm

[38] See the unofficial translation at http://www.indonesia-ottawa.org/news/abrogation-160999.htm

[39] Quoted in Richard Baker, "Indonesia-Australia: Relations Moving from Bad to Worse", *Comparative Connections: In E-Journal on East Asian Bilateral Relations*, published by the Pacific Forum of CSIS, 3rd Quarter 1999. http://www.csis.org/pacfor/cc/993Q.html

12

India and Maritime Security Environment in Southeast Asia

G. V. C. Naidu

The maritime security environment in the Asia Pacific in general and Southeast Asia in particular has undergone a major transformation in the post-cold war era. First, most of the disputes in the region are maritime-related by way of either dispute over the control of islands or unsettled offshore, maritime boundary issues. Second, what is noteworthy is that these disputes, which had remained dormant through most of the cold war period, have emerged almost suddenly. Third, most of the contested islands are supposed to be endowed with rich living as well non-living (mostly hydrocarbons) resources. Fourth, these islands have also enormous strategic importance. Fifth, despite best efforts, a viable solution to resolve these disputes seems to be very elusive. Finally, as a result, perhaps the most conspicuous development across the region is the acquisition of military hardware with the intent of building sophisticated naval forces. An emerging power with growing maritime, economic and strategic stakes in the region, India's interests will be affected by the developments.

The following study examines specifically the maritime dimensions of the Southeast Asian security in the contemporary context and evaluate the possible impact on, and role, for India. Thus, it is divided into various sections dealing with maritime disputes, with greater focus on the South China Sea, modernisation of the regional navies, and India's interests and concerns, especially in the Andaman Sea region.

Introduction

Geographically, among the ten countries of Southeast Asia, only, i.e., Laos, island-locked, while all others are either archipelagic nations or have long coastlines and substantial maritime interests. More importantly, barring a few exceptions, most of them have unsettled maritime boundaries or have claims for offshore assets, islands or seabed resources. Hence, sea power and maritime issues dominate the security concerns of the countries of Southeast Asia individually as well as collectively at the regional level. A clear manifestation of this can be seen in the attempts to develop the naval forces in the region.

Unlike in the past, and unlike the army and the air force, in modern times the navy is called upon to perform multi-faceted roles. Apart from repulsing an external aggression, a modern navy has the additional responsibility of protecting oceanic assets, undertaking explanatory missions, guarding the sea-lanes of communication, and as a major instrument of power projection. Hence, the navy of any power and its expansion (especially in the developing world) should not be viewed merely in a narrow military perspective. It is necessary to keep in mind the interests, concerns, aspirations and ambitions of developing navy while attempting its evaluation.

With the emerging technologies, classical modelling or strategies have little relevance in modern naval warfare. The advent of satellites and their critical role, and the invention of a wide array of missiles have fundamentally altered the concepts such as maritime strategy and naval warfare. Similarly, the technological advances have rendered the navy the most potent weapon to win wars or influence developments in distant regions. Thus, each navy has different capabilities, objectives, and ambitions depending on the resources a country can afford and the industrial/ technological base it possesses. Hence, it may be not be prudent to try and fit a navy into any categorisation, for each navy is unique in its own way.

With regard to Southeast Asia, an assessment of maritime security environment must also factor, in addition to the regional navies, the navies of Asian great powers, for these powers have historically played a significant role in shaping regional security and more recently their stakes in the developments in Southeast Asia have begun to grow considerably. While the traditional major naval powers, such as the United States, the former Soviet Union, the United Kingdom and France, are either stagnating or on the decline, there are new powers that are on the rise especially in Asia, for instance, China, Japan and India. One can add Indonesia, Taiwan, South Korea, Thailand and Australia as significant naval powers which are on the ascendance and possess capabilities that cannot be ignored. Nor far behind in their quest to build modern navies are other countries such as

Malaysia, Singapore, Vietnam, etc. All the above mentioned countries are on the path toward qualitative and quantitative expansion.

Apart from the overall increases in defence across the region (through temporarily halted by the financial crisis), there are perceptible changes in terms of quality and nature of equipment that is sought to be acquired. This process obviously entails effecting fundamental changes in strategic doctrines concurrently. Advanced and technologically sophisticated equipment and platforms are being acquired which more often than not tend to be offensive in nature with, of course, attendant power projection capabilities. Although it is difficult to categorise the present military modernisation in the Asian Pacific in terms of an "arms race" in the traditional sense, there is no denying the fact that there is a race for arms build-up.[1] While the defence expenditures in North America, Europe and the Middle East are on the decline, the Asia Pacific region has been witnessing a steady rise in real terms. It is estimated that in the next one decade, the expenditure on arms procurements in this part of the world would be worth about US$ 100 billion.[2] The current financial turmoil in the Asia Pacific may have dampened the earlier momentum, but it is widely considered to be a temporary phenomenon. To be sure, except for a few countries, the defence allocations of most have been cut and many planned acquisitions are kept on hold. Yet, given the geo-strategic realities of the Asia Pacific, this phenomenon is unlikely to last as a major feature.

Besides the general upgradation of defence forces, most of the countries have also embarked on enlarging their Research and Development (R&D) and defence-related industrial base. Rapid and substantial industrialisation of these economies in the recent past has further contributed to the above weaponry, greater emphasis on technology transfer and local production under licence is likely to be an important characteristic in the coming years. Generally depressed market conditions for arms exporters are expected to facilitate this process further.

Due to a qualitative difference in terms of implications on the rest of the region, the maritime issues of the Asia Pacific have acquired an important dimension in the emergent regional security for the following reasons.

First, most of the disputes in Southeast Asia (as well as in the larger Asia Pacific) are related to maritime boundary or offshore territorial claims and they completely overshadow other border and boundary disputes. These are:

1. The Paracel and Spratly Islands dispute involving China, Taiwan, the Philippines, Malaysia, Brunei and Vietnam in the South China Sea;
2. The gas-rich Natuna Islands group, again in the South China Sea, between Indonesia and Vietnam (over the demarcation line on the continental shelf);
3. The Natunas between Indonesia and China;
4. The dispute between Malaysia and Singapore over ownership of Pulau Batu Puteh Island in the Straits of Johore;
5. The dispute between Indonesia and Malaysia over Sipadan, Sebatik and Ligitan Islands in the Celebes Sea;
6. The province of Sabah and the water surrounding it between Malaysia and the Philippines.
7. Maritime boundaries in the gas-rich Gulf of Thailand portion of the South China Sea have not been clearly defined. Several companies have been signed

exploration agreement but have been unable to drill in a disputed zone between Cambodia and Thailand.

Second, the critical importance of the sea-lanes of communication. Full cognizance has been taken note of the fact that the ever-increasing global trade and economic interaction would automatically enhance the strategic significance of sea-lanes. This is particularly the case in the Asia Pacific region as most of these countries are critically dependent on sea-borne trade. Some of the world's busiest and most important sea-lanes are located in this region: the South China Sea, the Malacca and other straits in Southeast Asia, the Indian Ocean, etc. The ability to protect/control the sea-lanes in times of crisis would be the most crucial aspect of future naval development in the region. A related issue that has emerged as a major concern is the problem of piracy on high Seas. The waters of Southeast Asia are the most prone to piracy attacks than any other region in the world and this has been further aggravated by the economic turmoil that gripped the region.

Third, the oceanic resources. The ever increasing dependency on sea assets would only get aggravated as resources on land start diminishing and greater attention is paid to harness those sea resources. Although large-scale exploitation of seabed minerals may take quite some time (because of the heavy costs involved and lack of appropriate technology), the major concern would be to bring as much ocean space as possible under sovereign control which would entail immediate benefit in the form of fishing rights. There have been indications that in the cases of the South China Sea and Senkaku, reports of huge reserves of oil and gas may be exaggerated, but no one can deny the substantial and immediate benefit in terms of fishing and other activities that would accrue as a result of control of these islands. Protection of the Exclusive Economic Zone (EEZ) and the resources within it has become a major naval concern. The reported finding of massive seabed gas reserves in and around Natunas has already resulted in China extending its claims to this region too, thus forcing Indonesia to reappraise its security calculations.

Among the three recognised major flashpoints in the Asia Pacific-the Korean Peninsula, the China-Taiwan standoff, and the South China Sea, probably the most troublesome and tricky is the dispute surrounding the islands in the South China Sea. The contest for the islands in the South China Sea has already witnessed several bloody battles since 1974. Even as the disputants gear up their military capabilities, the involvement in, and the intensity of, any future conflict is anticipated to be much greater. It needs no underscoring that this problem would involve regional navies in a big way in the event of a conflict breaking out, in addition to the possibility of some major extra-regional navies getting entangled.

Given the limitations of the deterrent capabilities of Southeast Asian navies, notwithstanding the current effort at modernisation, and given clear signs of American disengagement from the region, the navies of the Asian great powers, viz. Japan, China and India, acquired added significance. These powers also happen to be some of the largest and fastest growing economies, have substantial defence industrial bases, and especially have experience in operating large, ocean-going navies. The problem is further compounded by the lack of transparency in their security interests and strategic doctrines. China maintains complete secrecy about its defence expenditure, security concerns and strategies, and India, although it publishes its defence expenditure details, does not publish any official documents on defence policies, and though Japan publishes an Annual Defence White Paper, it is not regarded to be very exhaustive. In the meantime, the Chinese Navy is undergoing a fundamental transformation in its modernsation by way of doctrinal changes, technological upgradation, and building power projection capabilities; the Japanese Navy continues to expand and remains technologically highly sophisticated; and the Indian Navy, despite recent setbacks because of funding and other constraints, continues to develop its indigenous base of ship-building and maintains limited power projection capability.

The South China Dispute

As far as regional security issues are concerned, now that domestic security has ceased to be of major concern, the most important issue is related to border and territorial disputes. Political turmoil continues unabated in Indonesia, and the issues of democracy and human rights have become major contentious points between ASEAN and the West, especially with regard to Myanmar. There are at least half a dozen other border or territorial disputes involving one or more Southeast Asian nations, which can be become very emotive in certain circumstances and have the potential to whip up strong nationalist sentiments. Needless to say that, among these, the contest for the South China Sea has already emerged as the biggest challenge. It needs to be recognised that the South China Sea is a complex issue with several dimensions to the disputes and hence it is not going to be easy to resolve this problem.

Territorial Dispute

First, there are four types of disputes involving at least seven nations:

1. Dispute between China and Vietnam over Paracel islands;
2. Dispute between China, Taiwan, Malaysia,[3] the Philippines,[4] Brunei and Vietnam over the Spratlys;
3. Dispute between Indonesia and Vietnam on demarcation line on the continental shelf near Natuna Island;
4. Dispute between China and Indonesia on the question of continental shelf around the Natunas.

Energy Resources

Second, it has been variously reported that these islands are sitting on vast quantities of hydrocarbons.

> "The focus of most attention regarding the South China Sea resources has been on hydrocarbons in general, and oil in particular. Oil deposits have been found in most of the littoral countries of the South China Sea. The South China Sea region has proven oil reserves estimated at about 7.5 billion barrels, and oil production in the region is currently over 1.3 million barrels per day. Malaysian production accounts for about one-half of the region's total. Total South China Sea production has increased gradually over the past few years, primarily as additional production from China, Malaysia and Vietnam in 1977, and oil was discovered in 1997 in Vietnam's Block 46 (southwest of Vietnam). The fact that surrounding areas are rich in oil deposits has led to speculation that the Spratly Islands could be an untapped oil-bearing province located near some of the world's largest future energy consuming countries. Such speculation has given the Spratly

Islands great strategic value, and has fueled disputes over ownership. In fact, there is little evidence outside of Chinese claims to support the speculation that the region contains extensive oil resources. Because of a lack of exploratory drilling, there are no proven oil reserve estimates for the Spratly or Paracel Islands, and no commercial oil or gas has been discovered there".[5]

As with oil, estimates of the South China Sea's natural gas resources vary widely.

"One Chinese report estimates that there are 225 billion barrels oil equivalent of hydrocarbons in the Spratly Islands alone. If 70% of these hydrocarbons were gas, total gas resources (as opposed to proven reserves) would be almost 900 Tcf. If the rule-of-thumb imply potential production levels for the Spratly Islands of almost 1.8 Tcf annually. Another Chinese report estimates that the entire South China Sea contains more than 2,000 Tcf of natural gas resources. By contrast, the most optimistic non-Chinese report has estimated total gas resources in the Spratly Island at 24 Tcf. If all of this were proven to be economically recoverable, this hypothetically could yield a peak natural gas production level for the Spratly Islands of 0.5 Tcf annually".[6]

Shipping

The third dimension to the South China Sea dispute is shipping.

"The South China Sea region is the world's second busiest international sea-lane. More than half of the world's supertanker traffic passes through the region's waters. More than half of the world's annual merchant fleet tonnage passes through the Straits of Malacca, Sunda, and Lombok, with the majority continuing on into the South China Sea. Tanker traffic through the Strait of Malacca leading into the South China Sea is more than three times greater than Suez Canal traffic, and well over five times more than the Panama Canal. Virtually all shipping that passes through the Malacca and Sunda Straits must pass near the Spratly Islands".[7]

It may be noted that the sea-lanes in the region carry the most critical element for the very survival of the economies of large industrialised nations such as Japan and South Korea (now increasingly China), i.e., energy from West Asia. There are alternate routes, but they are expensive. It takes much longer time and hence the need for more super tankers if South China Sea were to be avoided.

Piracy

The fourth dimension in a way related to the above is the security of sea-lanes by way of pirate attacks. This region is most prone to piracy on the high seas and it has emerged as a major menace. According to the International Maritime Bureau (IMB), reported incidents of piracy attacks tripled since the early 1990s. In 1999, the IMB's Piracy Reporting Centre (PRC) in Kuala Lumpur tracked two hundred and eighty-five piratical attacks — an increase of more than forty per cent compared to the previous year.[8] Joint patrolling and concerted action in a multilateral fashion involving regional navies is the only way this problem can be addressed. Indonesia, Malaysia and Singapore, for instance, are already undertaking joint anti-piracy activities, but it is limited to a small geographic area. Moreover, there are severe constraints because of their limited naval capabilities. Recognising the need to involve other nations in the regions, especially those that possess large navies and specialised agencies such as the coastguard, Japan convened a major conference in Tokyo in March 2000, specifically to discuss the problem of piracy and evolve ways to tackle it.

Strategic Significance

The sixth dimension is the strategic location of the islands of Spratly and Paracel in the South China Sea. The existence of large quantities of oil and gas reserves may be proven right or wrong, the piracy issue may be tackled, the shipping may not get disturbed after all, but no one can deny the fact that with the control of China, the entire security calculus would undergo a radical change. Southeast Asia would be virtually under the influence of Beijing. Moreover, China would be geographically part of Southeast Asia, which may even prompt China to become a member of ASEAN. This prospect would be very unnerving to most other great powers, which have developed considerable interests in the region, especially to Japan and the US and India.

Others

As noted, the major and immediate benefit that would accrue as a result of hold over the islands in the South China Sea is enormous economic advantages by way of exploitation of vast EEZ oceanic resources. Given the fact that the South China Sea is rich in vast variety of living resources, the economic benefit by way of fishing is enormous.

ASEAN Navies

A number of factors and developments in the last few years have spurred these nations to build up their navies whose tasks are not confined only to coastal defence. The foremost being the withdrawal of superpower presence from Southeast Asia in the early 1990s, a presence on whose backing the maritime external threats had been thwarted by the ASEAN nations. Second, all the ASEAN nations, especially after embarking on export-led development policies, are critically dependent on the seas for trade, in addition to a heavy reliance, for both living and non-living sources, on the seas. Third, after the agreement on Law of the Seas, maritime interests such as an Exclusive Economic Zone, Continental Shelf, etc., and the right to economic exploitation of these assets have imposed enormous responsibilities on the navies to guard these interest. Fourth, as mentioned in the beginning, all the ASEAN nations are confronted with a number of unresolved maritime disputes. Last but not least, in view of recent developments, most ASEAN countries are engaged in acquiring a sea power that is commensurate with their requirements.

The ASEAN countries seem to be adopting a broad strategy, which is primarily aimed at strengthening ASEAN solidarity *vis-à-vis* external powers. First, there has been a qualitative and quantitative increase in defence cooperation since the end of the cold war within ASEAN. Second, involvement in dialogue with all the powers that have some stake in the security of Southeast Asia (using the means of the "constructive engagement" policy where necessary) in the ASEAN-created forums — ASEAN-Post Ministerial Conferences (ASEAN-PMCs), the ASEAN Regional Forum (ARF), Joint Business Councils, etc. Third, forging new defence links through joint military exercises and MoUs with major external powers (the most notable being Australia and India). Last, gradually building military-related infrastructure to increase the level of self-reliance where collaboration and transfer of technology have become the buzzwords. It is believed that the defence industry as a technology-intensive and high-value added industry can boost national industrial development.[9] As the Malaysian defence minister has pointed out. "The days of straightforward procurement are over. We have to look in terms of industrial cooperation, collaboration and transfer of technology",[10] it appears, increasingly this is going to be the norm in the coming years.

Especially at the naval level, a common trend across ASEAN is the step-by-step approach, i.e., to develop naval power in a gradualist fashion, but with greater emphasis on high technology. Thus to start with, the most favoured ship in ASEAN is the fast attack craft armed with accurate and sophisticated surface-to-surface and surface-to-air missiles. These ships are not only highly manoeuverable but also extremely suitable to the shallow waters of the South China Sea. The second stage is to acquire larger ocean-going ships such as corvettes and frigates. Then follows interest in submarine capabilities. So far, Indonesia and more recently Singapore are the only nations that operate conventional submarines. However, at least a few other powers — Thailand and Malaysia in particular — have expressed plans to acquire a submarine arm. Once these plans are realised, the Southeast Asian maritime atmosphere will undergo a radical change.

There are moves at the individual, bilateral and multilateral levels to beef up strategic cooperation among the ASEAN nations. For instance, while the Philippines is trying hard to get closer to the Americans, Singapore and Malaysia have started conducting joint exercises, and in January 1995 an MoU was signed and a bilateral security dialogue (called Malaysia-Singapore Defence Forum) initiated to facilitate greater defence coordination and defence industrial cooperation.[11]

While most of the ASEAN countries are small in size and have limitations in building major navies, any attempt at greater defence cooperation and coordination is fraught with political sensitivity because of its implications on ASEAN's own political/diplomatic agenda and its dealings with external powers. Even an initiative to form an ASEAN regional grouping of a national defence industry association for limited cooperation was stalled, more for political reasons than financial ones.[12] As the biggest concern for most ASEAN nations is the dispute in the South China Sea and possible disruption of trade in that region, how far the ASEAN defence forces would be able to act in concert with each other will be a major political and strategic challenge for the member states in the coming years.[13]

China and South China Sea

In military terms, at present China does not seem to possess the wherewithal in terms of range and strategic lift to take over control of the Spratlys. The recently acquired Russian Su-27 (and the proposed MiG-31s) combat aircraft do give the PLA Air Force the reach, but not much manoeuverable time because of the long distance from the mainland. Thus, China either has to acquire refueling technology[14] or build an air base on one of the islands in the South China Sea. While trying to develop refuelling technology on its own, China for the time being appears to have preferred the latter option of building an air base, notwithstanding the limitations of space and other support systems to maintain large, sophisticated aircraft, by constructing a 2,700-metre airstrip on Woody Island in the Paracel group of islands.[15] From a naval point of view, the PLA-Navy is faced with serious limitations in terms of both sea control capabilities as well as solid ship-based air defence. If China were to occupy and establish an effective control over the Spratlys Islands through military means, it would have to acquire sea control ships such as aircraft carriers. Secondly, it would have to considerably enhance the navy's air defence so that it would not be vulnerable to air attacks by highly sophisticated strike aircraft of the F-16, Mig-29, F/A-18 or Hawk 1-8/208 type that many Southeast Asian nations currently possess.

In a scenario which China and the ASEAN countries together are engaged in a conflict, based on current capabilities, China would find it difficult to capture and sustain its hold over the Spratlys,[16] but it should be kept in mind that the South China dispute is very complicated:

1. Singapore and Thailand are not parties to any dispute in the South China Sea.
2. Indonesia's interests are limited to the Natunas and do not extend to the other islands either in the Spratlys or Paracel groups of islands.
3. Vietnam's claims are much larger than those of any other Southeast Asian nation, and include the whole of the Paracel group of islands in addition to the Spratlys, unlike those of other Southeast Asian countries.
4. The claims of Malaysia, the Philippines and Brunei are limited to a few islands in the Spratlys.

Against the above backdrop, if a small group of countries (the main Southeast Asian contenders for the Spratlys — Malaysia, Vietnam and the Philippines) are involved in a battle, even together they may find it difficult to confront the Chinese military might. In a worst-case scenario of a conflict breaking out, it is most unlikely that all ASEAN countries would plunge into the war in the name of ASEAN solidarity. China would certainly attempt a divide and engage policy in the event of a crisis. China may not even precipitate the tensions in the South China as long as it deems its military capabilities are insufficient and ineffectual. China has reasons to believe that time is on its side and by all indications, its influence and power will only increase rather than diminish in the coming years.

The Andaman Sea

From an Indian viewpoint, the other most significant maritime issues are the developments in the Andaman Sea region, especially the perceived growing nexus between China and Myanmar. India's Look East policy acknowledges that Southeast Asian affairs are of relevance to Indian security, but for its navy the immediate concerns are developments in the Andaman Sea. The Indian Navy became conscious of the danger the Andaman & Nicobar Islands faced during the 1965 India-Pakistan War, both from East Pakistan and from Indonesia. A series of events in the 1970s considerably enhanced the strategic significance of these islands from the Indian viewpoint. First, the sailing of the American carrier battle group *Enterprise* during the 1971 Indo-Pak War into the Bay of Bengal; second, the US decision to expand its presence in a big way at Diego Garcia in the Indian Ocean in 1978; third, fears of a Chinese nuclear submarine deployment in the Indian Ocean and a Beijing-Islamabad naval axis emerging; and finally, the 1979 UN-sponsored Law of the Sea Conference which provided for two hundred mile Exclusive Economic Zone (EEZ). The Andaman & Nicobar Islands alone constitute over one-third of India's total EEZ. The emergence of East Pakistan as separate political entity (as Bangladesh) and the change of leadership in Indonesia removed the threat from these sources. However, the 1971 *Enterprises* incident left a deep mark on naval policy-makers. The superpower naval build-up in the Indian Ocean, especially in the light of close links India has had with the former Soviet Union, had been a constant concern to India. Whether India liked it or not, as far Washington was concerned, during the period India belonged to the Soviet camp. Even the countries in Southeast Asia had a similar impression about India, whereas India was more worried about the ripple effect of the superpower rivalry and the close links among the US, China and Pakistan. These were factors that led to the strengthening of facilities at Port Blair in the Eighties, called Fortress Andaman (FORTAN).

From a strategic angle, the Andaman & Nicobar chain of islands are highly strategically located in the Bay of Bengal in close proximity to some of the busiest and important trade routes connecting the East with the West. For instance, estimated oil flows through the Malacca Straits in 1996 comprised 8.2 million barrels per day to Japan, South Korea, China and other Pacific Rim countries. If these straits were closed, nearly half of the world's fleet would be required to sail farther, more vessels would be required and freight rates would go up worldwide.[17]

Consisting of about five hundred islands (of which only thirty are inhabited) and spread over seven hundred and fifty km north to south, the Andaman & Nicobar Islands occupy an area of more than eight thousand sq. km., a coastline of two thousand km long, and an EEZ of 250,000 km.[18] While the northern most Landfall Island is just twenty nautical miles (nm) away from the Little Coco Island of Myanmar, Indira Point in Great Nicobar is only ninety-eight nm. from Northern Sumatra. The Malacca Straits are within three hundred nm. from the southern tip of Nicobar and the western shore of Thailand, and Malaysia is located five hundred and twenty to six hundred and forty km away from Port Blair; whereas, the closest point to the Indian mainland are at least one thousand two hundred km.[19] Despite the closeness to Southeast Asia, the maritime boundaries are clearly delineated and settled. With Indonesia, "the first agreement was signed in 1974, which settled the boundary between the Great Nicobar and Sumatra. In 1977, the boundary line was extended both into the Indian Ocean and into the Andaman Sea by another agreement. In the same year, the boundary between Indian and Thailand in the Andaman Sea was negotiated and an agreement was signed in June 1978 and came into force in March 1979".[20] The maritime boundary agreement with Myanmar was ratified in 1987.[21]

The China-Myanmar Factor

Andamans is once again in the news because of the Indian government's decision to create a new command at Port Blair called the Far Eastern Naval Command (FENC). The foremost reason that prompted the Indian Navy to upgrade the Andamans facility into a full-fledged command are the Chinese military activities in Myanmar close to these islands. The first hint of Chinese interest in Myanmar came in mid-1985 in an article written in *Beijing Review* by a former senior government official, which outlined the possibilities of using Myanmar as an outlet into the Indian Ocean.[22] That was also the beginning of a new Communist rebels fighting the military and started cultivating a new relationship. It started off as defence cooperation leading to two major deals in 1990 and 1994, worth nearly US$ 2 billion. As part of these agreements, China has supplied patrol boats and missile frigates to Myanmar.

Simultaneously, the Chinese started getting involved in the construction of a number of new ports in Myanmar. There have been persistent reports since 1992 that the Chinese have been assisting the Myanmarese regime in upgrading its naval and electronic facilities facing the Indian Ocean. "In late 1992, Western spy satellite detected a new, 150-foot antennae used for signals intelligence at a naval base on Coco Islands, a Burmese possession in the Indian Ocean. Suspicion that this equipment is likely to be operated at least in part by Chinese technicians has led to fears that Burma will allow Beijing intelligence agencies to monitor this sensitive maritime region".[23] This, Indians believe, lets China not only watch the strategic sea-lanes in the region, but also possibly monitor India's missile tests off the east coast. The Chinese are also engaged in "the construction of a new naval base on Hyianggyi Island at the mouth of the Bassein river, and the modernisation of existing naval infrastructure at Sitwe (Akyab), Mergui, and Great Coco islands."[24]

A second reason why the Chinese want a presence in Myanmar is related to the dispute in the South China Sea. In a scenario in which China and ASEAN are engaged in a conflict, based on current capabilities, China would find it difficult to capture and sustain its hold over the Spratlys. Second, China would be worried if the strategically located straits, such as Malacca, were closed in times of tensions. In the event of this happening, China would be cut off from both Southeast Asia and the larger Indian Ocean, Hence, China badly needs an alternate route.[25]

According to the Xinhua news agency, China and Myanmar entered into an agreement in early June 1997 on joint development of a new channel connecting the southwestern region of China with Myanmar major river, the Irrawaddy, extending along China's No. 320 National Road. This would provide direct access to China's Kunming region via Myanmar to the Indian Ocean.[26]

Even Southeast Asians seemed to be worried about Chinese activities in Myanmar. According to a Malaysian analyst, "There is a fear that the Chinese are coming in to Southeast Asia from the other side, via the Indian Ocean. This will give them access to the Straits of Malacca. If China has access through that area, it will give Beijing a better basis for power projection".[27] The Indonesians have also expressed similar views.

Chinese activities may be seen in the context of its growing dependency on the sea routes of the Indian Ocean for its trade and other defence links with the countries of West Asia. China's energy imports are not very substantial yet (it became a net importer of oil in 1995), but they are likely to grow in the future. China may feel vulnerable, but its capabilities are not large enough to confront the Indian Navy in the Indian Ocean. "In a worst-case scenario in the Indian Ocean, the Indian Navy would need to deal with a few modern guided-missile destroyers without adequate air defence or ASW systems, as also two or three missile-armed *Han* class nuclear-powered submarines which would have to surface to launch their anti-ship missiles. While such a Chinese naval force could threaten the Indian Andaman & Nicobar islands for purposes of coercive diplomacy, it would be at a considerable disadvantage in terms of the Indian Navy's range and extent of operations in the area, including missile strikes from the air, coordinated ASW missions, and overwhelming logistics support".[28] However, India is looking at Chinese activities from a medium to long-term point of view. In a scenario in which an invading power has to enter the Bay of Bengal through the straits of Southeast Asia, India would like to have a capability which can choke these entry points.

India also appears to be concerned about smuggling and gun running activities that take place in this region. The nagging northeast Indian armed militancy is sustained by the supplies of light weapons that have their origins in Southeast Asia. There have been several instances of the Indian Navy and coast guard intercepting the movements of weapons. In February 1998, in a combined operation involving the army, air force and navy, a huge consignment of light weapons was seized in a forty-eight hour operation, code named "Operation Leech", in the Andaman Sea which would probably have landed up in northeast India. It was confirmed that the arms consignment had its origin somewhere in Southeast Asia.[29]

The proposed FENC (the fourth one) would involve upgradation of existing facilities at FORTAN in a big way, such as "augmentation of military force levels and setting up of several surveillance and monitoring stations in the 750 km. long Andaman and Nicobar Islands".[30] "FORTAN, which is a tri-service defence and is commanded by a Vice Admiral. It is the Indian Armed Forces' only unified command where the Army, Air Force and Navy operate under an integrated command".[31] In an interview with a defence journal, the navy chief said: "The FENC has come into place because of India's growing geo-economic realities in the Andaman Sea and in accordance with the Government's Look East Policy".[32]

The establishment of a new command at the Andamans may act as a deterrent to future Chinese plans in the Indian Ocean. If China tries to check Indian influence in the Indian Ocean, India would not allow China to have unfettered control stretching from the South China Sea to the Malacca Straits.[33] The new command may, in a way, be measuring to the countries of Southeast Asia. In any case, as has been rightly pointed out, there is "fundamental consensus by Indian and Western analysts on the general operational doctrine and role for Fortress Andaman:

1. EEZ surveillance and policing, including control of refugees and piracy;
2. Contributing to sea-control and power-projection missions against any littoral state or navy within the Bay of Bengal or Andaman Sea. Under some circumstances these objectives could include destruction of locally attached units of extra-regional powers;
3. In conjunction with bases situated along the eastern Indian seaboard, exercising an effective deterrent or operational capability against extra-regional forays on the approaches to and within the Bay of Bengal or Andaman Sea. This sea denial orientation would be exercised through a layers defence, capable of progressively inflicting punitive and disproportionate damage to an intruder approaching the Indian mainland".[34]

Recent events, especially the growing defence links between India and several ASEAN nations, regular joint naval exercises between India and countries such as Indonesia, Singapore and Malaysia near the Andamans, and frequent visits by senior naval officers from these countries to the Andamans have further confirmed the defensive role of Indian naval forces based around this area. Despite so much attention being focused on FORTAN, perhaps the only major upgradation at the Port Blair base was the opening of a naval air station, called *INS Utkorsh,* in 1985 which, in theory, can offer facilities to operate both strike as well as interceptor aircraft.

Specifically with regard to Southeast Asia, the long-range TU-142M Bears of the Indian Navy have the range to conduct surveillance well into the South China Sea, but it is difficult to visualise a situation in which the Indian Navy takes an active part in a conflictual situation, especially in Southeast Asia. Undoubtedly, a peaceful and prosperous Southeast Asia is in India's interest, but, at the same time, India may not like the region to come under the strategic influence of any one great power. Now that the Southeast Asian countries do not have apprehensions about the Indian Navy any longer, and given the current atmosphere of close political, economic and strategic cooperation, India may be willing to extend all possible help to strengthen the defence forces of these countries. Enhanced strategic interaction could be expected in the coming years even as many ASEAN countries start acquiring advanced naval vessels, such as submarines, frigates, missiles boats, and aircraft carriers (in the case of Thailand).

A role for the Indian Navy in Southeast Asia may be viewed in terms of a threat stemming from that region which directly or indirectly impinges on its vital interests. The Andaman base facilities and their strategic location, however, do accord certain advantages. They provide the Indian Navy with the ability to monitor or perhaps even to close the Malacca Straits (of course, there are alternate sea-lanes, which offer access to the Indian Ocean). Against this backdrop, it is difficult to foresee a direct participation by the Indian Navy, for instance in a conflictual situation in the South China Sea. However, the Indian Navy would be in a position to influence developments in Southeast Asia by way of providing assistance to build up regional militaries through training and transfer of some technologies and weapon systems. From a Southeast Asian viewpoint, the fact that these countries are forging new defence cooperative arrangements with India might act as a deterrent to other major external powers.

Concluding Remarks

There is broad recognition that the security environment of Southeast Asia is overwhelmingly dominated by maritime issues, primarily related to disputes for islands and boundary problems involving not just the countries of the region but external powers as well. As a consequence, there has been a discernible tendency toward the modernisation of the regional navies. The trend is to acquire advanced platforms and missile-equipped ships and in some cases procurement of submarines as well. Among the several maritime-related disputes, the most significant one is connected to the control of islands in the South China Sea. As has been explained earlier, there are several dimensions to the issue and the number of countries that have staked claims, partly or fully, are large. Due to their strategic location astride some of the busiest sea-lanes of communication in the world and the reports of vast reserves of oil and gas beneath them, any settlement of the dispute is fraught with serious problems. China is already in occupation of the Paracel group of islands and has unequivocally extended its sovereignty claim to the Spratlys too. Malaysia, the Philippines, Brunei and Vietnam too have varying claims over the Spratlys islands and most of them have already deployed military forces. China's PLA-Navy is being rapidly modernised and the ASEAN countries individually will not be able match the Chinese military might. Collectively they may not be able to act together in the event of a conflict breaking out simply because some countries do not have claims. A negotiated settlement appears to be unlikely as long as China is reluctant to retract its position.

The second issue that directly concerns India is the Andaman Sea. India shares its second longest land and maritime boundary with Myanmar and the Andaman & Nicobar Islands lie close to Southeast Asia. Reported close proximity of the current military leadership in Myanmar and China and Chinese naval activities in Myanmar close to Indian-held Andamans have raised concerns in India. The Andaman base has been strengthened and plans have been announced to set up a new command, called Fast Eastern Maritime Command, in the region. Unlike the 1980s, the Indian navy is no more looked with suspicion by the Southeast Asians. As a result of a number of initiatives India has undertaken in the last few years, India has been gradually establishing military links with the select countries of Southeast Asia. Indian interests in Southeast Asia are growing and hence developments there will have considerable impact on India's security concerns. Although India is the only one that operates power projection capable ships such as aircraft carriers, it is unlikely to get involved in the event of conflict in South China Sea. Similar exercises with one or more countries of Southeast Asia are not ruled out. It would largely depend on the developments in South

China Sea and with active initiative coming from the countries of Southeast Asia.

Notes

1. It is obviously a futile exercise to pin-point any single-most important factor that is responsible for the current military build-up in the Asia Pacific. A combination of one or more of the following factors might be instrumental, specific to the individual country's real or perceived threat perception. These are: the super power, especially the US, military withdrawal/build-down as a result of the end of the cold war; a fundamental change in American strategy toward the Asia Pacific; rapidly growing economic prosperity which enables these countries to afford greater amounts on defence; changed orientation of threat perception of several countries, from internal/domestic to external; a large number of unsettled land and maritime boundary issues which have acquired a new dimension in the post-cold war atmosphere; the availability of advanced weapon systems at affordable prices; to maintain steady importation of defence equipment and technology so that the domestic defence industrial bases in most cases would remain as modern as possible, etc.
2. Carlyle A. Thayer, "Arms Control in Southeast Asia", *Defence Analysis,* Vol. 12, No. 1, April 1996, p. 77. Also, see Stockholm International Peace Research Institute (SIPRI) Report, 1994.
3. Many of Malaysia's natural gas fields located offshore Sarawak also falls under the Chinese claim.
4. The Philippines Malampaya and Camago natural gas and condense fields are in Chinese-claimed waters.
5. http://www.eia.doe.gov/emeu/cabs/schina.html
6. Ibid.
7. Ibid.
8. www.imp.org/imo/introd.htm
9. See Stewart Walters, "Will Asian Defence Industries Join the Big League", *Asian Defence Journal,* November 1995. The Singapore Shipbuilding and Engineering Ltd., is the most advanced among the ASEAN countries, which has exhibited its capabilities by successfully building corvette-sized ships and

patrol vessels (with some foreign assistance) and has developed indigenous designs to build the *Swift* class patrol vessels. Singapore has also upgraded naval vessels of several countries and has supplied patrol vessels to India, Brunei and Kuwait.

Indonesia's leading shipbuilder, PTPAL, has been upgraded to initially build fast patrol boats and later corvettes to foreign designs.

In Malaysia, the private sector Naval Dockyard at Lumut will be the prime contractor for the proposed 27 New Generation Patrol Vessels and, according to Malaysia's Defence Minister, Najib Razak, these vessels will have more than 50 per cent of local content. *Defence News*, 9April, 1995.

Thailand too has developed considerable shipbuilding capabilities at Itai Thai Marine and Royal submarines in the future will further boost these capabilities.

10 *Defence News*, 9 April, 1995.

11 *Jane's Defence Weekly*, 28 January, 1995.

12 Ibid.

13 ASEAN Navies have been discussed in detail in G.V.C. Naidu, *Indian Navy and Southeast Asia* (New Delhi: Knowledge World and IDSA, 2000), pp. 113–148.

14 Now that China has openly displayed the refuelling capability, its implications for South China Sea are obvious. Some unconfirmed reports have suggested that China acquired this technology from Iran (originally supplied by the US).

15 For details, see Felix K. Chang, "Beijing's Reach in the South China Sea", *Orbis*, Summer 1996, p.30.

16 As has been argued eloquently by Chang. Ibid., pp.352–374.

17 *U.S. Energy Information.* http://www.eia.doe.gov/emeu/cabs/choke.html

18 V. Suryanarayan, "The Relevance of Andaman and Nicobar Islands in India's Policy Towards Southeast Asia", in V. Suryanarayan and V. Sudersen, eds., *Andaman and Nicobar Islands: Challenges of Development*, (New Delhi: Konark Publishers, 1994), p. 173.

19 Ibid.

[20] S.P. Jagota, *Maritime Boundary,* quoted in ibid., p. 178.

[21] *Far Eastern Economic Review,* 8 October, 1987.

[22] Bertil Lintner, "Enter the Dragon", *Far Eastern Economic Review,* 22 December, 1994, p. 24.

[23] Ibid, p. 23.

[24] Rahul Roy-Chaudhury, "The Chinese Navy and the Indian Ocean", *Maritime International,* January 1995, p.22.

[25] G. V. C. Naidu, "South China Sea and China's Myanmar Connection", *Strategic Analysis,* August 1997, p. 809.

[26] Ibid., p. 807.

[27] Lintner, n.31, p. 23.

[28] Ibid., p. 21.

[29] *The Hindu,* 13 February, 1998.

[30] *Times of India,* 19 April, 1998.

[31] *Bharat Rakshak:* http://www.bharat-rakshak.com.

[32] *Jane's Defence Weekly,* 29 July, 1998.

[33] A former Indian naval chief states that "India's strategic frontiers broadly cover the entire Indian ocean up to West Asia including the Persian Gulf, the Red Sea and the western littorals, the Pacific up to the South China Sea. The importance of bolstering our reach up to our strategic frontiers becomes obvious..." *The Hindu,* 2 October,1998.

[34] D.N. Christie, *India's Naval Strategy and the Role of Andaman and Nicobar Islands,* Working Paper No. 291 (Canberra: Strategic and Defence Studies Centre, Australian National University, 1995), p.18.

Contributors

Shri K.C. Pant	Deputy Chairman, Planning Commission
Satish Chandra	Former Chairman, University Grants Commission
Baladas Ghoshal	Professor, School of International Studies, JNU, New Delhi
S.K. Singh	Former Foreign Secretary, Government of India
Ganga Nath Jha	Associate Professor, School of International Studies, JNU, New Delhi
V. Jayanth	Assistant Editor, *The Hindu*, Chennai
Dilip Chandra	Bahasa Indonesia, All India Radio, New Delhi
M. Ramstedt	Fellow at the International Institute for Asian Studies in Leiden, the Netherlands
K. Subramaniam	Joint Secretary (Retd.), Government of India
B. Bhattacharyya	Prof. & Dean, Indian Institute of Foreign Trade, New Delhi
Prithwis K. De	External Services Division, Head
B. Raman	Director, Institute of Tropical Studies, Chennai
G.V.C. Naidu	Research Fellow Institute for Defence Studies and Analyses, New Delhi